EZRA POUND & CHINA

Ezra Pound
& China

Edited by Zhaoming Qian

THE UNIVERSITY OF MICHIGAN PRESS
Ann Arbor

Copyright © by the University of Michigan 2003
All rights reserved
Published in the United States of America by
The University of Michigan Press
Printed and bound by CPI Group (UK) Ltd, Croydon, CR0 4YY

2006   2005   2004   2003   4   3   2   1

A CIP catalog record for this book is available from the
British Library.

ISBN13 978-0-472-09829-3 (cloth)
ISBN13 978-0-472-06829-6 (paper)
ISBN13 978-0-472-02435-3 (electronic)

To Hugh Kenner for his 80th birthday

Acknowledgments

Numerous people have helped make this volume possible. Beijing Foreign Studies University President Chen Naifang and Professors Zhang Jian, Qian Qing, Zhang Zhongzai, Chen Shu, Zhang Yun, Guo Qiqing, Li Ping-wei, and Wang Jiaxiang enthusiastically supported this project. So did the University of New Orleans former and current Vice Chancellors for Research Shirley Laska and Robert Cashner, Associate Dean of Multicultural Affairs Mackie Blanton, Department of English Chairman John Cooke, and Research Professor of English John Gery. I would also like to thank Wendy Stallard Flory and William Pratt, who read and commented on an early version of the introduction. I am especially grateful to Danniel Albright, George Bornstein, Reed Way Dasenbrock, William McNaughton, Mary de Rachewiltz, Tim Redman, and Richard Taylor for encouragement. I owe a great deal to the expert, collegial assistance of LeAnn Fields of the University of Michigan Press. Also, my thanks to Marcia LaBrenz for preparing the manuscript and Britton Gildersleeve for doing the index. Above all, I am indebted to the contributors to this volume for their remarkable collaboration.

ABCR *ABC of Reading.* 1934. New York: New Directions, 1987.
C *The Cantos.* 14th printing. New York: New Directions, 1998. References are to canto and page number.
CEP *Collected Early Poems.* Ed. Michael John King. New York: New Directions, 1976.
Con *Confucius: The Great Digest, The Unwobbling Pivot, The Analects.* 1951. New York: New Directions, 1969.
CWC *The Chinese Written Character as a Medium for Poetry,* by Ernest Fenollosa. Ed. Ezra Pound. 1936. San Francisco: City Lights, 1968.
GB *Gaudier-Brzeska: A Memoir.* 1916. New York: New Directions, 1974.
GK *Guide to Kulchur.* 1938. New York: New Directions, 1968.

Acknowledgments

J/M	*Jefferson and/or Mussolini.* London: Stanley Nott, 1935.
L/DP	*Ezra and Dorothy Pound: Letters in Captivity, 1945–1946.* Ed. Omar S. Pound and Robert Spoo. New York: Oxford University Press, 1999.
L/JQ	*Selected Letters of Ezra Pound to John Quinn, 1915–1924.* Ed. Timothy Materer. Durham: Duke University Press, 1991.
LE	*Literary Essays.* Ed. T. S. Eliot. New York: New Directions, 1968.
P	*Personae: The Shorter Poems.* Ed. Lea Baechler and A. Walton Litz. New York: New Directions, 1990.
P&P	*Ezra Pound's Poetry and Prose: Contributions to Periodicals.* Ed. Lea Baechler, A. Walton Litz, and James Longenbach. New York: Garland, 1991.
SL	*Selected Letters.* Ed. D. D. Paige. New York: New Directions, 1971.
SP	*Selected Prose, 1909–1965.* Ed. William Cookson. London: Faber and Faber, 1973.
SR	*The Spirit of Romance.* 1910. New York: New Directions, 1968.
YCAL	Unpublished material, Yale Collection of American Literature, Beinecke Rare Book and Manuscript Library, Yale University.

Contents

Introduction

ZHAOMING QIAN

Despite the proliferation of books about literary border crossings, the complex and intriguing interchange between Ezra Pound and China remains undervalued. To this day, many readers still find it puzzling that one of America's leading modernists spent a lifetime exploring Chinese modes of thought. In 1914, without any knowledge of Chinese, he undertook to retranslate the poems of Li Bo (701–62) and other masters that he found in the notebooks of Ernest Fenollosa (1853–1908). The result, *Cathay* (1915), earned him recognition as "the inventor of Chinese poetry for our time."[1] Inspired by this first success, he assayed the Chinese written character ("ideogram"), introducing it into his long poem *The Cantos* first symbolically and then in its original form. His way of absorbing Chinese culture and language into *The Cantos* is as bewildering as it is fascinating. Confucius, who enters the cantos early (in 1917)—"Confucius later taught the world good manners" (*P*, 233)—returns again and again, in the Confucian Canto, the Chinese History Cantos, and the Pisan, Rock-Drill, and Thrones sequences. The "Wind Song" of Song Yu ("Sō-Gyoku") in Canto 4—"No wind is the king's wind" (4/16)—is echoed throughout the poem, to its very last fragment:

> I have tried to write Paradise
> Do not move
>   Let the wind speak
>   that is paradise.
>
> (117/822)

To understand Pound's relation to China is to address one of the knottiest issues in poetic modernism. The career of this pivotal figure in the Anglo-American modernist movement is usually viewed in three periods: the early years (1908–20), defined by his imagism and vorticism, the middle years (1920–45), characterized by his "ideogrammic method" and enthusiasm for Mussolini's fascist economics, and the later years (1945–72), informed by his Confucianism. To a remarkable degree, his transitions from one stage to another parallel the shifts in his parleying with China. His rise from imagism to vorticism, for example, coincides with his study of Chinese poetry via the Fenollosa papers and the making of *Cathay*. His adoption of the "ideogrammic method" for *The Cantos* is directly linked to his preoccupation with Fenollosa's essay "The Chinese Written Character as a Medium for Poetry." His most "fascist" period corresponds to his work *both* with J. A. M. de Mailla's *Histoire générale de la Chine* and the *Book of Rites (Li Ji)* for the History Cantos *and* with his translations of two of Confucian China's "Four Books."[2] And finally, to account for his later cantos, one must grasp the importance of his postwar commitment to Confucius: his Confucian translations, *The Analects* (1951) and *The Classic Anthology Defined by Confucius* (1954), and his engagement with the *Book of Documents (Shu Jing)* and the *Sacred Edict (Shen Yu)* for the Rock-Drill and Thrones sequences.

Pound's lifelong interest in China raises questions central to debate about literary modernism in our own day, when politics, economy, philosophy, religion, literature, music, and art are brought into "the fold of cultural discourse."[3] What attracted Pound to China? Did he see the Self, the Other, or an odd combination of the two in Chinese culture and literature? How did China, as an "other," complicate and intensify Pound's modernism? Why did modernism need an "other" perspective to invigorate itself? How did the Other interfere with the self in Pound's *Cathay?* In what manner, precisely, did the interference affect his progressively modernist style? Why should Pound adopt the ideogrammic method for *The Cantos?* What new discovery did he make of Confucianism during his months as a prisoner at Pisa? How much of his Confucianism is missing from the published text of *The Pisan Cantos?* Is Pound interested only in Confucius? How does his non-Confucian Chinese material fit in with the themes of *The Cantos?* What problems does Pound's dialogue with China present to modernism? To contemporary poetics?

Pound's preoccupation with Chinese culture also raises questions important to current debate about Orientalism. Is Orientalism a monolithic and constant conception? Or is it a slippery and shifting process? Can Edward Said's seminal work on nineteenth-century British and French Orientalism be appropriated for our inquiry into Pound's relation to China?[4] If the answer is yes, how? Would our attempt benefit from acquaintance with the writings of Homi K. Bhabha, Lisa Lowe, and others that challenge and extend Said's theory?[5] To what extent was Pound influenced by what is generally referred to as Saidian Orientalism? In what way did Pound distinguish his Orientalism from the Orientalism of his predecessors?[6]

The present collection of essays is designed to examine or reexamine these controversial questions. Like earlier works on Pound and China, notably, Wai-lim Yip's *Ezra Pound's Cathay* (1969), John Nolde's *Blooms from the East: The China Cantos of Ezra Pound* (1983), and Mary Paterson Cheadle's *Ezra Pound's Confucian Translations* (1997), this book desires to keep the issues open and debatable, much like modernism itself. Whereas previous studies each focus on a particular theme, this volume attempts to deal with the interchange between Pound and China comprehensively. Pound's relation to China is such an intricate and multifaceted topic that it requires numerous scholars to work on it. For the student, who is not in a position to consult the wide range of pertinent materials in the time-consuming manner of the specialist scholar, this book conveniently incorporates a variety of fresh and authoritative accounts within one volume, providing both the updated scholarship required by the specialist and the condensed curriculum needed by the student.

The essays collected here were originally prepared for the Eighteenth International Ezra Pound Conference held in Beijing, China, July 16–19, 1999.[7] Our international conferences on Pound started in Orono, Maine, in 1975, with a group of scholars and friends commemorating the ninetieth birthyear of the poet.[8] This conference was followed by a second in Sheffield, England, the next year, exploring Pound's London period.[9] From 1975 through 1997 Poundians convened seventeen conferences, three in the United States, ten in England, three in Italy, and one in France.[10] In 1999, for the first time, an international colloquium on Pound took place outside Europe and America. With "Ezra Pound and the Orient" as its fitting theme, the Beijing conference brought together ninety participants from fifteen countries. Among the forty-five who delivered papers were many internationally recognized scholars. Much ground was covered, with subjects ranging from specific points of interpretation to broad theoretical concerns. The special setting facilitated by the conference's arrangements ensured that presenters could interact with their mainly Chinese audience while freely exchanging ideas among themselves. This defining characteristic of the occasion is captured in a participant's comment: "The coherence of the conference is due to the 'specialness' of the territory on which it took place. China is so different that it focused people's mind on the theme more than is usually the case. It was good for most of us to know that we were facing Chinese professors, to whom our remarks (if we were not careful) might seem very foolish."

This volume reflects the organization of the Beijing conference, which consisted of ten regular sessions, a multilingual poetry reading, a symposium, and a concluding keynote address given by Pound's daughter, Mary de Rachewiltz. The essays gathered here touch on all the points of the designated theme of "Ezra Pound and the Orient." By arranging them in chronological sequence, my intention is to illuminate an uninterrupted, career-long preoccupation with China that is centrally important to Pound's modernism. Although most subjects have been previously discussed, the contributors have sought to expand their boundaries by resurrecting forgotten primary materials, suggesting revised readings, and raising disturbing questions. Their mutual effort to reopen old inquiries follows a dictum Pound derived from China and adapted as his motto, "Make it new."

Starting with Pound's origins, Ira Nadel identifies particular American themes that prefigured Pound's lifelong passion for Chinese culture. The presence of Far Eastern fine and decorative arts in Philadelphia museums and households, what Nadel terms "Philadelphia Orientalism," "initiated an early but broadly based fascination and responsiveness to the Orient in Pound," which would lead to an "Orient of style" and an "Orient of text"—the visual field of *The Cantos*. Pound's reading of Longfellow, Emerson, and Whitman, on the other hand, prepared him for his encounters with China in London first through Laurence Binyon (1869–1943) and then through the notebooks of Ernest Fenollosa. Without his exposure to the American discourse about the Orient, Pound would not have crossed cultural borders so comfortably. To trace the roots of Pound's Orientalism, however, is not to confuse his Orientalism with his predecessors'. As Nadel notes, "whereas the nineteenth-century American construction of the Orient was of a passive and metaphysical kingdom, Pound's was active and alive, directly experienced through the notebooks of Fenollosa and re-created in the world of *Cathay* and the ideals of Confucius."

Barry Ahearn offers a fresh exploration of Pound's parleying with Chinese poets through Fenollosa, arguing that the style Pound adopted in *Cathay* can be partly attributed to his ambiguous stance toward translation. This stance arises from the common perception that translation is both necessary and necessarily flawed. It is necessary because we want a clear rendition of a text from a foreign language. It is necessarily flawed because so much of the original has no equivalent—or only an approximate equivalent—in the language of translation. Examining the *Cathay* poems from "Song of the Bowmen of Shu" to "The River-Merchant's Wife," Ahearn suggests that Pound's ambivalent stance appears when he implies that the Chinese originals are so like Western poems that the process of translation is simple, or when he inserts odd idioms and strange images that point to the ineluctably alien nature of Chinese poetry. The very title, *Cathay*, captures this dichotomy, since the term designates the mysterious and the remote, yet the name itself has for centuries been part of the vocabulary of the West.

In her account of the *Cathay* enterprise, Christine Froula turns her attention to the role it played in transforming Pound's English. She proposes that the incongruent grammars of classical Chinese poetry and modern English illuminate Wittgenstein's insight that "to imagine a language is to imagine a form of life."[11] As such radically different "forms of life" contend in the process of translation, the language of translation, in Lawrence Venuti's terms, either "domesticates" the language of the original or allows itself to be "foreignized" by it, its resources challenged and extended at the level of grammar and syntax.[12] Pound's encounter with China through the work of Fenollosa, as Froula shows, does not end with his creation of exquisite if sometimes erring English versions of Chinese poems but marks one of the sites of cultural interchange within which English poetry has evolved—from Caedmon's time through the twentieth century, the century that Fenollosa prophesied would open a new and startling "chapter" in the "book of the world," revealing "world-embracing cultures half-weaned from Europe," negotiating "hitherto undreamed responsibilities for nations and races" through their contending languages or forms of life (*CWC*, 3). Opening his English to the "foreignizing" influence of Chinese, Pound's encounter with Fenollosa is a microcosmic theater of twentieth-century history, consolidating the status of English as a global language and casting light on both Pound's "foreignizing" of the ideogrammic method and its experimental deviations from "domesticated" English grammar.

At the center of my reconsideration of Pound's Canto 49, generally known as the Seven Lakes Canto, are issues important to both Pound scholarship and cultural studies. Without taking into account all of the various resources Pound had access to, written and visual, we cannot appreciate this pivotal canto properly. I invite readers to examine the photographs of the eight painted scenes of Pound's sourcebook (courtesy of Mary de Rachewiltz and Richard Taylor) side by side with his transcript of an oral translation of the eight Chinese poems accompanying them. The result is a unique experience: we encounter (with Pound in 1928–30) the interaction of image and text firsthand and come to see the Seven Lakes Canto as conceived in response to two media striving to represent a monument of Chinese culture in their own ways. The "seven lakes," or rather the "eight views," had afforded a millennium of Chinese (and Japanese) poets and artists an apparatus through which to make statements about history and politics. In Canto 49, Pound places the traditional Chinese scenes in a pre–World War II European setting to offer his idea of government and economics.

The structure of *The Cantos* has perplexed many readers. In Pound's History Cantos (Cantos 52–71), Hong Sun charts a possible solution to this difficulty. Sun shows that Pound follows an underlying pattern, the pattern of the *Da Xue (The Great Digest),* one of the "Four Books," particularly, in its first three Confucian gradations: correcting the self, regulating the family, and governing the state. This pattern, in Sun's view, shapes not only the Chinese History Cantos, but also Late Cantos 74–117. It is in the Chinese History Cantos, nevertheless, that one discerns the recurrence of the three gradations most clearly. The mythology and history included appear to be illustrations for the *Da Xue* and the ideograms appear to be its exemplary figures. Some readers may find Sun's effort to make the poem fall into place controversial, but all will appreciate his fresh, interesting information about Chinese history and the *Da Xue.*

Peter Makin considers the ideogrammic method's consequences for Pound's use of the Confucian conception of "right naming." The theory of the ideogram, in Makin's view, is a theory of indirect communication, which holds that a writer, knowing something precisely, cannot usually call on a single term for what he or she wants to communicate, and so has to adduce a complex of things through which to achieve this purpose. "Right naming," by contrast, is a theory of direct communication stressing that writers have to know exactly the meanings of words from the common her-

6

itage of their language, and thus must be able to define them. Makin reminds us that in the later cantos Pound conducts a running campaign against "the loose users of words." According to Pound's theory of the ideogram, the term to be defined is usually a shortcut that leads to a loss of precision. Among the few who could define all their key words by means of other words were the medieval Schoolmen, whose example Pound frequently cites without apparently seeing that their kind of "precision" was precisely what the ideogrammic method seeks to avoid. Ultimately, Makin shows that a number of ambiguities in Pound's own words and conceptions led him into a trap. Right naming as he understood it seemed close to both his aesthetics and his metaphysics. But the consequences of Pound's campaign for right naming were probably regrettable.

Pound's rediscovery of China at Pisa is the concern of the next two essays. Wendy Stallard Flory's contribution documents a crucial shift in Pound's Confucian perspective that occurred during his months as a prisoner in the U.S. Army's Disciplinary Training Center. In place of an emphasis upon Confucian teachings about the governance of the state, which had tended to aggravate his political obsessiveness, he increasingly turned to Confucius's injunctions about self-governance under conditions of personal adversity. In addition to the Confucian Classics, Flory examines two unusual pieces of writing. The first is a two-page Confucian "manifesto" that Pound wrote, while still in the maximum security "cage," for the Roman Catholic chaplain who spent time with him each day during this period and whom Flory interviewed in 1981. The second is the series of Chinese characters that Pound inscribed in the margins of his copy of the *Catholic Prayer Book for the Army and Navy,* following his own suggestion to the chaplain that the Catholic prayer books in Chinese include "ideograms of [the] Confucian school." The characters added draw an analogy between Confucianism and Catholicism by identifying passages in the Confucian texts that make points similar to the passages in the Catholic liturgy that the characters stand beside. Tracing these characters to their exact Confucian sources by means of the glossary in James Legge's edition and *Mathews' Chinese-English Dictionary,* Flory follows a trial-and-error method comparable to Pound's own—one that draws attention to the intensity of his immersion in the Confucian texts and of his fascination with their characters and to the enduring validity of the insights that these ancient writings contain.

Ronald Bush's contribution grows out of his ambitious project on the composition of *The Pisan Cantos* that has yielded several previous essays.[13] Here Bush focuses on the obscuring of the imprint of Confucius on the sequence caused by the omission and garbling of fifty-odd sets of Chinese characters Pound inscribed in his Pisan typescript. After surveying the reasons for and history of this textual gap, Bush indicates that almost all of these sets of characters were taken from James Legge's bilingual edition of the Four Books that Pound had been allowed to carry to Pisa. Surprisingly, however, the majority of these characters are not from the *Da Xue* and the *Zhong Yong*, whose translations *(The Great Digest* and *The Unwobbling Pivot)* Pound completed at Pisa, but from the *Lun Yu* or *The Analects.* It is "in the variegated moods and voices of *The Analects,*" Bush points out, "that Pound finds expression for both sides of some of his most fundamental artistic and emotional ambivalences." Indeed, without the missing characters, the importance of Confucius to Pound at Pisa—not just the familiar Confucian assertions, but the extraordinary Confucian comfort, counterpoint, and allusions—is nearly invisible. To conclude, Bush usefully reproduces the fifty-odd sets of characters in the context of *The Pisan Cantos,* followed by Legge's translations of the Confucian passages Pound alludes to, Pound's translations in *Confucius,* and occasional brief commentary.

Rarely do scholars accord Pound's use of non-Confucian Chinese material any serious attention. For most Poundians, Pound's treatment of Buddhism and Daoism is anything but positive. In Britton Gildersleeve's estimate, Pound's argument with both religions centers not on doctrinal issues, but rather on corrupt institutionalization of belief, mirroring his dissatisfaction with comparable Western institutions. Pound's "Kuanon" (Guanyin), Gildersleeve contends, cannot be seen as a Chinese version of Kore. She appears to embody for Pound what she has embodied for Chinese Buddhists—compassion. For Pound, Kuanon—in addition to her traditional functions within the Buddhist pantheon—is a female figure who eludes easy delineation, one who draws upon a legacy of androgyny and Orientalist perspectives to embody *yin* and *yang,* male and female, being and becoming. Pound juxtaposes Kuanon with Greco-Roman female deities in the same way that his ideogrammic method relies on multiple images to establish paradigmatic meaning. Kuanon ultimately becomes a feminine ideogram conjoining Eleusinian and Eastern mysticism as well as the enigma at the heart of Pound's flawed journey-quest toward mystic union with the divine.

Among the strange and beautiful elements in Pound's final cantos, *Drafts & Fragments*, are certain rites and ceremonies and customs of the Naxi ("Na Khi"), a Chinese minority tribe living near the Tibetan border in the town of Lijiang. Readers tend to think that the Naxi were an ethereal fiction and Lijiang a fantasy place on another planet. A recent visit to the area, with a Naxi man as guide and a Naxi woman as driver, taught Emily Mitchell Wallace otherwise. Her essay, accompanied by photographs taken in Lijiang, shows that the paradisical atmosphere is real: "the waters of Stone Drum" (101/746), the Jade Dragon Snow Mountain, the alpine meadows, "the pomegranate water, / in the clear air / over Li Chiang" (112/804), surround beautiful people living in peace and harmony. Pound did not exaggerate, which means that his source, Joseph Rock, did not misrepresent the place and the people. Today at the entrance to the New Town a large sign proclaims, in English, that Lijiang is the model for Shangri-La, the utopia in James Hilton's *Lost Horizon*, named after a street, Shangra, in the Old Town. UNESCO placed the Old Town of Lijiang on its World Heritage List in December 1997, and a sign at the entrance to the Old Town "confirms the exceptional and universal value of a cultural and natural site, which requires protection for the benefit of all humanity." This honor occurred mainly because of Joseph Rock's persistent and arduous efforts to record the world of the Naxi, as our poet says: "And over Li Chiang, the snow range is turquoise / Rock's world that he saved us for memory / a thin trace in high air" (113/806). Reviewing the reasons Pound admired the eccentric genius of Rock as well as the ways he used the material that Rock collected, Wallace makes evident that the spirit of the Naxi religion, the core of which is the pre-Buddhist religion of Tibet known as the Bön, chimes with Pound's youthful interest in Plotinus, an ancient mentor he returned to in his old age because of his belief that "the universe is alive" (94/657).

Without overlapping, the essays all strive to assert the dynamic nature of Pound's interchange with China. Taken together, they mark a significant step toward revised readings of Pound, readings that place his poetry and poetics more firmly in international and multicultural contexts. Concluding the volume are two texts that endorse this orientation. The first is a selection of poems from several languages and cultures that reflect the sustained impact of Pound on contemporary poetry throughout the world. The second is Mary de Rachewiltz's afterword based on her lecture "From Pisa to Taishan," meant to be delivered in China. Once in China, de Rachewiltz realized that the voice that had a right to be heard was Pound's. So she played a tape of Pound's reading of the Confucian Odes instead. Here, in the present volume, we are finally able to hear her own voice.

NOTES

1. The phrase is T. S. Eliot's in his introduction to *Selected Poems of Ezra Pound* (London: Faber and Faber, 1928), xvi.

2. Pound's Italian translations of the *Da Xue* and *Zhong Yong* were published in 1942 and his English translations *(The Great Digest* and *The Unwobbling Pivot)* in 1947.

3. Geoffrey Hartman, *The Fatal Question of Culture* (New York: Columbia University Press, 1997), 61.

4. Edward Said, *Orientalism* (New York: Random House, 1978). In Said's most radical definition, Orientalism is "a Western style for dominating, restructuring, and having authority over the Orient" (3).

5. For broader understandings of Orientalism, see Edward Said, "Orientalism Reconsidered," in his *Reflections on Exile and Other Essays* (Cambridge: Harvard University Press, 2000), 198–215; Homi K. Bhabha, "Difference, Discrimination, and the Discourse of Colonialism," in *The Politics of Theory*, ed. Francis Barker et al. (Colchester: University of Essex, 1983), 194–211, especially 199–201; Lisa Lowe, *Critical Terrains: French and British Orientalism* (Ithaca: Cornell University Press, 1992), 4–5; Zhaoming Qian, *Orientalism and Modernism: The Legacy of China in Pound and Williams* (Durham: Duke University Press, 1995), 1–5.

6. Although the book's contributors do not generally respond to this issue, the materials they provide seem to indicate at once linkage to, and revolt against, hegemonic Orientalism, what we now call Saidian Orientalism.

7. See William McNaughton, "A Report on the Eighteenth International Conference on Ezra Pound, Beijing, China, 16–26 July 1999," *Paideuma*, forthcoming.

8. See Barbara Eastman, "The Ninetieth Birthyear Symposium," *Paideuma* 4, nos. 2–3 (1975): 519–28.

9. Philip Grover, ed., *Ezra Pound: The London Years, 1908–1920* (New York: AMS Press, 1978).

10. A listing of the first thirteen international conferences on Ezra Pound is given in *Ezra Pound and Europe*, ed. Richard Taylor and Claus Melcheor (Amsterdam: Rodopi, 1993), vii. The fourteenth to the seventeenth conferences were held in Brunnenburg, Italy, 16–18 July 1991; Rapallo, Italy, 13–16 July 1993; Brantome, France, 18–21 July 1995; and Brunnenburg, Italy, 12–15 1997, respectively.

11. See Froula, note 3.

12. See Froula, note 12.

13. See Ronald Bush, "Towards Pisa: More from the Archives about Pound's Italian Cantos," *Agenda* 34, nos. 3-4 (1996-97): 89-124; "'Quiet, Not Scornful'? The Composition of *The Pisan Cantos*," in *A Poem Containing History: Textual Studies in "The Cantos,"* ed. Lawrence Rainey (Ann Arbor: University of Michigan Press, 1997), 169-212; and "Late Cantos LXXII–CXVII," in *The Cambridge Companion to Ezra Pound*, ed. Ira B. Nadel (Cambridge: Cambridge University Press, 1999), 109-38.

Constructing the Orient:
Pound's American Vision

IRA B. NADEL

A three-storied house in a Philadelphia suburb was only one of many lo-
cales for Pound's introduction to the Orient. But there, on Fernbrook Av-
enue in Wyncote, Pennsylvania, the young Ezra Pound encountered his
first Chinese object: a Ming dynasty vase. At Aunt Frank Weston's in
New York, he saw a remarkable screen book, a sequence of oriental
scenes adorned with poems in Chinese and Japanese ideograms.[1] The
oriental collections in the museums of Philadelphia provided additional
exposure to Chinese culture, preparing Pound for his later absorption in
Orientalism developed through the work of Laurence Binyon, Ernest
Fenollosa, Nō drama, and his own study of Chinese.

Pound, himself, displayed an early interest in things oriental. At one of
his first public appearances, he chose an oriental disguise. He was sixteen
and attending a Halloween party in Philadelphia where he met Hilda
Doolittle, later the imagist poet H.D., for the first time. He wore a green
robe that appeared to be Chinese, although he said it was acquired in
Tunis some years earlier with his aunt (it was—he went there in 1898 with
Aunt Frank). "This robe was much discussed," writes H.D. "I suppose it
was something Indo-Chinaish. It went with Ezra."[2]

Family interest in China originated in Homer and Isabel Pound's con-
cern with the work of Christian missionaries in China. Accounts of travel,
religious work, and trade formed part of the family's reading, encouraged
by their involvement—from teaching to administration and regular atten-
dance—with the Calvary Presbyterian Church in Wyncote.[3] But the orien-
tal objects in the Pound home indicate more than homage to a foreign cul-
ture or curiosity with things Chinese for the young Pound. They represent
Philadelphia's continuing attraction to the material culture of China, which
had a formative role in Pound's earliest conception of the Orient.

Chinese decorative and fine art formed Pound's initial encounter with
China and contributed to his likely being the first major American writer
to respond more to oriental art than to its literary tradition. Chinese paint-

ing and imagery acted as a catalyst for his writing and formation of his work. Although this vision would overlook some of the harsher aspects of Chinese life, generally absent in the imagery of China represented through the visual arts, and neglect some of the more violent aspects of contemporary Chinese history such as the Boxer Rebellion of 1900, Pound nevertheless found in the cultural heritage of Philadelphia's celebration of China the beginnings of a lifelong preoccupation with the country.

Philadelphia, where the Pounds had moved in 1889, was at the center of America's response to the Orient, reflecting a national fascination with oriental art. The city's link with China originated in eighteenth-century trade, and Philadelphia soon became one of the earliest repositories of Chinese art and decorative objects, the bounty of traders, collectors, and importers. America's supposedly first sinologist, Robert Waln Jr., author of an important 475-page history of China (published 1823), was from Philadelphia. The prominent China merchant Benjamin Chew Wilcocks of Philadelphia was known for his Oriental collection, which included a mezzotint of a famous Canton merchant, Houqua, symbolizing a link between the commerce of China and Philadelphia, intensified when it was discovered that Beijing and Philadelphia shared the same latitude (forty degrees). This led some to believe that Chinese silk and tea could easily be cultivated in Pennsylvania. In 1828 construction began of a one-hundred-foot pagoda with a Chinese garden and pavilion in Philadelphia's Fairmont Park (where the Philadelphia Museum of Art would be located), a copy of a tower in Canton. It was popularly known as "The Temple of Confucius."

The 1839 opening of Nathan Dunn's museum of Chinese objects confirmed Philadelphia's importance as a site for Oriental culture. Dunn, a merchant who had spent more than twelve years in China, returned with some twelve hundred Chinese craft items, from dress to tools and furniture, all wonderfully arranged. Standing alone among the fifty-three display cases was a facsimile of an apartment of a wealthy Chinese merchant's palace. Dunn's collection offered the first large-scale public exhibition of Chinese materials in the United States. Between 1839 and 1841, some one hundred thousand people reportedly visited the exhibit, while more than fifty thousand copies of his *Descriptive Catalogue* were sold.[4] A second, even larger, Chinese museum opened in Philadelphia in 1847, organized by John Peters. Oriental art and culture had a significant

13

presence in Philadelphia before and during Pound's residence there. The Philadelphia Centennial Exposition of 1876, the first international exposition ever held in the United States, had two impressive exhibits that fascinated the public: the Chinese and Japanese pavilions, which increased the popularity of Oriental objects and the desire to have such objects in the home.[5] The publications, lectures, and sponsored travel of the American Philosophical Society, founded in Philadelphia, also contributed to the city's interest in the Orient. The so-called Orientalists of the organization included its founder, Benjamin Franklin, and its secretary, Peter Duponceau, a student of Chinese. Andreas van Braam and Nathan Dunn, both of whom spent many years in China, would become members of the society.[6]

In 1890, Ernest Fenollosa returned from the Orient to become curator of the new Oriental Department of the Boston Museum of Fine Arts and within a few years began a series of widely popular lectures on Chinese and Japanese art, history, and literature that introduced the East to many Americans. The growing private collections of Oriental art by American entrepreneurs, travelers, and importers, most of which found their way into museum collections like the Peabody in Salem, Massachusetts, set the pattern for the popularity of Chinese porcelain, lacquerware, and bamboo furniture in many American homes. Importing Chinese silk, tea, and other commercial goods to America meant a constant cultural, as well as commercial, exchange between the two countries. Domesticating China soon found a natural outlet, as well, via Chinese horticulture, which soon marked the American landscape, whether it was the Chinese elm, gingko, azalea, magnolia, peony, gardenia, or formal garden.

In the neighborhood of the Pounds in the Philadelphia suburb of Jenkintown, preceding their move to Wyncote, lived a number of the nouveau riche, eager to include elements of the Orient in the decor of their homes and collection of artworks. Cyrus Curtis, publisher of the *Saturday Evening Post*, George H. Lorimer, journalist and then editor of the *Post*, J. B. Stetson, the hat manufacturer, and John Wanamaker, merchant, all wealthy or at the least well-to-do men, lived within a short radius from the Pounds. Several of these neighbors even dined at the Pound home. The 1907 fire at Lyndehurst, the Wanamaker mansion, where Pound and his father rushed to rescue several (faked) old masters, vividly remained in Pound's imagination. There may well have been some Oriental objects saved.

One result of the growing collections of Oriental art among Philadelphians was the development of the Asian collection at the Philadelphia Museum of Art. Capitalizing on the presence of Oriental furniture, ceramics, lacquerware, and other decorative arts from the Chinese, Japanese, and Indian exhibitors at the 1876 Philadelphia Centennial Exhibition, the museum rapidly expanded its Oriental holdings. Donations by others enhanced the collection; the appointment of the distinguished Orientalist Langdon Warner as director of the museum in 1917 meant the establishment of the Division of Eastern Art, which in 1923 alone acquired over 750 Chinese ceramics, including a set of tomb figures. The expansion of the Oriental department meant that by 1928, when the new building opened, the museum could display an evocative Chinese scholar's study as well as a Japanese ceremonial teahouse.[7] The following year the museum purchased a large group of Chinese paintings—and Homer and Isabel Pound decided to remain permanently in Rapallo, where their son had moved. Notifying a neighbor to send the silver and portraits, they auctioned off the rest of their goods. The house itself was sold in July 1930.

What would Pound have seen in looking at Chinese art in the parlor or museum? In landscapes, called in Chinese "mountain and water pictures," he could discover an art of wild solitudes and wide prospects with possibly a contemplative figure in a secluded pavilion. Exhilaration, through the action of nature from torrents to peaks, combined with a sense of peace. The Chinese convention was to lift the viewer above the earth, the high horizon of the painting filled with mountain forms and the absence of detail in the foreground. Liberating spaces lead the eye. Importantly, as Pound's later friend and scholar of Chinese painting Laurence Binyon wrote, "painting for the Chinese is a branch of handwriting"; all the brushstrokes must flow. Such art, Binyon added in a comment apt for Pound, "is concerned with relations rather than with objects."[8] Placing an object in relation to another, or to space, transforms it from a fact to an idea; this transformation Chinese painting repeatedly performs, as does Pound, who in the later parts of *The Cantos* has empty space dominate through gaps between lines or indentations. Pound met Binyon in February 1909, attended his lectures on Oriental and European art the following month, and frequently visited him at the British Museum with his soon-to-be wife, Dorothy Shakespear, who often copied Chinese paintings while Binyon and Pound talked.

The images of China depicted on the paintings, porcelain, silks, and lacquerware, which re-created a mythical and mysterious China, reproduced in the Chinese landscape environments around Philadelphia, were idyllic and exotic. In execution the art was also focused, precise, clear, objective, elegant in detail, and in harmony with nature. Such visual imagery of China influenced Pound's own response to matters and objects Chinese, whether through wallpaper, furniture, teapots or woodcuts, written characters or paintings. Contradicting anti-Oriental sentiment expressed in other parts of the country (and formalized in the notorious exclusion laws renewed by the U.S. Congress in 1904–5), the widespread materiality of China in Philadelphia, where the culture of the Orient was held in high regard, strongly affected Pound's vision of this world.

The culture of China, expressed through its imagery and art, goods and skills, initiated an early but broadly based fascination and responsiveness to the Orient in Pound that would soon take form in his poetry, from *Cathay* to *The Cantos*. His later appreciation of Confucius through Fenollosa and literature through James Legge, H. A. Giles, and others had its grounding in his culturally situated "Philadelphia Orientalism."[9] To state matters concisely: the genealogy of Pound's Orientalism originated in Philadelphia.

The modest Oriental art that inhabited the Pound household was not, then, unusual. Throughout America, Oriental objects and furniture, art and silks, found a place. Pound's reaction to it informed his imagination, not only in such practical ways as drawing the Seven Lakes Canto (Canto 49) from a small book of Chinese and Japanese poems made of silk and rice paper that unfolded like a screen with accompanying Oriental paintings, but in his broader response to the Chinese prints, arts and crafts, and calligraphy he likely saw or was aware of as he grew up in Philadelphia.[10] This awareness led to an "Orient of style," as well as an Orient of text, forms of inscribing the East that originated in America's interest in Chinese art and culture.

"Restraint . . . drives the master toward intensity and the tyro toward aridity," wrote Pound in *The Spirit of Romance* (*SR*, 18). His comment refers to language and the value of the Orient as a style. This concentration on intensity relates to Pound's understanding of the function of language, combining what he read in Emerson with what he understood in Fenollosa to create an "Orient of style."[11] It begins with Pound's view of nature, where language is constituted entirely by particular signs for which translation into verbal terms is not adequate:

> In nature are signatures
> needing no verbal tradition,
> oak leaf never plane leaf.
>
> (87/593)

This emulates Emerson's view of language in "Nature." He, too, understood not only that nature precedes language but that "a leaf, a drop, a crystal, a moment of time is related to the whole, and partakes of the perfection of the whole. Each particle is a microcosm, and faithfully renders the likeness of the world."[12] In Emerson's concept of language Pound discovered a blend of Oriental and American symbolism: "From the colour the nature / & by the nature the sign!" (90/625), he writes in Canto 90. Combining this view with Confucian concentration resulted in an aesthetic Pound summed up in this 1939 statement about his writing: "There is *no intentional* obscurity. There is condensation to maximum attainable. It is impossible to make the deep as quickly comprehensible as the shallow" (*SL*, 322–23).

For Emerson, "words are signs of natural facts" ("Nature," 20). For Fenollosa, reading Chinese was like "watching *things* work out their own fate."[13] Emerson prepared for Pound's Oriental imagism and understanding of the function of language, charting the way for his acceptance of Fenollosa. Pound, quoting Aquinas, echoes this shared reading: "Names are the consequence of things" (*GB*, 92). Earlier, to Harriet Monroe, Pound declared that "language is made out of concrete things" (*SL*, 49). Chinese for Pound meant the recovery or reinvention of Adamic speech, "in which words contain the essence of the things they name," a return to the world Emerson had outlined.[14] Chinese was for Pound the restitution of what Emerson saw as the special requirement of language: to "fasten words again to visible things."[15]

In "Poetry and Imagination," Emerson actually articulates a method Pound, especially in *The Pisan Cantos*, relied on:

> While the student ponders this immense unity, he observes that all things in
> nature, the animals, the mountain, the river, the seasons, wood, iron, stone,
> vapour,—have a mysterious relation to his thoughts and life . . . he is com-
> pelled to speak by means of them.[16]

Pound, in terms less connected to nature but equally intense, wrote,
"When one really feels and thinks, one stammers with simple speech" (*SL*,
49). Or conversely, as he writes in Canto 74/448, "A lizard upheld me."

Seeing and responding to this world is a mutual process activated by
Emerson's "transparent eyeball: I am nothing; I see all; the currents of the
Universal Being circulate through me" ("Nature," 10). In Pound this be-
comes the light and sun of Canto 83 of *The Pisan Cantos* and the "acorn
of light" of Cantos 106 and 116 (106/775, 116/815). And for Pound, "Where
love is, there is the eye," quoting the Neoplatonist Richard of St. Victor
(90/629). The eye, as Emerson wrote, "is the first circle; the horizon
which it forms is the second" ("Circles," 403).

But if there is an Orient of style, there is also an Orient of text—in the
case of Pound, the establishment of a visual fabric that relates to the verbal
matter of his poems. His response to Oriental art, originating in "Philadel-
phia Orientalism," may be the source of this awareness, later supple-
mented by his instruction from Binyon, work on the Fenollosa notebooks,
and his response to Nō theater. Again, *The Cantos* demonstrate this most
clearly, not only with their incorporation of actual visual elements such as
literal signs (see 22/103 or 34/171 or 71/418), musical notations and the sym-
bols from a deck of cards, but in the Chinese ideograms (entire pages are,
of course, devoted to them: see Cantos 77/487, 85/573), illustrated capitals,
and elegant typography of the text. What I am calling the "Orient of text"
occurs when the visual interacts—and sometimes dominates—the linguis-
tic. These signifying functions form a bibliographic code that at times con-
tests the linguistic code of the work, but at other times reinforces it.[17]
Meaning is transmitted through their exchange.

The "Orient of text" joins two forms of perception, Pound presenting
a visual image at the same time he outlines a rhetorical function. Different
fonts and sizes establish different codes or strategies for reading; as he ex-
plains in a letter, "ALL typographic disposition, placings of words *on* the
page, is intended to facilitate the reader's intonation, whether he be read-
ing silently to self or aloud to friends" (*SL*, 322). This combination of ap-
pearance and meaning, or text and sound, is Pound's "phanopeia,"

loosely defined as constructing the page as a visual field. The decorative materials in *The Cantos*, whether elaborately presented as in *A Draft of XVI Cantos* with elegant illustrations by the artist Henry Strater from the Three Mountains Press in Paris (1925), a work recalling the ornamental books of William Morris, or in finely printed late editions of his work, such as the 110 copies of *Redondillas* (1968), each copy with Pound's signature, demonstrate Pound's concern with the physical form as well as the linguistic meaning of his writing.

Further examples of the "visual field" in Pound's texts are those individual pages of *The Cantos* where ideograms compete with linguistic statement in several languages, marrying the world of borders with limitless horizons, to echo Emerson. The East and West unite, visually demonstrating what Emerson, as well as Fenollosa, desired. The visual and the verbal function cognitively and imagistically, parallel to what occurs in Oriental art. Melopoeia of the ideogrammic page is subtlely presented via the superscript numbers, which are the conventional signs used by linguists to indicate the tonal values to be given to the phonetic equivalents of the ideographic characters (see, for example, Canto 93/649). In simple terms, Pound's "Orient of the text" resides in its spatial relations, something he was aware of as early as 1913, when he experimented with the form of his most famous haiku, "In a Station of the Metro." As is well documented, the imagistic poem took various shapes before it reached its final spatial form of two distinct lines.[18]

Spatial relations structure texts and their meaning, and in his creation of textual arabesques, Pound drew on traditions that he believed enhanced each other. Chinese art is one of those traditions, for as Binyon in his 1935 essay on Chinese painting remarked, "the spacing of Chinese design . . . is its most original factor" (12). The empty part of a painting is not something left out but a vital, integral element, "although symmetry is deserted" (12). This in many ways summarizes *The Cantos*. Pound knew that how we see a text, that is, how and where it is printed, determines how we understand its meaning. "In the 'Metro' hokku, I was careful, I think, to indicate spaces between the rhythmic units, and I want them observed," he instructed the editor of *Poetry* magazine, Harriet Monroe (*SL*, 17). The materiality and form of a text in the hands of Pound demonstrate his effort to link the Orient with the Occident.

The shape of a text visually and materially codes its reading; the physical shape of a book or essay on the page embodies a code of meaning that readers decipher, with the graphic and the linguistic interacting in the form of type, paper, size, pictures, and even binding. How we understand a text is often a function of how we literally see it. A series of American texts—illustrated, carefully designed and presented, such as the various and reordered editions of Whitman's *Leaves of Grass*—shows that this, too, was an element of American writing witnessed by Pound.[19]

American poetry, which also contributed to Pound's idea of the Orient, took early note of the East, drawn to its mysterious potential. The first American ship to sail to the East made its journey in 1784. To mark its departure, Philip Freneau published a poem that anticipated the treasures it would discover, one verse reading

> From thence their fragrant TEAS to bring
> Without the leave of Britain's king;
> and PORCELAIN WARE, enchas'd in gold,
> The produce of that finer mould.[20]

Whitman's "Passage to India," some eighty-nine years later, sustained the romance of the East.

Pound was said to be Longfellow's grandnephew; regardless, the young poet knew the elder poet's work. In fact, it was read to him often by his maternal grandmother, Mary Weston, a descendant of the Wadsworths (hence the family connection to the distinguished poet), whenever she visited. Objects again linked the Pounds with Longfellow: a grandfather clock stood in the parlor of the Wyncote home, having been in the Wayside Inn of Longfellow's popular (and favored by Pound) poem "Tales of a Wayside Inn."

While there are few direct references to the Orient in Longfellow's poetry, the rhythms and exoticism of the East are present. "Sandalphon," focusing on Talmudic legends and ancient lore of the Near East, or the tales of the Spanish Jew in "Tales of a Wayside Inn," suggest the presence of East in the narratives of the travelers. The student in that poem declares in fact that the stories of the Spanish Jew have transported all to the Orient:

> Your glittering caravan
> On the road that leadeth to Ispahan
> Hath led us farther to the East
> Into the regions of Cathay.[21]

Longfellow's late poem "Kéramos," dealing with a potter in the Near East, parallels Fitzgerald's *Rubayait,* while his "Hermes Trismegistus" celebrates the magical powers of the East, which Longfellow found poetically suggestive and alluring. He acknowledged the importance of the Orient as early as his inaugural lecture as professor of poetry at Bowdoin College. Titled "Origin and Growth of the Languages of Southern Europe and of Their Literature" (1830), the lecture emphasized the "oriental pomp and magnificence of expression" that characterized the Spanish language and traced the origins of French drama and chivalric romances to Oriental ideas.[22]

Other examples of Longfellow's Oriental awareness appear in his popular terza rima translation of Dante's *Divine Comedy,* a translation Pound likely read at some point, given its popularity, his early appreciation of Longfellow, and his developing interest in Italian and Dante's work. In Canto I of *Purgatorio,* Longfellow identifies the sun as possessing the "sweet colour of the Oriental Sapphire, / That was upgathered in the cloudless aspect / Of the pure air." Later, in *Paradiso,* Canto XXXI, Longfellow writes, "I lifted up mine eyes, and as at morn / The oriental part of the horizon / Surpasses that wherein the sun goes down." Longfellow's sense of the Orient was related to anticipation, emergence, and light, combined with a sense of the exotic. Longfellow's interest in the Orient continued throughout his career, from reading a comparative study of Confucius and Mahomet, to James Legge's account of Mencius. Books on voyages to China and on Buddhism rounded out his investigations.[23] But it may have been Longfellow the translator that appealed most to Pound: in *Confucius to Cummings,* Pound includes Longfellow's translation of Santa Teresa d'Avila's poem "Bookmark."[24]

Another poet immensely popular during Pound's youth was James Whitcomb Riley, who found midwestern life and Hoosier dialect the key to his fame. It was poetry as informal speech, filled with natural if ungrammatical expressions, as in the widely successful "Little Orphan Annie." Pound found some of Riley's poetry in an anthology of popular poetry at the Disciplinary Training Center outside Pisa and asked in Canto 80, "wd/Whitcomb Riley be still found in a highbrow anthology" (80/530)? Yet Riley, for all his naturalistic, dialect poetry, also found his way into Pound's Orient. In *The Classic Anthology Defined by Confucius,* Pound borrowed Riley's style for several Confucian Odes; one translation reads

Yaller bird, let my corn alone,
Yaller bird, let my crawps alone,
These folks here wont' let me eat,
I wanna go back whaar I can meet
the folks I used to know at home,
　　　I got a home an' I wanna git goin'.

Another reads, "Ole Brer Rabbit watchin' his feet, / Rabbit net's got the pheasant beat." Pound's ear overlaid the eccentric spellings, dialect, and idiosyncratic format of Riley's work on that of Confucius, giving the classic Chinese Odes a distinctly American flavor. Pound's appreciation of Riley also meant his inclusion of the poem "Good-By er Howdy-Do" in the *Confucius to Cummings* anthology.[25]

Pound did not formally study American literature: he took courses in English literature, Anglo-Saxon, and Romance languages at the University of Pennsylvania and Hamilton. Informally, however, he read Whitman with H.D., and Emerson at Hamilton College. Both writers, of course, elaborate ideas of the Orient and further aided Pound's emerging concept of the East.

Pound's early encounters with these figures were not always positive, but the lasting effects of such confrontations appear everywhere—from individual essays such as "What I Feel about Walt Whitman," to citations of these American writers throughout *The Cantos*. Like other young university students at the beginning of the twentieth century, Pound's study of the major writers of nineteenth-century America was haphazard. But so, too, was his reaction to them, one of dismissal, rejection, and critique—especially if one had ideas of reshaping and restructuring American expression. American masters were to be overthrown; anyone with avant-garde, soon-to-be imagist ideas needed to criticize those who went before. So praise is damning and only sometimes faint. In his essay on Robert Frost, for example, Pound grudgingly writes that "Even Emerson had sufficient elasticity of mind to find something in the 'yawp.' One doesn't need to like a book or a poem or a picture in order to recognize artistic vigor" (*LE*, 384). The "yawp" reference is to Whitman, with whom Pound had a complicated association.

In 1909, Pound would declare, "Mentally I am a Walt Whitman who has learned to wear a collar and a dress shirt" and that "Whitman is to my fatherland . . . what Dante is to Italy" (*SP*, 145, 146). But by June 1913,

Pound could write his father from London that "Whitman is a hard nutt. The *Leaves of Grass* is the book. It is impossible to read it without swearing at the author almost continuously" (*SL*, 21). In August 1918, he would tell John Quinn, "I have always insisted that I was Walt, no doubt about our identity, epluribusunum, Walt and I are, were, etc." (*L/JQ*, 160). However, a tension always existed between the two: "Personally," writes Pound,

> I might be very glad to conceal my relationship to my spiritual father and brag about my more congenial ancestry—Dante, Shakespeare, Theocritus, Villon, but the descent is a bit difficult to establish. (*SP*, 145–46)[26]

The strain between Pound and Whitman is symptomatic of his reading and response to his nineteenth-century American predecessors—although he would likely have been pleased to learn that selections from Confucius were read at Whitman's funeral.[27] But these American masters remained part of Pound's literary psyche, even as he rejected and criticized them, Emerson no less so.

Emerson established a typology of difference between the worlds of the West and the East. Pound, however, challenged this separation as he discovered through poetry how the world of the East—its language, forms, imagery, and reference—could enhance and enlarge the history, action, and values of the America he would construct most notably in *The Cantos*. And let there be no doubt about Pound's identity: "I don't have to *try* to be American. . . . Am I American?" he asks. "Yes, and buggar [*sic*] the present state of the country, the utter betrayal of the American Constitution." Reflecting his union between America and China, Pound declares that "An Ars Poetica [for America] might in time evolve from the *Ta Hio*" (*SL*, 322).

Emerson's essay "Plato," found in *Representative Men* (1850), further clarified American literary Orientalism. In his celebration of Plato as the great unifier of East and West, Emerson offers some defining contrasts:

> The unity of Asia, and the detail of Europe; the infinitude of the Asiatic soul, and the defining, result-loving, machine-making, surface-seeking, opera-going Europe,—Plato came to join, and by contact, to enhance the energy of each. ("Plato," 640)[28]

Here, the opposition between East and West is clear and, for a young writer, distinct. But Plato, to his credit, could also discriminate: "he leaves with Asia the vast and superlative; he is the arrival of accuracy and intelligence" ("Plato," 637).

Unity and variety become the defining strategies of these two complementary but distinct worlds. Differences once more are drawn:

> The country of unity, of immovable institutions . . . of men faithful in doctrine and in practice to the idea of a deaf, unimplorable, immense fate, is Asia. . . . On the other side, the genius of Europe is active and creative. . . . If the East loved infinity, the West delighted in boundaries. ("Plato," 640)

Representation of the practical ethics of Confucius, as seen in the work of Emerson and others, partially shaped Pound's admiration for the Confucian notion of the guiding leader who evolves into the patron and political strongman. Malatesta and Mussolini stand as examples. Emerson's representation of Confucius and Mencius as establishing a government that regulates society by philosophic principles was fundamental to Pound. The importance of morally founded regulations also appealed to Pound, who understood that for the American transcendentalists, "the Orient was the home of the oldest philosophic truths; [but] to the British Romanticists it was a source of poetic glamour."[29] Confucius asks a question that Emerson copied in his journal of 1843 and that summarizes Pound's later position: "If I follow not men, whom shall I follow? If the world were in possession of right principles, I should not seek to change it." This, to Pound, was a cry to action. But what would appeal to Pound even more strongly than the convergence of idealism and politics is Emerson's further statement on the Chinese philosopher: "Confucius, sage of the Absolute East, was a *middle* man. He is the *Washington* of philosophy, the *Moderator* . . . of modern history."[30] "Washington" is an eponymous pun, referring to both George Washington, the first American president, and the nation's capital.

A further Confucian idea noted by Emerson of immense importance to Pound is that "the accomplished scholar is not a utensil!" which Emerson expressed in this way: "we are not pans and barrows, nor even porters of the fire and torch bearers, but children of the fire, made of it" ("The Poet," 447).[31] To elevate the scholar in society was of great importance for Pound. Also of importance was sincerity, crucial for Confucius, because it leads to what is right and important for Emerson. Correct behavior, in Pound's later writing, reaches forceful if not strident heights. And through Emerson on Confucius, Pound might have conceived the following paradigm: sincere thoughts lead to clear hearts, which lead to cultured people. They, in turn, lead to regulated families and then to a state rightly governed. This means a happy and orderly and morally just empire.[32] For Pound, Emerson's presentation of Confucius meant ethics.

While Emerson outlined philosophic exchanges between the West and the East, and in his later writings explored the metaphysical connection between transcendentalism and Oriental religions, another form was affecting the literary ethos of nineteenth-century Americans: the Oriental tale.[33] This popular genre became significant from the 1780s onward with the opening of trade in the Indian Ocean and China Sea and the proliferation of magazines. It dramatically affected the work of Poe, Hawthorne, Emily Dickinson, and Melville. Such tales were "philosophically enriching and aesthetically liberating." Whitman in "Passage to India" explained that one of his literary goals was to "Eclaircise the myths Asiatic, the primitive fables . . . eluding the hold of the known, mounting to heaven!"[34] The unusual term "Eclaircise" means to clear up or enlighten or clarify the marvelous myths of the East, which would, in turn, free North Americans from the restraints of puritanism and regulation.

Oriental fiction transposed to America found expression in short stories by Poe like "Psychic Zenobia" and in Hawthorne's novel *The Blithedale Romance* (1852) with the dark, mysterious, and Oriental woman Zenobia (also the heroine of William Ware's best-selling novel of 1838, *Zenobia*) the center of intrigue and romance. This Oriental tale mixed secular adventure with Eastern philosophy, drawing on the Syrian princess of the same name. Oriental devices competed with Oriental thought to motivate the American literary imagination in the nineteenth century. Such devices aestheticized writers' work and provided their visionary fiction and allegorical tales with new resources and forms of stylization.[35]

Pound absorbed the American topos of the Orient before he left for Europe in 1908—and such an American orientation guided him through his encounter with Fenollosa, study of Oriental masterworks, and the shaping of such texts as *The Pisan Cantos* and his anthology *Confucius to Cummings*, where Melville and Whitman vie with Whittier and Bret Harte. But Oriental art, as much as Fenollosa or Confucius, constructed Pound's East. Furthermore, the early picture of Confucius presented in these American texts also prepared the way for his later understanding of this great thinker.

Supplementing Pound's knowledge of the Orient, rooted in the fine and decorative arts introduced to him in Philadelphia, was Pound's sketchy reading of nineteenth-century American literature and its presentation of the philosophic, religious, and moral concepts of the East. This second-stage Orientalism—the first being his encounter with Chinese art—prepared him for his later entanglement with the Orient, encountered again in London through Laurence Binyon and then the work of Ernest Fenollosa. More specifically, Pound's "Philadelphia Orientalism" and awareness of American literary Orientalism prepared him to accept Nō theater and Confucius. As he announced in 1915, "this century may find a new Greece in China."[36]

Prefiguring Pound's obsession with ideograms, minimalist expression, and order, emerging from his study of Fenollosa, Nō, and Confucius, was his response to an earlier American discourse of the Orient that was material as well as exotic, but atmospheric rather than poetic. As Mary de Rachewiltz remarked in a different context, "wherever we find *The Cantos,* there we find America."[37] This is no different for Pound's conception of the Orient.

Collectively, what those American writers who represented the Orient did for Pound was construct an Orient and a language that provided an "Other—first glimpsed in its art"—for the young and ambitious writer. But whereas the nineteenth-century American construction of the Orient was of a passive and metaphysical kingdom, Pound's was active and alive, directly experienced through the notebooks of Fenollosa and re-created in the world of *Cathay* and the ideals of Confucius. But Oriental art in an American context provided the first step, theorized by Edward Said when he wrote that "space acquires emotional and even rational sense by a kind of poetic process, whereby the vacant or anonymous reaches of distance are converted into meaning for us here."[38]

Pound sought to conquer the distance between himself and the Orient not through sustaining an "imaginative geography" but through the direct absorption of a world manifested and made possible through his immediate engagement with its imagery and symbolic language, later formalized in his study of Fenollosa, Nō drama, and Confucius.[39] Pound did not reject the Orient of Philadelphia, or of Longfellow, Emerson, or Whitman. He seized it to frame an entrance to a much larger and encompassing room.

NOTES

1. Hugh Kenner in *The Pound Era* (Berkeley and Los Angeles: University of California Press, 1971), 265, and James J. Wilhelm in *The American Roots of Ezra Pound* (New York: Garland, 1985), 68, attribute the picture book to Hiram Walker, Pound's great-great-grandfather on the Weston side of the family. It was supposedly given to him by a Chinese merchant when Hiram was a seaman. Zhaoming Qian in "Pound and Chinese Art in the 'British Museum Era,'" in *Ezra Pound and Poetic Influences*, ed. Helen Dennis (Amsterdam: Rodopi, 2000), however, has determined that the book originally belonged to "Aunt Frank," according to Richard Taylor and Mary de Rachewiltz, whose authority is Pound. In a discarded fragment for *The Cantos*, Pound wrote, "and my gt aunt's third husband / received in ms / from a friend / the 49th canto." The volume became a key source for the Seven Lakes Canto, Canto 49. See also Qian's essay in this volume.

2. H.D. in Wilhelm, *American Roots*, 102.

3. Noel Stock, *The Life of Ezra Pound* (1970; San Francisco: North Point Press, 1982), 176.

4. Ellen Paul Denker, *After the Chinese Taste: China's Influence in America, 1730–1930* (Salem, Mass.: Peabody Museum of Salem, 1985), 21; see also Jonathan Goldstein, *Philadelphia and the China Trade, 1682–1846* (University Park: Pennsylvania State University Press, 1978), 78. Earlier, in 1796, the merchant Andreas van Braam, a Dutch-born American China trader, arrived in Philadelphia with an entourage of Chinese servants and a large collection of Chinese goods. He settled in Croydon, Pennsylvania, and built China Retreat, a home in the Chinese style with a cupola in the form of a pagoda. In addition to furnishings, van Braam's collection included more than eighteen hundred Oriental drawings.

5. Denker, *After the Chinese Taste*, 43.

6. Goldstein, *Philadelphia and China Trade*, 7. Interestingly, the young country also sought to construct its cultural evolution in the East, whether Near or Far. When the new America chose symbols for its *Novus Ordo Seclorum* (new order of the ages) on its one-dollar bill, it turned not only to the fasces of Rome but beyond, to the pyramids of Egypt. On the left-hand side of the back of every American one-dollar bill is an unfinished Egyptian pyramid of thirteen layers—one for each original colony, as there are thirteen letters in the Latin motto above the American eagle on the right-hand side of the dollar, *E Pluribus Unum* (out of many, one). On top of the pyramid is an all-seeing eye, "The Eye of Providence," forming a smaller pyramid staring out from the pinnacle at the top. The phrase on the banner beneath the pyramid is, indeed, *Novus Ordo Seclorum*. The East meets the West on green-colored paper. Orientalism—Egyptian, Turkish, Chinese, and Indian—indisputably pervaded the literature and symbols of America in the nineteenth century.

7. For details on the Oriental collection, see *Philadelphia Museum of Art: Handbook of the Collections*, ed. Sherry Babbitt (Philadelphia: Philadelphia Museum of Art, 1995), 24–48.

8. Laurence Binyon, "Painting," in *Chinese Art: An Introductory Handbook*, ed. Roger Fry et al. (London: B. T. Batsford, 1935), 7, 12. On Pound's poetic concepts drawn from Binyon's explication of Chinese art, see Woon-Ping Chin Holaday, "Pound and Binyon: China via the British Museum," *Paideuma* 6 (1977): 27–36. Binyon in *Painting in the Far East* (London: Arnold, 1908), the first work of its kind in English to interpret the aims of Oriental painting, stresses that painting in East Asia is the art of line, not color. He also emphasizes that a copy is not an imitation. In *Guide to an Exhibition of Chinese and Japanese Paintings* (London: British Museum, 1910), Binyon states that "not to render the external aspect but the animated spirit, the character the genius of things, is the artist's aim" (10). Pound, of course, would share this view.

9. Explicitly, I refer to Binyon's *Painting in the Far East*, Ernest Fenollosa's notebooks and "The Chinese Written Character" *(CWC)*, and Herbert A. Giles's *A History of Chinese Literature* (New York: Appleton, 1901). Of course, many other works contributed to Pound's grasp of China's language and culture. Interestingly, Philadelphia appears throughout *The Cantos*. See especially Cantos 62, 70, 89.

10. For detailed descriptions of the screen book, see Zhaoming Qian's essay in this volume; Daniel D. Pearlman, *The Barb of Time: On the Unity of Ezra Pound's Cantos* (New York: Oxford University Press, 1969), appendix B, 304–11; and Sanehid Kodama, "The Eight Scenes of Sho-Sho," *Paideuma* 6 (1977): 131–45.

11. The phrase is Beryl Schlossman's. See *The Orient of Style: Modernist Allegories of Conversion* (Durham: Duke University Press, 1991). The term partly originates in Proust's description of beautiful representation as the "poetic dazzle of the Orient." The phrase implies the emergence of writing "as a work of style that masks the author's sentiments" (5), giving some form of poetic expression.

12. Ralph Waldo Emerson, "Nature," in *Essays and Lectures* (New York: Library of America, 1983), 29–30. Unless otherwise indicated, all further citations to Emerson's prose are to this edition.

13. Fenollosa quoted in Robert Kern, *Orientalism, Modernism, and the American Poem* (Cambridge: Cambridge University Press, 1996), 11.

14. Murray Cohen, *Sensible Words: Linguistic Practice in England, 1640–1785* (Baltimore: Johns Hopkins University Press, 1977), 143.

15. Kern, *Orientalism, Modernism*, 22.

16. Emerson quoted in ibid., 29.

17. The terms are Jerome McGann's. See *The Textual Condition* (Princeton: Princeton University Press, 1991), 56–57. See Canto 87/591 where, within three lines, an ideogram, English, and Greek visually and linguistically compete for meaning. Pound even incorporates hieroglyphics, as in Canto 93/643, 644, 647, 651. On the subject of hieroglyphics and American writing, see John T. Irwin, *American Hieroglyphics: The Symbol of the Egyptian Hieroglyphics in the American Renaissance* (New Haven: Yale University Press, 1980), especially part 1 on Emerson, Thoreau,

and Whitman, 3–42. For Pound's development of these devices, see Nadel, "Visualizing History: Pound and the Chinese Cantos," in *A Poem Containing History: Textual Studies in "The Cantos,"* ed. Lawrence Rainey (Ann Arbor: University of Michigan Press, 1997), 151–66.

18. The form of the poem as it first appeared in *Poetry* for April 1913 was

The apparition   of these faces   in the crowd:
Petals   on a wet, black   bough.

The form of the poem, as it appeared in *Lustra* (1916), differed:

The apparition of these faces in the crowd;
Petals on a wet, black bough.

19. "Passage to India," for example, was not integrated into the full text of *Leaves of Grass* until the 1881 edition, although it had appeared as an "annex" to the 1871–72 edition. Similarly, Pound kept revising, adding, and correcting elements of *The Cantos* throughout his life—and what constitutes the ending of the poem still remains in dispute.

20. Freneau quoted in Denker, *After the Chinese Taste*, 17.

21. Henry Wadsworth Longfellow, "Tales of a Wayside Inn," in *The Poetical Works of Longfellow*, Cambridge edition (Boston: Houghton Mifflin, 1975), 248.

22. Longfellow quoted in Luther S. Luedtke, *Nathaniel Hawthorne and the Romance of the Orient* (Bloomington: Indiana University Press, 1989), 146.

23. On Longfellow's reading, see the entries in Kenneth Walter Cameron, *Longfellow's Reading in Libraries* (Hartford, Conn.: Transcendental Books, 1973), nos. 238, 273, 340 411, 553, 594, 685.

24. See *Confucius to Cummings: An Anthology of Poetry*, ed. Ezra Pound and Marcella Spann (New York: New Directions, 1964), 127. Pound also cites Longfellow in "Patria Mia," *SP*, 124.

25. *The Classic Anthology Defined by Confucius*, trans. Ezra Pound (Cambridge: Harvard University Press, 1954), 100, 35. For a recent account of Riley and his importance, see Elizabeth J. van Allen, *James Whitcomb Riley: A Life* (Bloomington: Indiana University Press, 1999). See also *Confucius to Cummings*, 276–77.

26. Ezra Pound, "What I Feel about Walt Whitman," *SP*, 145–46. See also Hugh Witemeyer, "Clothing the American Adam: Pound's Tailoring of Walt Whitman," in *Ezra Pound among the Poets*, ed. George Bornstein (Chicago: University of Chicago Press, 1985), 81–105.

27. See Gay Wilson Allen, *The Solitary Singer: A Critical Biography of Walt Whitman* (New York: New York University Press, 1967), 543.

28. On American literary Orientalism, see Beongcheon Yu, *The Great Circle: American Writers and the Orient* (Detroit: Wayne State University Press, 1983), 15–22; Luedtke, *Nathaniel Hawthorne*, 63–67; Marwan M. Obeidat, *American Literature and Orientalism* (Berlin: K. Schwarz Verlag, 1998).

29. Arthur Christy, *The Orient in American Transcendentalism* (1932; New York: Octagon Books, 1978), 50.

30. Emerson, *The Journals and Miscellaneous Notebooks,* ed. Ralph H. Orth and Alfred R. Ferguson (Cambridge: Belknap Press of Harvard University Press, 1971), 8:410; 9:318.

31. See Confucius, *The Analects,* in *The Chinese Classics,* trans. James Legge (London: Trubner, 1861), 2:12.

32. See Christy, *Orient in American Transcendentalism,* 135–36.

33. On Emerson's philosophic and religious use of the East, see Carl T. Jackson, *The Oriental Religions and American Thought* (Westport, Conn.: Greenwood Press, 1981); and Carl T. Jackson, "Oriental Ideas in American Thought," in *Dictionary of Ideas,* ed. Phillip P. Wiener (New York: Scribners, 1973), 3:427–39.

34. David Reynolds, *Beneath the American Renaissance* (New York: Knopf, 1988), 41; Whitman, "Passage to India," in *Complete Poetry and Collected Prose* (New York: Library of America, 1982), 531.

35. Reynolds, *Beneath the American Renaissance,* 45–53.

36. Pound, "The Renaissance," in *Poetry* 5, no. 5 (1915): 228; reprinted in *P&P,* 2:10. At the end of part 1, Pound adds the following: "Undoubtedly, pure color is to be found in Chinese poetry, when we begin to know enough about it; indeed a shadow of this perfection is already at hand in translations. Liu Ch'e, Chu Yuan, Chia I, and the great *vers libre* writers before the Petrarchan age of Li Po, are a treasure to which the next century may look for as great a stimulus as the renaissance had from the Greeks" (*LE,* 218; *P&P,* 2:13).

37. Mary de Rachewiltz, "Afterword: *Ubi Cantos, Ibi America,*" in Rainey, *A Poem Containing History,* 269.

38. Edward Said, *Orientalism* (1978; New York: Vintage, 1979), 57, 41.

39. See Derek Gregory, *Geographical Imaginations* (Cambridge, Mass.: Blackwell, 1994), 171.

Cathay: *What Sort of Translation?*

BARRY AHEARN

It is a bold man who will undertake to render into English a language he does not know. But Ezra Pound dared to be bold when the occasion demanded. In the autumn of 1914, while the newly mobilized armies of Europe tested each other's resolve on the battlefield, Pound essayed the mysterious, alluring Chinese poems in the Fenollosa papers. Much was at risk; in *Cathay* the celebrated (or infamous) imagist and vorticist would add further luster to his career—or demonstrate how badly he could fall on his face. Unless Pound could offer to the public a convincing document, what barbs mightn't his detractors plunge into his reputation—and make them stick? And there were detractors hovering in London. Pound's *Sonnets and Ballate of Guido Cavalcanti* (1912) had drawn fire from the *Times Literary Supplement*. Its reviewer, deeming Pound's versions inferior to those of Dante Gabriel Rossetti, made some ugly comments about the young American: "He is sometimes clumsy, and often obscure, and has no fine tact about language."[1] What would the *Times* say when Pound ventured beyond the Romance languages?

The odds seemed against him. For several centuries the standards for sucessful translation had been set rather high. Perhaps the most succinct summary of those standards appears in John Dryden's "Preface to the Translation of Ovid's Epistles" (1680):

> No man is capable of translating poetry, who, besides a genius to that art, is not a master both of his author's language, and of his own; nor must we understand the language only of the poet, but his particular turn of thoughts and expression, which are the characters that distinguish, and as it were individuate him from all other writers.[2]

This definition—or something comparable—remains the standard by which most critics assess translators. Consider, then, the difficulty that faced Pound when he took up the job of editing the late Ernest Fenollosa's manuscripts for publication. Dryden had stipulated that being "a genius to [the] art" of poetry amounted to one qualification, and Pound felt—despite the aspersions of *Times* reviewers—that in this respect he filled the bill. In regard to other requirements, however, he was woefully wanting. Hitherto Pound's translations had been restricted to European languages, living and dead, in which he had been trained at Hamilton College and the University of Pennsylvania. He could claim with some justification that, first, he knew the languages of Lope de Vega, Arnaut Daniel, Cavalcanti, and Bertran de Born, and, second, that he could follow their "particular turn of thoughts and expression." With respect to Chinese masters, however, Pound lacked the requisite expertise. Through the medium of the Fenollosa papers he could glimpse some of the characteristics of Chinese poetry, but he certainly could not produce a translation that Dryden would have found worthy of the name. What then could he do to avoid being pilloried in the press?

Hugh Kenner, Wai-lim Yip, Zhaoming Qian, and Ming Xie have each addressed this question of whether and to what degree the poems in *Cathay* may be considered translations. They have not, however, approached the issue from the perspective of Pound's obvious difficulty in the winter of 1914–15: that it would have been advisable for him to find some way, or ways, to prevent potential attacks on his qualifications as a translator. In this essay I hope to show that some features of *Cathay* can be attributed to Pound's intention to defuse the issue of his qualifications. Even though Pound spoke of the poems in *Cathay* as translations, and put his name on the title page, we also find him shifting the responsibility from his shoulders. The style achieved in *Cathay* can be partly attributed to Pound's intention to evade the burden of responsibility for the translation.

Before examining the style of *Cathay*, however, it will be fruitful to examine the ways in which Pound himself touched on the question of translation in regard to the poems in the Fenollosa papers. In various ways, he insisted that much of the work of translation had already been done. Pound's efforts to minimize his role as translator are evident in the first edition of *Cathay*, in the form of two commentaries. One appears at the beginning of the volume, the other at the end. The first of these is familiar to all readers of the poems because it has consistently been reprinted as a headnote: "For the most part from the Chinese of Rihaku, from the notes of the late Ernest Fenollosa, and the decipherings of the professors Mori and Ariga." The existence of this note (or should we call it a subtitle?) can be partly attributed to Pound's interest in documenting provenance. Pound frequently alerted readers to the fact that the words on the page have a history, that they exist as the latest link in a chain of transmission. The note implies that the production represents a collaborative effort, combining the labors of Mori, Ariga, Fenollosa, and Pound. Thus Pound appears to shift from his shoulders the sole responsibility for what has been produced. In this instance, however, the way he documents it raises an interesting problem; the note seems to cast doubt on the quality of the transmission. The initial and rather vague phrase, "For the most part," can, of course, be taken to mean that these are mostly Chinese poems—with the obvious exception of "The Seafarer." Most readers, however, probably understand the phrase as meaning that *(a)* the words of the poems are largely indebted to Chinese verse, but that *(b)* the author makes no claims to be a sinologist and is therefore uncertain to what extent the words he puts before his readers are faithful to the originals. Furthermore, as Hugh Kenner notes in *The Pound Era,* the reference to the contributions of Mori and Ariga as "decipherings" leaves the reader wondering about the professors' abilities.[3] "Deciphering" suggests the patient and attentive labor required to alter something obscure into something familiar. We decipher that which we do not know well. Thus Pound not only suggests that his role in the process of translation has been minimal, but calls into question the qualifications of two of his fellow translators. We are left, then, with the impression that the two Westerners responsible for *Cathay* hardly know any Chinese at all, and that the two Easterners involved have to grope for meaning. From whence, then, comes the authority for the translations? Why should the reader have any confidence that the poems that follow are worth reading?

When we turn to the afterword Pound wrote for the first edition, we find that the authority for the translation no longer rests with any particular translators. Rather, Pound implies that the authority comes from the poems themselves. The Chinese originals, he intimates, have certain qualities that enable Pound and company to ease the poems across a linguistic divide. These qualities, though never clearly specified, make the poems already comparable to Western poems. The afterword also reflects a somewhat ambiguous stance toward Pound's own status as a translator. It begins by noting that further poems remain unpublished, and suggests that Pound withholds them partly because his skills are not quite sufficient for the task. "I have not come to the end of Ernest Fenollosa's notes by a long way, nor is it entirely perplexity that caused me to cease from translation."[4] Nevertheless, Pound goes on to cite some lines from poems still in manuscript that he treats as if they present no difficulty to him. "True, I can find little to add to one line out of a certain poem: 'You know well where it was that I walked / When you had left me.' In another I find a perfect speech in a literality which will be to many most unacceptable. The couplet is as follows: 'Drawing sword, cut into water, water again flows: / Raise cup, quench sorrow, sorrow again sorry.'"[5] In this case Pound is not perplexed; he withholds the poem not because of his failed perception, but because some readers are not ready for it. Pound takes up most of the afterword to declare that the "personal hatred in which I am held by many" would spoil the reception of the poems. (This protestation again diverts attention from the issue of Pound's qualifications as a translator of Chinese.) Pound presents himself as a defender of the Chinese poems, of which he is publishing only a fraction. This fraction, he says, consists "only [of] those unquestionable poems." But what does Pound mean by "unquestionable"? He seems to mean that the nature of these poems—when translated into English—will be similar enough to English verse that English readers will find them acceptable. Pound leads his readers to believe that the original Chinese verses are of such high quality that even inexpert translators cannot greatly harm them. Pound has lowered the bar for translators, at least in respect to certain Chinese poems.

Pound's subsequent essay "Chinese Poetry" (1918) suggests an explanation for what he means by "unquestionable." That essay represents a sustained attempt to elide the differences between European and Chinese poetry. Pound indicates the poems he chose for *Cathay*, selected from a large body of poetry, are those with characteristics comparable to Western poetry. Here is another claim Pound can make for his abilities as a translator. He can be most successful with this particular selection because the poems already are, in significant but unspecified ways, like Western poetry. These poems have already gone halfway to meet his abilities.

In "Chinese Poetry," Pound cites two poems from *Cathay* as examples of how Chinese and Western poetic practices share common ground. In respect to "The Jewel Stairs' Grievance," Pound illustrates how the Western reader should approach the poem.

> I have never found any occidental who could "make much" of that poem at one reading. Yet upon careful examination we find that everything is there, not

merely by "suggestion" but by a sort of mathematical process of reduction. Let us consider what circumstances would be needed to produce just the words of this poem. You can play Conan Doyle if you like. (*P&P*, 3:85)

Pound begins his comment by noting how baffling the poem initially seems. By the end of his remarks, however, he likens the process whereby Western readers will acquaint themselves with the poem to that employed by Sherlock Holmes. Conan Doyle's stories, Pound supposes, have had such wide currency that the reader will find familiar the logical exercise required to unravel "The Jewel Stairs' Grievance." In other words, the Western reader's difficulty stems from his or her bringing to the poem reading habits that are ineffectual. The reader must switch to the practices suitable to a different genre—the detective story—before the poem reveals itself. What appears to be the most puzzling of the poems in *Cathay* turns out to be the one most available to the Western reader.

Pound's other example in "Chinese Poetry" is "The River-Merchant's Wife: A Letter." Here he also tries to convince us that East can meet West. He invokes Browning as a key to the mysteries of Chinese poetry.

Perhaps the most interesting form of modern poetry is to be found in Browning's "Men and Women." This kind of poem ... has had a curious history in the west. You may say it begins in Ovid's "Heroides," which purport to be letters written between Helen and Paris or by Œnone and other distinguished persons of classical pseudo-history; or you may find an earlier example in Theocritus' Idyl of the woman spinning at her sombre and magic wheel. From Ovid to Browning this sort of poem was very much neglected. It is interesting to find, in eighth-century China, a poem which might have been slipped into Browning's work without causing any surprise save by its simplicity and its naive beauty. (*P&P*, 3:108–9)

(Pound then prints "The River-Merchant's Wife: A Letter.") In his commentary Pound dismisses the differences between much Chinese and Western poetry. The Chinese, he asserts, have a long tradition of dramatic monologues. And so does the West. Pound tries hard to create a Western cousin to this Oriental tradition, although his remark that the Western one was "very much neglected" indicates that the tradition may be necessary fiction rather than ascertainable fact. Whether such a tradition exists in the West is beside the point. Pound needs such a tradition to create common ground between the West and Chinese poetry, a ground the translator can more easily cross.[6]

Thus far we have identified two ways in which Pound minimizes his job as translator. First, he shares the burden with Fenollosa, Mori, and Ariga (though on closer inspection, he calls their abilities into question and transfers credit to the poems themselves). Second, he contends that the poems in *Cathay* have qualities (some of which he specifies and some of which he does not) that make them amenable to translation. There is also a third strategy Pound employs to divert the reader's attention from his role as translator.

This third strategy is to include images in the poems that will strike the reader as recognizably Chinese because these images already seem Chinese, thanks to existing Western preconceptions about China. Since Pound depends upon such images being *obviously* taken as Chinese in nature, it is easy to extract them from the text. So easy, in fact, that one example will suffice. (Readers of *Cathay* can readily supplement them with their own.) "Taking Leave of a Friend" stipulates that the old acquaintances "bow over their clasped hands." Pound is depending on the Western presumption that when meeting or parting, the Chinese would behave in just this fashion. The friends in this poem must be Chinese because their posture is familiar as well as appropriate to the moment. Yet who can say whether the original poem must be translated just so? Herbert A. Giles's earlier version of the same poem renders the action differently: "To wave a last adieu we sought."[7] No bowing, no clasped hands. Could it be that Giles, whose knowledge of Chinese far surpassed Pound's, is closer to the truth? But in this case, as in others one could cite, getting closer to Li Bo's meaning produces a translation that the Western reader might well find less convincingly Chinese.

So far we have listed three ways in which Pound evades the burden of responsibility as translator. All of them have one thing in common. Each strategy implies that the original Chinese poems are quite comparable to modes of expression familiar to Western readers. To that extent, Pound's strategies seem consistent with what Lawrence Venuti describes as Western translation's tendency to postulate "the existence of a public sphere governed by universal reason."[8] Such a postulate, as Venuti says, produces translations that valorize "transparent discourse."[9] Indeed, our investigation of the poems thus far shows Pound implying that these "foreign" poems are not all that foreign. What ultimately results from the process of translation is a text supposedly conveying almost without deviation the original intention of the translated author. The reader falls for the "illusion that this is not a translation, but the foreign text, in fact, the living thoughts of the foreign author."[10]

Yet there is an alternative form of translation, albeit one seldom employed. This is the "foreignizing translation" that "signifies the difference of the foreign text."[11] This kind of translation disrupts the reader's expectation that the original is readily translatable into easily understood terminology. It is a method the translator uses in acknowledgment of the difference between the original text and the language with which the reader is conversant. The translator refuses to fold the original text into the linguistic practices of his own time and space. It is, in short, a way of respecting the integrity of the original.

Such a strategy, it might be thought, would also have the effect of bringing the translator into the foreground. Since such a translation often depends upon an archaic or unconventional vocabulary, the reader may be more aware that someone (the translator) is deliberately creating the translation. Yet in this case, as in others one could cite, the translator is revealed as someone who—like the reader—has a somewhat distant relation to the original text. To put it another way, the "foreignizing" translation brings the translator and the reader closer together. Both are revealed as facing an original that is pointedly not in their own tongue. Even as the translator becomes more visible to the reader, this translator becomes less and less the traditional sort of translator: the invisible adept who expertly straddles two languages.

What is remarkable about *Cathay* is that Pound uses both modes of translation. As we have seen, he adopted various strategies to suggest the virtual identity of Chinese poetry and Western literary forms. But he also "foreignized" the translations to remind his readers that there were unavoidable differences. Pound uses complicated means to make his translations seem authentically "foreign"—complicated because they depend upon delicate adjustments of diction. To put it succinctly, the poems of *Cathay* are often meant to sound like a slightly alien form of English. Perhaps the best way to illustrate what I mean is to once again compare two translations of a poem, one by Pound and one by someone who had a much better claim to being considered an expert on Chinese culture: W. A. P. Martin. Martin was a scholar and educator who worked in China for much of his life. For several years he was president of the Foreign University in Beijing. He also wrote several books about China.

In one of these, *The Lore of Cathay or, the Intellect of China* (1901), Martin published a translation of a poem by Li Bo, the same one that Pound was to translate a few years later as "The River-Merchant's Wife: A Letter." Martin, however, used a different title. Here is the first half of his version.

A SOLDIER'S WIFE TO HER HUSBAND

'Twas many a year ago—
  How I recall the day!—
When you, my own true love,
  Came first with me to play.

A little child was I,
  My head a mass of curls;
I gathered daisies sweet,
  Along with other girls.

You rode a bamboo horse,
  And deemed yourself a knight—
With paper helm and shield
  And wooden sword bedight.

Thus we together grew,
  And we together played—
Yourself a giddy boy,
  And I a thoughtless maid.[12]

With the sole exception of "bamboo" in line 9, the first half of Martin's translation would be indistinguishable from a dramatic monologue spoken by an English lass. The rest of the poem similarly takes pains to avoid non-Western discourse. Martin has discarded almost every detail that would render the poem foreign, including the title. The occupation of a soldier is a universal one, but that of a "river-merchant" will only be found in a country with broad rivers that stretch for hundreds of miles. (The fact that Pound has to hyphenate in order to indicate the husband's profession simply indicates that it is a neologism in English.) Martin also has eliminated the oriental reticence from the poem, thus transforming the speaker into someone who says exactly what is on her mind. Moreover, she speaks in familiar, well-worn terminology. Martin's translation provides no indication of what difference there might be between the Chinese and the Westerner. The translation seems entirely unaware that there might even be differences.

When we turn to Pound's version, we find a different strategy.

While my hair was still cut straight across my forehead
I played about the front gate, pulling flowers.
You came by on bamboo stilts, playing horse.
You walked about my seat, playing with blue plums.
And we went on living in the village of Chokan;
Two small people, without dislike or suspicion.[13]

Pound retains place-names and details specific to China, such as that re-
ferred to in the first line: tonsorial custom as it pertains to children. The
third line, which specifies the material from which the stilts are made
(bamboo), also shifts the poem into a local rather than a universal context.
Even more suggestive of an alien sensibility, however, are the strange
choices Pound makes with respect to diction. Consider, for example, the
phrase "pulling flowers." Martin's version of this act is simple and famil-
iar: she "gathered daisies." Pound, however, has selected an unconven-
tional participle. A look at the *New Oxford English Dictionary* shows
that Pound has not invented a new way of describing the action of re-
moving a flower from the ground or from its stalk. English does indeed
have a history of using *pulling* in that sense. Nevertheless, the most com-
mon choice in the early twentieth century would be to write *picking* or,
perhaps, *plucking*. Pound, in short, has inserted a word that, although it
has the dictionary for its authority, is decidedly less than idiomatic in this
context—as if chosen by a Chinese scholar who, laboring to render the
poem in English, has become bewildered by the multiplicity of choices
offered by his English dictionary and settles on *pulling* by mistake.

Another glance at "The River-Merchant's Wife" reveals further odd
verbal choices. Consider line 4, "You walked about my seat, playing with
blue plums." Many readers, one presumes, suppose that "seat" in this in-
stance means the surface of a chair or stool. Nothing in the poem, how-
ever, requires that we accept only this reference. "Seat" could refer not to
a portion of furniture, but to her immediate surroundings (as in Duncan's
remark in *Macbeth:* "this castle hath a pleasant seat"). But once again—if
we posit the phantom Chinese translator casting about for English equiv-
alents—he has selected a somewhat archaic noun, one that dropped from
common usage a century ago. (Pound would also have been aware that
the use of *seat* to describe a geographical location persists in the United
States only in such expressions as *county seat*.)

One final example will, I think, demonstrate sufficiently that our phantom translator has difficulty assessing the proper uses for simple English verbs. In "Taking Leave of a Friend," the third line ends with a curious phrase: "Here we must make separation." In customary English usage, the meanings for *make* usually involve the production of something tangible, or (if the something is intangible) the overcoming of a rift (as in *to make amends*), or (again, if the something is intangible) a positive result (as in *to make good*). The pairing in English of *make* with negatives is most uncommon (*I can make nothing of it* is an exception).

In his attempt to make the language of *Cathay* an occasionally bizarre form of English, Pound does not limit himself to nouns and verbs. Pound well knew that some of the most perplexing problems for a novice translator arise from some of the simplest words. Consider, for example, that the word *set* has so many different uses in English that a full explanation of these uses takes seven pages in the *NOED*. *Set* and other similarly simple but variously used words present a series of pitfalls for the translator not altogether comfortable with English idioms. Someone who wished to translate the first of Pound's *Cantos* would have to grapple with the fact that *set* appears three times, but with slight variations in meaning at each occurrence.

With the problematic nature of common words in mind, let us turn to some features of "The River Song." Its first lines are straightforward. Although the nouns designate Asiatic materials, the sentence structure and syntax are conventionally English: "This boat is of shato-wood, and its gunwales are cut magnolia, / Musicians with jewelled flutes and with pipes of gold / Fill full the sides in rows." Yet the end of this sentence is puzzling: "and our wine / Is rich for a thousand cups."[14] To boast that one's wine is rich presents no problem, but to specify that it is "rich for a thousand cups" does give pause. Here again we come upon phrasing that sounds vaguely appropriate, but which, when we ask what the poem exactly means, becomes slippery. Does the poem mean that the supply of wine is rich in the sense of being abundant enough to fill so many cups? Has the translator been searching for an English equivalent of a Chinese character meaning "plentiful"? Has he then been misled by the sense in which *rich* is sometimes used to indicate quantity? (As in *the situation was rich with possibility*.) The problem in interpreting the end of that first sentence is primarily created by that innocuous preposition, "for." Does it mean "intended for"? That is, the wine is sufficiently abundant so that a thousand cups can be filled? Or does the poem want us to read "for" in the sense of "good enough for"? That is, the wine is of such excellent quality that one person could drink one cup after another and the wine would not pall. We cannot say which of the two readings should be preferred. To posit the possibility that both readings are legitimate in the original Chinese poem is one way out of the dilemma. Such a conclusion, however, only emphasizes Chinese poetry as a poetic markedly different from English poetry, in the sense that ambiguity is more characteristic of Chinese verse than English verse.

The effect of such verbal perplexities in *Cathay* is to produce a strange impression, the impression that this translation has been produced not by Ezra Pound, but by a native speaker of Chinese whose command of English is less than fluent. When faced with a variety of words that might be used to describe the action of gathering flowers, this phantom translator has wavered among various synonyms. Having an imperfect command of English, he has mistakenly selected inapt ones. Most of Pound's readers in 1915 would have been reminded of their own schooldays, when attempts to translate Latin classics into English would have produced similarly clumsy expressions. Pound inserts a sufficient number of odd expressions in the poems of *Cathay*, with the intention of leaving the reader with the impression that even though these English versions may be imperfect, there must lie behind them a superior Chinese original. Pound exploits the hallmarks of inferior or near-miss translation to suggest the existence of a more perfect translation hovering just at the edge of the poems as printed. One reason why the poems of *Cathay* are a success is that they *seem* to point to or circle near a brilliant—but just out of reach—translation.[15]

One reviewer of *Cathay* (Arthur Clutton-Brock) was alert to Pound's manipulation of diction, recognizing how much it differed from that found in contemporary English usage.

> There is a strong superstition among us that a translation should always seem quite English. But when it is made from a literature very alien in method and thought, it is not a translation at all if it seems quite English. Besides, a literal translation from something strange and good may surprise our language into new beauties. If we invite a foreigner of genius among us, we don't want to make him behave just like ourselves; we shall enjoy him best and learn most from him if he remains himself. So we think Mr. Pound has chosen the right method in these translations, and we do not mind that they often are "not English."[16]

Clutton-Brock recognizes that Pound's versions of Chinese poetry deliberately retain elements of the "alien" while simultaneously exhibiting "new beauties." I shall return to the paradoxical nature of *Cathay* later, but for the moment I want to emphasize the assertion that the language of *Cathay* produces the effect of seeming "not English."

It is worth noting that the poems frequently appear to be "not English" in their early lines. Pound wastes no time in alerting the reader that something is amiss. The curious expression, "rich for a thousand cups," appears in line 4 of "The River Song." "Pulling flowers" is in the second line of "The River-Merchant's Wife." "Trees fall" in the third line of "Lament of the Frontier Guard." Other oddities might be adduced, such as "close garden" ("The Beautiful Toilet," 1. 2) and "to cut the heart" ("Poem by the Bridge at Ten-Shin," 1. 3). The placement of curious expressions at the beginning of the poems alerts the reader immediately to an alien sensibility.

The examples offered so far have only addressed the issue of the extent to which some of Pound's verbal choices strike one as not English in the sense that they are not contemporary English. There are, however, other distortions that Pound employs. In "The Lament of the Frontier Guard" we find many images that present no difficulty to the contemporary reader of English. Lines such as "there is no wall left to this village" would resonate with those who had heard of the recent consequences of the war. The remarks in the poem's fourth line about climbing towers would also remind readers of the fact that tall structures such as cathedral towers in northern France were preferred vantage points for artillery spotters. The mention of "barbarous kings" would also surely remind the British reader of the German "policy of *Schrecklickeit* which burned whole towns and massacred hundred of inhabitants as at Louvain, Andenne, and Dinant."[17] Yet mixed with these familiar—indeed, painfully familiar—details are verbal oddities that infuse the poem with the air of the alien. In this landscape, with the arrival of autumn, the leaves do not descend from the trees; rather, "Trees fall." One might suppose that what is being described is the felling of trees for the construction of winter quarters or the laying in of a supply of firewood, or both. But in the absence of clarification, the phrase suggests an alien sort of vegetation. This is all the more remarkable since the version of the poem from which Pound was working, the one in the Fenollosa papers, specifies that in this portion of the poem the poet means—and the reader is to understand—that leaves are falling. Still other details in the phrasing indicate a landscape vividly seen in the original, but projected in a mystifying fashion in the translation. What are we to make of "Bones white with a thousand frosts, / High heaps, covered with trees and grass"?[18] Setting aside the indication that the bones are white because colored by frost, it is even more peculiar that the sharply pictured bones are, in the next line, specified as "covered." How can they be seen if they are under the trees and grass?

Pound's treatment of the poems in the Fenollosa papers adopts a divided stance: the Chinese poems are like Western ones; the Chinese poems are in many respects alien. One result of this division is the reader's frequent perception of these poems as simultaneously familiar and strange. With this paradoxical effect in mind, let us see if we can account for one other aspect of *Cathay*—its title. At first glance it does not seem an obvious choice for a book of translations of Chinese poetry. Wai-lim Yip lists a series of translations preceding Pound's, only one of which contains the word in its title: W. A. P. Martin's *The Lore of Cathay*. Martin's book, however, is a survey of Chinese culture. It devotes only one chapter to poetry. The word *Cathay* does not even appear in Martin's commentary. What about *Cathay* prompted Pound to light upon this particular title?

One way of approaching this problem is to estimate what the word *Cathay* signified to English and American readers in 1915. Perhaps the best way to make that estimation is to look at its usage in English and American poetry in the several generations leading up to 1915. For the most part, that usage is remarkably consistent. At its simplest level, *Cathay* signifies an extremely remote place, as in Robert Louis Stevenson's "Ticonderoga," in which a regiment carries the Union Jack around the globe, starting in Germany and Flanders, but then proceeding elsewhere: "Through Asiatic jungles / The tartans filed their way, / And the neighing of the war-pipes / Struck terror in Cathay."[19] In this and in other poems of the nineteenth century, Cathay represents the utmost distance one can travel and yet remain in the civilized world.

Other poets supplement Cathay's physical remoteness with a degree of cultural remoteness. Its distance offers these poets the chance to figure Cathay as a place whose qualities are intriguingly different. In some cases that difference can be construed favorably; *Cathay* can suggest a repository of alien wisdom. Oliver Wendell Holmes, in the poem he recited at a Boston banquet for Chinese ambassadors in 1868, honors them with this stanza.

> Land of wonders, fair Cathay,
> Who long hast shunned the staring day,
> Hid in mists of poet's dreams
> By thy blue and yellow streams,—
> Let us they shadowed form behold,—
> Teach us as thou didst of old.[20]

The poem depicts China as mysterious, but nonetheless surely "fair," with its "blue and yellow streams." Undiscovered deposits of intellectual or spiritual treasure are to be found there, along with portions of China already familiar to the West.

The most consistent treatment of China under the rubric of *Cathay* is not simply its remoteness and exotic or unknown qualities. As Holmes's poem suggests, *Cathay* stands for a paradoxical quality: it is simultaneously alien yet familiar. The various ways in which poets use Cathay in this bifurcated fashion deserves some attention, if only to demonstrate its frequency. Limitations of space, however, permit only a glance at two such usages.

My first example is Hartley Coleridge's "Address to Certain Gold Fishes" (1831). The fish in this poem are more than just creatures with gills. The poem associates them with their place of origin, the East. Coleridge remarks that they are "Keener than the Tartar's arrow" and likens their color to that of "golden flowers / Such as we fetch from eastern bowers / to mock this murky clime of ours." Having established these fish as alien importations, Coleridge proceeds to speculate whether their motion as they swim in captivity signifies happiness or "weary pain." He ultimately concludes that the fish are inscrutable. Coleridge cannot determine what their movements represent; he is reduced to wishful thinking: "I fain would dream / That ye are happy as ye seem, / Deck'd in Oriental pride, / By homely British fire-side." Part of the value of the goldfish lies in their illegibility. They become bright hieroglyphs, partly familiar and partly mysterious. Coleridge therefore can project meaning upon them. These goldfish, as it turns out, become metonyms for the East. And the East, for Coleridge, is reducible to two states of being. He is torn between seeing the goldfish as subject to "weary pain" provoked by "endless labor," and supposing that they are

> As gay, as gamesome, and as blithe,
> As light, as loving, and as lithe,
> As gladly earnest in your play,
> As when ye gleam'd in far Cathay.[21]

Coleridge's perspective reflects two common Western views of China. On the one hand, it connotes elegant gardens, beautiful pavilions, and courtly pleasures such as those found in the pages of Marco Polo. On the other hand, it suggests the grinding, endless toil of the peasantry, doomed from generation to generation to backbreaking labor: the life of the coolie. Even as he raises these commonplace aspects of the Western perception of China, Coleridge nevertheless fancies that the fish—and, by extension, their homeland—lie outside his comprehension. For Coleridge, Cathay represents something as familiar as the domestic fishbowl and as strange as the mysterious East.

The simultaneous association of Cathay with both the extremely remote and the extremely familiar occurs also in Christina Rossetti's sonnet sequence "Later Life." This series of introspective lyrics depends partly for its effect on contrasts between the speaker's past and present circumstances. At the beginning of sonnet 17 the speaker's memory is mysteriously aroused.

> Something this foggy day, a something which
>   Is neither of this fog nor of today,
>   Has set me dreaming of the winds that play
> Past certain cliffs, along one certain beach,
>   And turn the topmost edge of waves to spray:
>   Ah pleasant pebbly strand so far away,
> So out of reach while quite within my reach,
>   As out of reach as India or Cathay![22]

Nothing in "Later Life" indicates the particular significance of the beach to the speaker, but the rest of sonnet 17 implies that the beach represents (or at least is associated with) a happy or placid state of mind. Unfortunately that mental peace has been lost, perhaps irrecoverably. In the rest of the sonnet the speaker laments that she is "sick of self." The remembered beach is not just distant in miles or years, but emotionally removed as well.

Thus it is as "out of reach as India or Cathay." Nevertheless, it is available to some extent to her memory. She can recall that place and its associations, although she cannot revive them. Cathay becomes the apt metaphor for a mental state the speaker longs for but cannot recover, because it connotes a place both extraordinarily distant and alien yet present in both its artifacts and the history of British contact with China.

Pound depends upon his readers understanding that *Cathay* signifies something with which they are already acquainted, yet which is also elusive. It stands for something that readers of *Cathay* know only partly; the remainder intrigues by its enticing, enigmatic air. The title therefore captures the paradoxical combination of the strange and the familiar.[23] This combination, as we have seen, has been woven into the book. Pound has carefully managed the ambiguous presentation, which emphasizes Chinese poetry's common ground with Western verse while also leaving the impression that much has been missed in the translation. Many readers considered *Cathay* a faithful rendering of Chinese poetry, not realizing that it seemed so accurate because it mirrored Western conceptions of China.

NOTES

1. John Bailey, "The Poems of Cavalcanti" (unsigned review), reprinted in *Ezra Pound: The Critical Heritage*, ed. Eric Homberger (London: Routledge and Kegan Paul, 1972), 91.

2. W. P. Ker, ed., *Essays of John Dryden* (Oxford: Clarendon Press, 1900), 241.

3. Hugh Kenner, *The Pound Era* (Berkeley and Los Angeles: University of California Press, 1971), 222.

4. Ezra Pound, *Cathay* (London: Elkin Mathews, 1915), 32.

5. Ibid.

6. Referring to Pound's 1918 essay on Chinese poetry, Hugh Witemeyer notes that Pound wants to suppress the differences between European and Chinese poetry: "Pound is determined always to deal with world literature as a single body of material with certain artistic and spiritual unities which transcend differences in time and place of origin" (*The Poetry of Ezra Pound: Forms and Renewal, 1908–1920* [Berkeley and Los Angeles: University of California Press, 1969], 151). Yet it is also true that Pound sometimes retained elements emphasizing a text's foreign nature. There is evidence that in 1915 Pound was interested in the problems associated with inspecting a distant time and place. "Near Perigord," published in the same year as *Cathay*, is a remarkable meditation on the difficulty—perhaps the impossibility—of knowing another person or another period adequately. Ronald Bush also finds in *Cathay* some indication of Pound's attention to the difficulty of transmitting thoughts and emotions: "The heart of Pound's sequence lies in its progression from a desperate suspicion to a melancholy acknowledgment that shared experience is beyond the power of

language to effect" ("Pound and Li Po: What Becomes a Man," in *Ezra Pound among the Poets*, ed. George Bornstein [Chicago: University of Chicago Press, 1985], 40). Eliot also touches on the strangeness of the *Cathay* poems when he compares them to Pound's Nō translations: "The Noh are not so important as the Chinese poems (certainly not so important for English); the attitude is less unusual to us" (*Ezra Pound: His Metric and Poetry* [New York: Knopf, 1917], 27).

7. Herbert A. Giles, *Chinese Poetry in English Verse* (London: Bernard Quaritch, 1898), 70.

8. Lawrence Venuti, *The Translator's Invisibility: A History of Translation* (London: Routledge, 1995), 76.

9. Ibid.

10. Ibid., 61.

11. Ibid., 20.

12. William Alexander Parsons Martin, *The Lore of Cathay; or, The Intellect of China* (New York: Fleming H. Revell, 1901), 84.

13. *Cathay*, 11.

14. Ibid., 8.

15. Donald Davie was the first to discuss Pound's use of apparently clumsy translation, but only with regard to *Homage to Sextus Propertius*. Davie says of *Cathay* simply that it amounts to "beautiful translations." *Ezra Pound: Poet as Sculptor* (New York: Oxford University Press, 1964), 36.

16. Arthur Clutton-Brock, "Poems from Cathay" (unsigned review), *Times Literary Supplement*, April 29, 1915, 144.

17. C. R. M. F. Crutwell, *A History of the Great War, 1914–1918*, 2d ed. (New York: Oxford University Press, 1969), 16.

18. *Cathay*, 16.

19. Robert Louis Stevenson, *The Works of Robert Louis Stevenson* (London: William Heinemann and Charles Scribner's Sons, 1922), 8:328.

20. Oliver Wendell Holmes, *The Complete Poetical Works of Oliver Wendell Holmes* (Boston: Houghton Mifflin, 1908), 200. Paradoxically, the best-known instance of the word *Cathay* in the poetry of the nineteenth century is one that uses it as a term of contempt. Tennyson, in "Locksley Hall," has his young speaker remark, "Through the shadow of the globe we sweep into the younger day: / Better fifty years of Europe than a cycle of Cathay." *The Poems of Tennyson*, ed. Christopher Ricks (London: Longmans, 1969), 698. Cathay becomes synonymous with that element of obstinate complacency which the British perceived in contemporary China. Hugh Honour credits the disillusionment of the West with Cathay to encounters diplomatic and military in the late eighteenth and early nineteenth centuries. "Finally the advent of British troops in 1857 as reprisal for the burning of a factory at Canton turned the exquisite vision of Cathay into the problem of modern China." *Chinoiserie: The Vision of Cathay* (London: John Murray, 1961), 28. My argument in this essay is partly based on the assumption that older, idealized versions of Cathay persisted in a literary setting, and that Tennyson's reference represents an anomaly.

21. Hartley Coleridge, *Poems* (Oxford: Woodstock Books, 1990), 113–14.

22. R. W. Crump, ed., *The Complete Poems of Christina Rossetti* (Baton Rouge: Louisiana State University Press, 1986), 2:145.

23. Harold R. Isaacs makes this point in respect to American attitudes toward China, but it is also pertinent to British perspectives. "China occupies a special place in a great many American minds. It is remote, strange, dim, little known. But it is also in many ways and for many people oddly familiar, full of sharp images and associations, and uniquely capable of arousing intense emotion." *Scratches on Our Minds: American Images of China and India* (New York: John Day, 1958), 66.

The Beauties of Mistranslation: On Pound's English after Cathay

CHRISTINE FROULA

> Great literature is written in a sort of foreign language. To each sentence we attach a meaning . . . often a mistranslation. But in great literature all our mistranslations result in beauty.
> —Marcel Proust, *By Way of Sainte-Beuve*

> [T]o imagine a language means to imagine a form of life.
> —Ludwig Wittgenstein, *Philosophical Investigations*

> This twentieth century not only turns a new page in the book of the world, but opens another and a startling chapter. Vistas of strange futures unfold for man, of world-embracing cultures half-weaned from Europe, of hitherto undreamed responsibilities for nations and races.
> —Ernest Fenollosa, *The Chinese Written Character as a Medium for Poetry*

> How many people today live in a language that is not their own? Or no longer, or not yet, even know their own and know poorly the major language that they are forced to serve? This is the problem of immigrants, and especially of their children, . . . of minorities, . . . of a minor literature, but also a problem for all of us: how to tear a minor literature away from its own language, allowing it to challenge the language and making it follow a sober revolutionary path? How to become a nomad and an immigrant and a gypsy in relation to one's own language?
> —G. Deleuze and F. Guattari, *Kafka: Toward a Minor Literature*

> many of the things the words were about
> no longer exist
>
> the noun for standing in mist by a haunted tree
> the verb for I
> —W. S. Merwin, "Losing a Language"

> I am luckier than Pound—I was born into Chinese. He had to struggle against what his language imposed. *The Cantos* are complete only in their Chinese translation.
> —Yang Lian, in conversation, Beijing, July 21, 1999

The great ages of English literature, as Pound often observed, have been great ages of translation. Bede recounts that an unlettered herdsman named Caedmon, attached to the monastery of Whitby, created the earliest

49

recorded English poem when he received the gift of song in a dream and melded the great Germanic oral poetic tradition to his employers' Roman Christian cosmos in his "Hymn" (ca. 658–80 C.E.). Caedmon's use of "pagan" meters—the Anglo-Saxon prosodic system in which he must have been fluent, and to which Pound's "Seafarer" fits an archaized modern English—to praise the "Wuldor-Faeder"'s Creation in the vernacular in-augurates the long, dynamic emergence of English poetry and the English language from intercultural crossover, reinvention, and fusion. In this his-tory, textual translation is a springboard to an inspired freehand cultural translation integral to processes of cultural self-fashioning.[1] Chaucer's graceful embrace of French influences upon "Engelond"'s vernacular, Wyatt's chiaroscuro adaptations of Petrarch's idealizing love sonnets to the brooding eros and violence of Henry VIII's court, Milton's audacious self-portrait after Moses on Mount Sion, in which he receives a far more elab-orate revelation of the Western creation story in English than was vouch-safed to Moses in Hebrew: all these moments exemplify the cross-cultural borrowings and hybridizing inspirations that move English language, po-etry, and culture toward ever-widening horizons.

Ezra Pound's long adventure with Chinese poetry marks another lin-guistic and cultural crossroads, an encounter—some Sinologists say, a vi-olent, scandalous collision—between a twentieth-century American poet's cosmopolitan English and the ancient written language of classical Chinese poetry.[2] Knowing no Chinese, I shall draw on Sinologists' stud-ies of *Cathay* to pursue a different question, in the spirit of Wittgenstein's insight that "to imagine a language is to imagine a form of life."[3] How does Pound's decades-long encounter with ancient Chinese poetry and culture participate in the future of English, that borderless, exploratory, accretive, imperial, colonizing language whose twentieth-century advance toward a global destiny Fenollosa foresaw? What kinds of force does an-cient Chinese grammar exert upon the English of *Cathay* and of Pound's modern epic, *The Cantos*—a work in part inspired by Fenollosa's vision of "world-embracing cultures half-weaned from Europe"? How does Pound—who, as Hugh Kenner remarks, "never translates 'into' some-thing already existing in English"[4]—make a language that had burgeoned from Caedmon's islanded vernacular to the frontiers of global dominance hospitable to that different "form of life"?

Such questions shift the emphasis from Pound's fidelity or lack thereof to the ancient Chinese originals toward the impact of Chinese—or an idea of Chinese—upon his English and, more broadly, upon the multifarious poetic practices by which he spectacularly exploits his language's un-policed borders, across which pan-global influences travel freely in all directions. These questions align Pound's Orientalism with Caedmon's, Chaucer's, Wyatt's, and Milton's respective exoticisms and situate his project within the multicultural origins and history of an English whose "world-embracing" processes display translation's complex role in cultural interchange, from mediating economic and cultural imperialism to facilitating cosmopolitan self-fashioning to catalyzing the fortuitous beauties and inventions sparked by the mutual influences of different forms of life.[5]

Pound was about to embark on *The Cantos*, his internationalist-modernist English epic, when he came upon Fenollosa's prophecy of the dawning century's new and startling "chapter" in the "book of the world" from which would issue "strange futures," "world-embracing cultures half-weaned from Europe," "hitherto undreamed responsibilities for nations and races."[6] Fenollosa's vision springs from his immersion in translation, but what does translation mean in this context? Translations of poems of any depth, Pound contends, do not properly exist but at best are either "the expression of the translator, virtually a new poem," or "as it were a photograph, as exact as possible, of one side of the statue."[7] But what interests Fenollosa, Pound, and many translation theorists is less translations as objects than translation as function; less translation's ontological impossibility than the consequent animation of figuration, myth, tropes, twists and turns in the processes of translation, including all the ways that the translated original "sur-vives," as Derrida puts it—lives not just longer but "more and better, beyond the means of its author."[8] Walter Benjamin's idealist meditation locates a translation's value not in its concrete utterance but in its power to gesture, ever provisionally, toward "coming to terms with the foreignness of languages": in its always unfulfilled intention we glimpse "the predestined, hitherto inaccessible realm of reconciliation and fulfillment of all languages"—a univocal paradise not before but beyond Babel. Benjamin's translator seeks to produce not a simulacrum of the original's "meaning" but a peculiar "echo" of its language such that both languages seem "fragments" of a third, "greater language"; "to release" in the language of the translation "that pure language which is under the spell of another."[9]

If "to imagine a language is to imagine a form of life," the form of life peculiar to a given language would seem to be bound up with the incommunicable "something" that Benjamin distinguishes from "information" and finds best evoked through "a literal rendering of the syntax" (78–79). Such a translation, by enabling the original to imprint a mark of difference upon the host language, corrects what Rudolf Pannwitz diagnoses as (in this case, German) translators' "'wrong premise'": "'They want to turn Hindi, Greek, English into German instead of turning German into Hindi, Greek, English'"; to preserve the state in which their language "'happens to be'" instead of permitting the "foreign tongue" to affect it.[10] In the same spirit, Gilles Deleuze and Claire Parnet celebrate the strange futures that translation's ontological impossibility brings into play in preferring the term *mistranslations*, which are to be valued insofar as they do not "consist in interpretations" but "create another language inside" their own.[11]

The incommensurable forms of life inscribed in the grammars of classical Chinese poetry and English must surely have struck Pound as he studied the collaborative (mis)translations in Fenollosa's notebooks, as they must strike any English speaker who studies Chinese scholars' mappings of Chinese-to-English translation strategies. Pound's "mistranslations" of Chinese exploit this differential, seeking less to recast the Chinese poem in the alien grammar of English (as, for example, Arthur Waley does) than, in Pannwitz's terms, to turn English into Chinese, or, as Lawrence Venuti puts it, to "foreignize" English, to refashion it in the image of that difference.[12] They aim less for a fluent transparency that renders the act of translation "invisible" than for an English subtly altered under the influence of the Chinese poem's different form of life. More generally, influenced by Fenollosa, Pound pioneered modernist translation practices that bend English toward the different forms of life embodied in other languages. Within the geopolitical history of English, Venuti argues, such foreignizing translation interrupts and complicates the appropriative dynamics of traditional "fluent" translation: "the ethnocentric violence that every act of translating wreaks on a foreign text is matched by a violent disruption of domestic values that challenges cultural forms of domination, whether nationalist or elitist. Foreignizing undermines the very concept of nation by invoking the diverse constituencies that any such concept tends to elide" (147).

From the classical Chinese poems that Pound found sketchily translated in Fenollosa's notebooks emanates a "form of life" alien to English as to the other major European languages. Even we who know no Chinese can sense the radical incongruence between the grammars of English and classical Chinese poetry through translators' notes and Sinologists' descriptions—for example, Wai-lim Yip's translation glosses on Li Po's "Taking Leave of a Friend":

青	山	横	北	郭
白	水	繞	東	城
此	地	一	爲	別
孤	蓬	萬	里	征
浮	雲	遊	子	意
落	日	故	人	情
撣	手	自	兹	去
蕭	蕭	班	馬	鳴
green	mountain(s)	lie-across	north	outer-wall-of-city
white	water	wind-around	east	city
this	place	once	make	separation
lone	tumbleweed	ten-thousand	miles	travel
floating	cloud(s)	wanderer		thought (mood)
setting	sun	old	friend	feeling
wave	hand(s)	from	here	go
hsiao	hsiao*	parting	horse	neigh

* onomatopoeic words for neighing.

> Green mountain(s) lie across (the) north wall.
> White water wind(s) (the) east city.
> Here once (we) part,
> Lone tumbleweed(;) (a) million miles (to) travel.
> Floating clouds (;) (a) wanderer('s) mood.
> Setting sun(;) (an) old friend('s) feeling.
> (We) wave hands(,) (you) go from here.
> Neigh, neigh goes (the) horse at parting.

(12–13)

Translators of classical poetry, Yip explains, run into difficulties less through ignorance of the Chinese language or text than through "their failure, as translators," to grasp the "special mode of representation of reality constituted . . . by the peculiarity of the Chinese language itself" and given in "the linguistic structure of the line" (12). Yip's "word-for-word translation" into English immediately below the ideograms highlights the two languages' constitutive peculiarities. This translation, though made of English words, is not yet, or not quite, "in" English because it has not been subjected to the exigencies of English grammar—except lightly, in the recognition that English nouns have number: mountain(s), cloud(s), hand(s). Trying to make out the poem from the English words, an English-speaking reader may wonder, as it were, "Where am I? Is this the Grand Canyon?" If she cannot make out the poem from this austerely literal translation, it is neither because she cannot read Chinese (is this not a translation?) nor because she cannot read English (the words are clear enough) but because she cannot "read" the form of life that has so powerfully foreignized Yip's word-for-word English translation, refracting the original's essential "something" through "a literal rendering of the syntax."

James Liu compares the different modes of being in the world, and of representing reality, that come into conflict and into play in English mistranslations of classical Chinese poems. "Chinese, being a completely uninflected language, is not burdened with Cases, Genders, Moods, Tenses, etc.," he writes. This grammatical openness fosters concentration and concision even as it "leads easily to ambiguity," as illustrated in his word-for-word translation of lines by Wang Wei:

> *Yueh ch'u ching shan niao*
> Moon rise surprise mountain bird
> *Shih ming ch'un chien chung*
> Occasionally cry in spring valley.

Because Chinese nouns are free of such "irrelevant details" as number and tense, the poet can evoke "the spirit of a tranquil spring night among the mountains" "almost *sub specie aeternitatis*": rather than "watch a particular spring night scene viewed by a particular person," we "are invited . . . to feel the quintessence of 'spring-night-ness.'"[13] George A. Kennedy notes that the Chinese are "'most casual'" about the grammatical subject "indispensable" to Western grammars: "'It is often omitted in ordinary conversation, and a good deal of fine prose lacks it.'"[14] A poem that specifies no particular subject of a verb, Liu observes, creates a "sense of timelessness and universality" (40), as in this Wang Wei quatrain:

> *K'ung shan pu chien jen*
> Empty mountain not see people
> *Tan wen jen yü hsiang*
> Only hear people talk sound

Fan ying ju shen lin
Reflected light enter deep forest
Fu chao ch'ing t'ai shang
Again shine green moss upon.[15]

(40–41)

Eliding the lyric speaker whose perspective serves to "focalize" the scene, as English readers expect, these lines convey "the presence of nature as a whole"; "the mountains, the human voices, the sunlight, the mosses" co-exist in flux within a plenitude of potential relationships, none of which grammatically excludes the others (41).[16] By rendering the grammatical subject implicit—not absent but open, unfixed—the poet refrains from obtruding a singular, univocal perspective upon the scene; the subject "can be . . . anyone," even any *thing*. Beside Chinese poetry, with its negligible grammatical subjects, Liu argues, "much Western poetry appears egocentric and earth-bound. Where Wordsworth wrote '*I* wander*ed* lonely as *a* cloud,' a Chinese poet would probably have written simply 'Wander as cloud.'" Whereas Wordsworth describes "a personal experience bound in space and time," Liu's spare Chinese mistranslation grammatically domesticates the unique and solitary Western self to Chinese norms, despecifying person, number, and tense to suggest a timeless "state of being with universal applications" (41).

Classical Chinese poems may omit not only nouns and pronouns but verbs, Liu observes, along with the connectives (prepositions, conjunctions, particles) that prose grammar—even Chinese prose grammar—ordinarily requires. He gives as example a thirteenth–fourteenth-century poem by Ma Chih-yuan in which a verbless scene "unfolds" as if in "a scroll of Chinese painting," creating "a sense of stillness in movement, as if these objects had been arrested in time and frozen in an eternal pose" (42):

Withered vines, old trees, twilight crows,
Little bridge, flowing water, people's house,
Ancient road, west wind, lean horse

To make this effectively foreignized English mistranslation "read more smoothly," Liu domesticates it with "a few verbs and prepositions":

Withered vines, aged trees, twilight crows,
Beneath the little bridge *by the* cottage *the* river flows.
On the ancient road *and* lean horse *the* west wind *blows.*

(41)

Overlaying English prepositions, particles, and verbs upon the translated words, Liu locates the poem's objects in spatial relation to one another *(beneath, by, on)*. In doing so, he generates an implied viewer's singular perspective that—even as it placates the Western reader's "Where am I?"—has no existence in the Chinese poem. Minor, subtle, even necessary though these grammatical operations seem, Liu's smooth, fluent, "invisible" mistranslation is paradoxically far less neutral than his word-for-word mistranslation into an English foreignized by that literal rendering of syntax which, for Benjamin, best approximates the incommunicable something that it is the translator's task to evoke. As Liu's two translations move from the relatively foreignized to the relatively fluent, "something" of the Chinese poem's form of life that "sur-vives" in the first is obscured by the monological perspectivism of Western grammar in the second.

This perspectivism, and the subject/object relationships it inscribes, inform not only the grammar but much of the painting of the West as well as its objectivist science. Comparing translations of "Taking Leave of a Friend," Yip remarks that the Chinese poem depicts "things in nature, like objects in a painting"; he judges that Pound, Ayscough/Lowell, and Obata more or less preserve this "drama of things," while Giles, Bynner, and Gautier substitute "analysis at work" through "intellectual, directional devices" (16, 19). By contrast with the "architectural" modality of western European grammars, Liu likens the fluidly signifying ideograms of ancient Chinese poetry to "chemical elements that form new compounds with great ease. A Chinese word cannot be pinned down to a 'part of speech,' 'gender,' 'case,' etc., but is a mobile unit which acts on, and reacts with, other units in a constant flux." Its freedom from grammatical inflection—and so from such "accidental trappings" and limitations as monological perspective—is the condition of this semiotic fluidity and openness (46–47). The baffled English speaker's "Where am I?" comes, then, from left field. Whereas the Lamborghini-like grammatical machine of English addresses that question precisely, the Chinese form of life that we glimpse through these word-for-word English translations overleaps it altogether. Even Liu's light veneer of English grammar dramatizes the incommensurability of these forms of life and the incommunicable "something" at stake in efforts to mistranslate one into the other.

Liu also points to the different ways of being that are mediated, respectively, by the subject/object relations of Western perspectival grammar and the indeterminate relationality of the classical Chinese poems in the contrast between Western dualism and the Chinese word for nature: "*tzu-jan*, or 'self-thus'" (pinyin: *ziran*) (Liu, 49). "Self-thus": self like, as, continuous with, integral with nature? Liu's etymological gloss suggests that the ideogram figures mind and nature as immanent in, transparent to, one another, not differentiated and disjunct as in the dominant Western mind/nature or mind/ body duality. In *Science and Civilization in China*, Joseph Needham argues that Western science began absorbing Chinese representations of the organic continuity and transparency of mind and nature in the seventeenth century, when Leibniz encountered neo-Confucian thought through "the greatest of all Chinese thinkers, Chu Hsi" (twelfth century C.E.) in translations by Jesuit missionaries. Chu Hsi's influence on Leibniz, he writes, was an early force in "the great movement of our time" beyond "the mechanical Newtonian universe" toward awareness of the organic interconnectedness of nature, "a better understanding of the meaning of natural organization." As Hugh Kenner notes, Needham traces this vast conceptual sea-change—which encompasses "all modern investigations in the methodology and the world-picture of the natural sciences," from Marx and Engels to Whitehead and quantum physics— back "through Hegel, Lotze, Schelling and Herder to Leibniz" and thence through the Jesuit mission to Chu Hsi.[7] In Needham's view, modern Western science owes to China, and to the idea of the Tao as "a field of force" within which "[a]ll things orient[] themselves . . . without having to be instructed to do so, and without the application of mechanical compulsion" (293), the initial impetus for its transformation of Newtonian objectivism (paralleled in our subject/object grammar) into the mysterious, logic-defying quantum universe—"as though," marvels Kenner, "the east, with centuries-long deliberation, were writing the macro-history of western thought" (231).

Kenner relates *The Chinese Written Character as a Medium for Poetry* to Needham's East-West intellectual genealogy by way of the New England Transcendentalists, whom Fenollosa was teaching to his Japanese students. (Thoreau, Kenner notes, had translated the "Confucian anecdote that opens Canto XIII," 230.) Ralph Waldo Emerson's etymological concept of poetic language famously excavates the originary "brilliant picture[s]" buried in the dead metaphors of English, and his self-portrait as "transparent eyeball" in his essay "Nature" has affinities with

Chinese *tzu-jan/ziran/* "self-thus" as glossed by Liu: "Standing on the bare ground—my head bathed by the blithe air and uplifted into an infinite space—all mean egotism vanishes. I become a transparent eyeball; I am nothing; I see all; the currents of the Universal Being circulate through me."[18] *The Chinese Written Character as a Medium for Poetry* critiques the subject/object dualism of English grammar in terms that parallel the modern developments in natural science, philosophy, and social thought that Needham remarks. Approaching this essay not as a scholarly treatise on the Chinese ideogram but as a twentieth-century manifesto for English poetry, we observe the ways Fenollosa deploys the different form of life encoded in the grammar of classical Chinese poetry to critique Western grammar's subject/object logic from within.[19]

Fenollosa attacks the nouns and verbs of Western grammars as misleading reifications that represent discrete, stable entities (nouns, subjects, objects) and abstract acts and motions, whereas in nature there exist only things-in-motion, things-in-relation, things indistinguishable from actions and processes. "A true noun, an isolated thing, does not exist in nature," he writes. "Things are only the . . . meeting points, of actions" (10). Nor is "a pure verb, an abstract motion, possible in nature. The eye sees noun and verb as one: things in motion, motion in things, and so the Chinese conception tends to represent them" (10). This inseparability of matter and motion underlies the apparent universality of the sentence. All languages have it, he argues, not because it represents a "complete thought," for "in nature there is *no* completeness"; "[a]ll processes in nature are interrelated," and "motion leaks everywhere, like electricity from an exposed wire"; thus no "complete" sentence could exist "save one which would take all time to pronounce" (11). Nor does the grammarian's idea that the sentence unites a subject with a predicate explain its universality, for any sentence thus conceived is "but an accident" of the human "conversational animal," not a manifestation of any "truth" (11). Rather, Fenollosa asserts, "All truth has to be expressed in sentences because all truth is the *transference of power*"; because the "*act* is the very substance . . . denoted. The agent and object are only limiting terms" of an action-in-process that they embody and so make visible (12–13).

Fenollosa's "etymosinology" recalls Emerson's concept of an English word as a "metaphorical composition" that inscribes not a discrete object or action but a dynamic relation, as in "*transgression, the crossing of a line*" ("Nature," 31). Fenollosa argues that the ideogram's pictographic structure and resistance to grammatical stabilization locate it "close to nature," in semiotic affinity to nature as movement, process, power, potential. Echoing Nietzsche's "I fear we are not rid of God because we still believe in grammar"—and anticipating Derrida's critique of Western onto-theology in *Of Grammatology*—Fenollosa inquires rhetorically, "Are there pronouns and prepositions and conjunctions in Chinese as in good Christian languages?" As nature knows no grammar, the Chinese ideograph knows no grammar, at least not in the Western sense; it is "not exclusive of parts of speech, but comprehensive; not something which is neither a noun, verb, nor adjective, but something which is all of them at once and at all times." In Chinese, "A part of speech is what it does"; "parts of speech grow[] up, bud[] forth from one another" (17–18), by contrast with the fixed grammatical functions of words in English sentences.

The ideogram's materiality and its relative freedom from grammatical inflection contribute to Fenollosa's apprehension of it as closer to nature—less meta-physical—than Western grammars. He translates his apprehension of it as a form of life that mimes a nature that "knows no grammar" (17) into a visionary *Western* poetics of fluid noun-verbs that would bend English grammar toward the post-Newtonian nature then emerging in Einstein's revolutionary theory of the mutual convertibility of matter and energy. The decomposition of the noun in Fenollosa's poetics ("relations are more real and more important than the things which they relate," 22) parallels the dissolution of the object—and with it, of Newtonian subject/object relations—in relativity and quantum physics, as it foreshadows affinities between quantum physics and Eastern philosophies—both of which, Gary Zukav argues, posit the insubstantiality of the sensible world and a fundamental "unbroken wholeness" in nature beneath the play of appearances.[20]

According to Liu, only perhaps 10 or 20 percent of ideograms function in the "etymosinological" way Fenollosa and Pound describe. But that perhaps 80 or 90 percent do not does not cancel the force of *The Chinese Written Character as a Medium for Poetry* as a critique of Western objectivism and a manifesto for a poetics aligned with Fenollosa's vision of a "world-embracing" language—"whether Chinese exemplifies it or not," as he says, in effect acknowledging his Orientalism.[21] He is concerned with the Chinese character less in itself, and less even as a poetic "medium" whose qualities he would import into English, than as the inspiration for a visionary poetics that would help to move the objectivist grammars of European languages toward the transcultural horizon his opening sentences conjure—toward the "strange futures" he foresees as cultures "wean" themselves from Europe in response to "hitherto undreamed of" challenges "for nations and races" in the twentieth century (3).

Foregrounding the intercultural translation—translation not just of words but of forms of life—that must mediate that global future, Fenollosa warns of the dangers our habituation to Western grammars conceals: "We should be ware of English grammar, its hard parts of speech and its lazy satisfaction with nouns and adjectives"; we must resist mindlessly deploying "all the weaknesses of our own formalisms" in our mistranslations; we would do well to remember translation's impossibility and seek to break through our habituated form of life to "attain the inner heat of thought that melts down parts of speech and recasts them" (17, 28, 30). At the dawn of the twentieth century, Fenollosa envisions Western thought's awakening to the limits of the objectivist modalities its grammars inscribe and its search for a poetics not trapped within subject/object dichotomies, whether at the level of grammar or of international, interracial, intercultural, and geopolitical interchange.

Pound, Fenollosa's first audience, wrote toward such a future English by means of foreignizing practices that evoke that historical horizon. As he was publishing *Cathay* and *The Chinese Written Character as a Medium for Poetry*, Pound was designing his great half-century epic project as a kind of laboratory for what he would later name the "ideogrammic method," which he exemplifies by signaling the color red through juxtaposing rose, cherry, iron rust, flamingo (*ABCR*, 22). This method—assemblages of images and vignettes that mime the semiotics of certain Chinese characters—assimilates his encounter with Chinese to *The Cantos'* very structure. Further, following Fenollosa's global extension of ideogrammic poetics, Pound incorporates thematic and linguistic materials from Europe, North America, Africa, Asia, and Australia—including untranslated floating fragments of other languages—into his poem, even as he makes foreignizing translation integral to it from *Three Cantos* (1917) on, disrupting the dominance and transparency of the poem's English ground. If Pound's glimpse of a different form of life in Fenollosa's notebooks and essay was not the only inspiration for *The Cantos'* foreignized English, it may have been the most salient; so, at any rate, his invocation of Chinese in much later comments on Mary Barnard's draft translations of Sappho suggest: "'utility of syntax? waaal the chink does without a damLot'" and "'it is now more homogene/it is purrhapz a bit lax. . . . it still reads a bit like a translation/ what is the maximum abruptness you can get it TO?' "[22] Cosmopolitan and time-traveling from its first page, *The Cantos'* self-foreignizing operations, at once experimental and virtuosic, make it a microcosmic register of modernity's shrinking globe.

In fact, Fenollosa's theory converged with a modernist poetics that Pound was already vigorously honing when he received the notebooks in 1913. "The Return" (1912), in its Vorticist abstraction, frees language of the semiotic specificity imposed by Western grammar's "hard parts of speech"; it destabilizes solid objects, blurs perspectival subject/object relations, subordinates the "utility of syntax" to sculpted rhythms, and dissolves the lyric I into an unspecified, mobile subject transparent to nature and the world.[23] Yeats judged it "the most beautiful poem that has ever been written in the free form, one of the few in which I find real organic rhythm," and wrote that it seemed to have been "translated at sight from some unknown Greek masterpiece."[24] In fact, "The Return" *is* a free (mis)translation of sorts, as Yeats must have known: René Taupin reported that Pound composed it in fifteen minutes with Henri de Régnier's Symbolist poem *"Les Médailles d'Argile"* (The Clay Medallions) to hand.[25] Likening it to Vorticist sculpture, Pound describes "The Return" as an "objective reality" with "a complicated sort of significance, like Mr. Epstein's 'Sun God' or Mr. Brzeska's 'Boy with a Coney'"—in other words, as a translation of a modernist aesthetics from the medium of sculpture to that of language (*GB*, 85).

Pound's remarks frame "The Return" as a (mis)translation from French to English, Symbolism to Vorticism, sculpture to poetry. Yet in what sense is it a translation at all? Its twenty lines omit nearly everything in Régnier's fifty-one. From Régnier's speaker's dreamlike narrative of tremblingly engraving on medallions of metal and fragile clay an invisible *"Face divine,"* whose many forms emerge *"une à une"* from his desire *"pour vivre en eux qui sont nous divinement,"* "The Return" abstracts a drama of verbal rhythms. Conceived as a free verse sculpture—in Pound's words, an "absolute rhythm," "form cut into TIME," as Gaudier and Epstein cut spatial form into stone—the poem's rhythmic patterns make it an "object" the more solid as the experience it captures is mysterious and unexplained (*ABCR*, 198). Cutting Régnier's explicit *je* along with his narrative, and delaying the grammatical antecedent "Gods" of the first line of *"Médailles,"* "The Return" foregrounds a different kind of "reality," an autonomous rhythmic object ("one, and by one") freed from even such semantic weight as the Symbolist poem carries. As Régnier casts a dreamlike thematic narrative into *vers libre*, Pound abstracts vision from narrative and sculpts it into sound, his ghostly revenants inseparable from the poem's materiality. The speaker who stamps his dreaming desire on figures of metal and clay in *"Médailles"* becomes in "The Return" a speaker whose deictic gestures meld vision to a verbal art "absolute" in itself.

The explicit first-person speaker in *"Médailles"* also serves to locate the reader—to tell us, in the manner of Western grammars, where we are—even as it describes the smiling gaze of an indeterminate *vous: "vous les comptiez en souriant, / Et vous disiez: Il est habile; / Et vous passiez en souriant."* "The Return" condenses Régnier's I/*je* and its indeterminate addressee(s)—which include the reader—in the single word "See," whose succinct imperative at once aligns all gazes and projects what is in *"Médailles"* an inward vision out into the world. Gesturing toward an apparitional "they," the small word "See" merges the perspectives of Régnier's *je* and *vous* and bridges inward vision and outward reality, subject (subjective vision) and object (the addressee, the visible "they"). Seer, seeing, and what is seen—the solid objects of Western dualism—dissolve into interdependent, interpenetrating mind/nature, self/other, subject/object, noun/verb. Even as it defers the noun *"Dieux"* of Régnier's first line until after "they" have materialized as rhythmic "Movements, . . . the slow feet, / The trouble in the pace and the uncertain / Wavering," and then identifies them only by ancient epithets ("the 'Wing'd-with-Awe,' / Inviolable, // Gods of the wingèd shoe!"), "The Return" does not cause us to wonder who "they" are. "They" just are, immanent; they "exist" in the poem as though in Fenollosa's Emersonian, etymo-imagist sense of "standing forth"—existence as "a definite act," in the spirit of his glosses on English *is*, from an Aryan root that means to breathe; and on *be*, from *bhu*, to grow; and on Chinese *is*, "actively 'to have,'" from an ideogram he reads as "to snatch from the moon with the hand" (15).

At about the time Fenollosa's notebooks came into Pound's hands, he published "Fan-Piece, for Her Imperial Lord" (February 1914), a three-line abstraction of Ban Jieyu's "Song of Regret," in which the poet, once the favorite concubine of the Han emperor Cheng, laments her displacement by a young rival in an address to her fan, in whose fate she sees her own and her rival's. Pound's "Fan-Piece" stands at much the same creative distance from H. A. Giles's ten-line English mistranslation as does "The Return" from *"Médailles."* As in "The Return" Pound mistranslates French to English, Symbolist to Vorticist aesthetics, sculpture to poetry, in "Fan-Piece" he mistranslates a Chinese poem glimpsed through the murky glass of Giles's Victorian English into an intensely dramatic and expressive elliptical form that seems inspired equally by haiku and by Vorticist abstraction.[26] Again Pound carves away almost everything except the speaker's evocation of the fan's pure beauty and swift abandonment, adding the small, telling word *also:*

> O fan of white silk,
>   clear as frost on the grass-blade.
> You also are laid aside.

The speaker's apostrophe to her fan condenses subject and object; the lyric I, her rival, and the fan; inward vision with objective history and circumstance. As "The Return" translates Régnier's thematic narrative into "form carved in TIME," the three lines of "Fan-Piece" allude formally to the love triangle and to the repetitive (prospective, retrospective) patterned fall from favor to abandonment, the turn deftly caught in the "frost" of line 2. The crucial "also" crosses the speaker's past with her rival's future, her reticent autobiography with the delicately ironic prophecy of the fan's fate. In translating Giles's future tense ("autumn chills / . . . / Will see thee laid neglected on the shelf") into present tense ("you also are laid aside"), Pound arrays the women's identical phased histories within a timeless now—form cut into time, a pattern abstracted from their interchangeable fates, a flowing dance of power and desire from which the dancer discovers she is not inseparable. Composed during the days when he was "getting orient from all quarters," "Fan-Piece" displays Pound's mistranslation of Giles's mistranslation of a Chinese poem into a modernist/Imagist/Vorticist aesthetic that projects the fluid subject/object dynamics he was simultaneously discovering in Fenollosa's writings.

Analyzing the influence of Pound's encounter with classical Chinese poetry and the ideogram on *The Cantos*, Ming Xie observes that "what Pound thought he had learned" was

> a paratactic movement in phrases to articulate and propel the natural rhyth-
> mic flow of verse-lines: "ply over ply, thin glitter of water; / Brook film bear-
> ing white petals" (C4), "prow set against prow, / stone, ply over ply" (C17);
> "With sound of pipe against pipe / The sound ply over ply" (C40); "cloud
> over cloud" (C79), "Leaf over leaf, dawn-branch in the sky / And the sea dark,
> under wind" (C23) . . . "And the waves like a forest / Where the wind is weight-
> less in the leaves / But moving / so that the sound runs upon sound" (C27).[27]

Ming Xie proposes such phrases as examples of what Donald Davie calls "a poetry of the noun rather than the verb," accurately enough, since what verbs there are mostly lapse into participles and copulas (56). In light of Fenollosa's essay, such phrases also suggest nouns-becoming-verbs, verbs-becoming-nouns, words performing forms of life in which grammatical and lyric subjects unfold within nature, *ziran*/self-thus, rather than articulate themselves against it—are literally im*pli*cit, en-folded "ply over ply" in nature's translucent moving web. *Ply:* a noun (fold); a verb (to fold); fold over fold, the redoubled noun im-plying movement, change, temporality: one after, over, against, under, another in verb/nouns that multiply, move, fold, "run," exist, stand forth, in mu-tual im-pli-cation: matter, motion, and time caught in the paradoxically stilled movement of the poem's continuous present. Whether or not such verse-lines mime a *natural* rhythmic flow, as Ming Xie argues, their muting of grammatical inflection recalls Fenollosa's critique of the meta-physics attendant on "hard parts of speech" in the name of a physics/nature he posits as act inseparable from substance.

In 1920, the year after he published Fenollosa's essay, Pound deployed such verbless paragrammatical movements to close *Hugh Selwyn Mauberley*'s elegy for Gaudier-Brzeska and the war dead:

> Charm, smiling at the good mouth,
> Quick eyes gone under earth's lid,
>
> For two gross of broken statues,
> For a few thousand battered books.

"Charm" and "quick eyes" would be grammatical subjects if there were a verb, but there isn't; or rather, there is but it's "gone"—a fragment or rem-nant of a verb, its auxiliary *(have)* gone missing and eloquent in absence.

Instead of fixing a completed action securely in the past, the lost *have* leaves hanging a reverberating elegiac participle ("gone") that prolongs the shock of loss into the present in a spectral afterimage, a perpetual movement downward "under earth's lid," which does not conceal what it covers. The broken verb that renders "Charm" and "Quick eyes" grammatical subjects *manqué* also makes them nouns-in-motion, brilliant traces of lives shattered by objects moving in time and space, transferring power; by a "botched" civilization's self-destructive violence, subjects versus objects, we against "them."

In the implied lyric I/eye that captures this afterimage we sense the I/eye of *The Cantos:* there yet unspoken, nowhere, everywhere, eluding the exact perspectival location conferred by person, number, tense; felt though not seen in the oddly suppressed yet somehow not absent grammatical subject of the poem's opening lines: "And then went down to the ship / Set keel to breakers, forth on the godly sea." It surfaces briefly in the plural ("and / We set up mast and sail on that swart ship"), then dives into and under the verb to emerge on the other side as object ("Bore sheep aboard her, and our bodies also, / Heavy with weeping, and winds from sternward / Bore us out onward with bellying canvas") to lose itself again in the muted orison of the sentence's appositive close: "Circe's this craft, the trim-coifed goddess." Would these opening words, "And then went down to the ship," not ordinarily make us ask, "Who? I? we? you? he? they? Where am I?" Yet do we wonder where the subject has gone and why? Or does its implicit if unspecified presence conduct us almost imperceptibly across a linguistic threshold into an unfamiliar form of life, mediated by an experimental English engaged with other grammars and refracting itself through them, saved from solecism by its power to situate us differently, at home somewhere in the endless expanses of Fenollosa's nature (self-thus), that uncompletable sentence that would take all time and more to pronounce ("And then went . . . So that:")? Does *The Cantos'* vanishing subject perform a different way of being in the world, folded into and unfolding in time, as the Western epic's subject-in-process slips into, out of, among, and behind verbs-becoming-nouns-becoming-verbs?

On the watch for a lyric I/eye that vacates its grammatical place for a different form of life, we recall Eliot's word for Pound's translations— "translucencies."[28] Rather than invent Chinese poetry for English speakers, as Eliot claimed, does Pound not invent, after Emerson, Fenollosa, and those countries of the mind he called Cathay, a translucent I/eye for a twentieth-century English epic? Dismantling the solid-state, positivist, monological (or monotheistic) Western "I" through its subversions of English grammar, does *The Cantos* in some sense invent a verb for an I/eye that stands forth or *bhu* / grows within a protean nature, in the image of Fenollosa's noun-verbs? Does the poem, then, track a "Mind like a floating wide cloud,"[29] borne on a speaking wind toward a horizon of undreamed responsibilities for nations and races, encountering its century's epic terrors, beauties, evils—self-thus, translucent even to its worst mistakes?— now a camera eye, seeing not seen; now errant, dislocated, lost—the capsized "being we call human, writing- / master to this world," writing "error / with four Rs"[30] (the translator's condition, as it is the epic wanderer's); now, having cast off specificity and "persona-lity" (in Fenollosa's gloss, not the soul but the soul's mask), a decapitalized existential subject-in-process that "is," stands forth, in what it sees, does, performs, feels?

And in this connection, does *The Cantos'* self-foreignizing English enable speakers born into this global language to experience something of what it is like to live in a language not one's own, or no longer or not yet to know one's own and to "know poorly the major language" one is "forced to serve"—the problem not just of immigrants, minorities, and their children but of "all of us"? Reading *The Cantos*, do we sense something of what it is to be "a nomad and an immigrant and a gypsy" in one's own language; something of what it might be to lose—or to gain—"the noun for standing in mist by a haunted tree, / the verb for I"; something of what it means to be born into English, or Chinese?[31]

NOTES

1. I build on Wai-lim Yip, who distinguishes between textual and cultural translation in comparing Pound's ("While my hair was still cut straight across my forehead") and Waley's ("Soon after I wore my hair covering my forehead") translations of "The River-Merchant's Wife," observing that "Pound has crossed the border of textual translation into cultural translation and Waley has not, though he is close enough to the original" (*Ezra Pound's* "Cathay" [Princeton: Princeton University Press, 1969], 90).

2. See Yip, chap. 3, on the reception of *Cathay* as translation.

3. Ludwig Wittgenstein, *Philosophical Investigations*, trans. G. E. M. Anscombe, 3d ed. (New York: Blackwell and Mott, 1958), sec. 19 (8e).

4. Hugh Kenner, introduction to Ezra Pound's *Translations* (New York: New Directions, 1963), 9.

5. In a similar vein, Eugene Chen Eoyang judges Pound "perhaps the most protean of post-Babelian writers, for not only did he translate actively from many languages but he incorporated what he translated, often in its original form, in his *Cantos*. His creative impulse was multicultural (even if his politics were reactionary and his poetic accents determinedly American); more than any other author, he tried to understand the literatures of the world in any language, to see from the perspective of another culture, and to speak, in his own voice, as many 'other' languages as he could" (*The Transparent Eye: Reflections on Translation, Chinese Literature, and Comparative Poetics* [Honolulu: University of Hawaii Press, 1993], 10).

6. *CWC*, 3. Fenollosa died in 1908; Pound found the manuscript in the notebooks Mary Fenollosa gave him in late 1913 and edited and published the essay in 1919.

7. Ezra Pound, unpublished introductory note to his Cavalcanti edition, cited in David Anderson, *Pound's Cavalcanti: An Edition of the Translations, Notes, and Essays* (Princeton: Princeton University Press, 1983), 5.

8. Jacques Derrida, "Des tours de Babel," trans. Joseph F. Graham, in *Difference in Translation*, ed. Graham (Ithaca: Cornell University Press, 1985), 165, 179.

9. Walter Benjamin, "The Task of the Translator," in *Illuminations*, ed. Hannah Arendt, trans. Harry Zohn (New York: Schocken, 1969), 75, 76, 78. See also Paul de Man, "Walter Benjamin's 'The Task of the Translator,'" in *The Resistance to Theory* (Minneapolis: University of Minnesota Press, 1986), 73–105; and John Johnston, "Translation as Simulacrum," in *Rethinking Translation: Discourse, Subjectivity, Ideology* (London: Routledge, 1992), 42–56.

10. Cited in Benjamin, "Task of the Translator," 80–81.

11. Gilles Deleuze and Claire Parnet, *Dialogues*, trans. Hugh Tomlinson and Barbara Habberjam (New York: Columbia University Press, 1987), 5.

12. Analyzing Pound's and others' translation practices, Lawrence Venuti distinguishes between "'foreignizing' translation" and "the forced 'invisibility' or 'transparency' of 'fluent' or 'domesticating' translation" in *The Translator's Invisibility: A History of Translation* (London: Routledge, 1994), 148. Venuti ascribes ideological valences to these principles, framing foreignizing translation as "a dissident cultural practice" that "maintain[s] a refusal of the dominant by developing affiliations with marginal linguistic and literary values at home, including foreign cultures that have been excluded because of their own resistance to dominant values"—which even so enact "an ethnocentric appropriation of the foreign text by enlisting it in a domestic cultural political agenda, like dissidence" (148).

13. James J. Y. Liu, *The Art of Chinese Poetry* (Chicago: University of Chicago Press, 1962), 40.

14. George A. Kennedy, *Selected Works*, ed. Tien-yi Li (New Haven: Far Eastern Publications, 1964), 480, cited in William McNaughton, "Chinese Poetry in Untranslation," *Delos* 1 (1968): 196.

15. Cf. discussion of "impersonality, timelessness, and a sense of the universal," by J. D. Frodsham and Ch'eng Hsi in *An Anthology of Chinese Verse* (Oxford: Clarendon, 1967), cited by McNaughton, "Chinese Poetry in Untranslation," 195.

Disputing such inferences of timelessness and universality, McNaughton delineates six "parts of speech in classical Chinese": "substitutes, connectives, particles, interjections, negative verbs, and 'full words,'" which "can function in any primary position in the sentence or as the adjunct of any word that functions in a primary position, including the second. Although this sixth word-class is subdivided in English and other European languages, it is scarcely accurate to say that Chinese lacks definite parts of speech" (195).

16. For "focalize," see Mieke Bal, *Narratology: Introduction to the Theory of Narrative* (Toronto: University of Toronto Press, 1997).

17. Joseph Needham, *Science and Civilization in China* (Cambridge: Cambridge University Press, 1956), 291; see Hugh Kenner, *The Pound Era* (Berkeley and Los Angeles: University of California Press, 1971), 230-31. On the influence of China and Confucius on the European Enlightenment, see Zhang Longxi, "The Myth of the Other: China in the Eyes of the West," *Critical Inquiry* 15 (1988): 108-31.

18. Ralph Waldo Emerson, "Nature," in *Selections*, ed. Stephen E. Whicher (Boston: Houghton Mifflin, 1960), 24.

19. Sinologists' dismay at Fenollosa's perpetration of "etymosinological myths" about the origins, structure, and meaning-functions of Chinese ideograms coexists in the essay's reception with its influence as a modern *Ars poetica* to stand with Sidney's and Shelley's defenses of poetry, beginning with Pound's reading of it as "a study of the fundamentals of all aesthetics" (3). For "etymosinological myths" see Achilles Fang, "Fenollosa and Pound," *Harvard Journal of Asian Studies* 20 (1957): 213-38. For bibliography and commentary on critiques of the Pound-Fenollosa poetics and translations, see Yip, *Ezra Pound's "Cathay,"* 3-7.

20. Gary Zukav, *The Dancing Wu Li Masters: An Overview of the New Physics* (New York: William Morrow, 1979), 313, 54; cf. the twentieth-century discoveries, from *within* Western science, that "there is no substantive physical world" (Henry Stapp, "S-Matrix Interpretation of Quantum Theory," *Physical Review* D3 [1971]: 1303); that "[m]ost particles or aggregates of particles that are ordinarily regarded as separate objects have interacted at some time in the past with other objects"; that "in some sense all these objects constitute an indivisible whole. Perhaps in such a world the concept of an independently existing reality can retain some meaning, but it will be an altered meaning and one remote from everyday experience" (Bernard d'Espagnat, "The Quantum Theory and Reality," *Scientific American* 241 [November 1979]: 158, 181). For fuller discussion of Fenollosa's and Derrida's critiques of Western grammar in relation to the challenge to ordinary language presented by quantum physics, see my "Quantum Physics/Postmodern Metaphysics: The Nature of Jacques Derrida," *Western Humanities Review* 39 (winter 1985): 287-313.

21. Fenollosa's etymosinology would seem to have something in common with "The Wonderful and Mystical Chinese Characters" promoted by the Beijing International Chinese Characters Study Association of Jiangxi Normal University and Jiangxi TV Station, which describes the ideogram as "a mysterious image, a unique sign, a demonstration of noble spirit, a crystallization of wisdom. . . . Each word . . . is a series of musical notes, a picture in motion. Once you have mastered its conno-

tation and denotation, you will have endless associations . . . [and] images" (*People's Daily*, November 11, 12, 14, 15, 1991, translated and cited by Guiyou Huang in "Ezra Pound: [Mis]Translation and [Re-]Creation," *Paideuma* 22, no. 3 [1993]: 101 n. 7).

22. Mary Barnard, *Assault on Mount Helicon: A Literary Memoir* (Berkeley and Los Angeles: University of California, 1984), 283; the letter dates from late 1951 or early 1952.

23. "The Return" dates from the year before Pound met Mary Fenollosa and found himself "getting orient from all quarters" (*Ezra Pound and Dorothy Shakespear: Their Letters,* ed. Omar Pound and A. Walton Litz [New York: New Directions, 1984], 264). For a detailed history of Pound's encounters with Chinese art, see Zhaoming Qian, *Modernism and Orientalism: The Legacy of China in Pound and Williams* (Durham: Duke University Press, 1995), chaps. 1–2. Qian dates Pound's "exploration of Chinese literature" from 1913–14 and notes that Pound learned from Herbert Allen Giles's *A History of Chinese Literature* of Qu Yuan's invention of Chinese free verse some two millennia earlier (25, 28).

24. William Butler Yeats, introduction to *The Oxford Book of Modern Verse, 1892–1935* (Oxford: Clarendon, 1936), xxvi.

25. See appendix. René Taupin, *L'Influence du symbolisme français sur la poésie americaine (de 1910 à 1920)* (Paris, 1929): "*Entre* Apparuit *où Pound a étudié la structure de la strophe, en s'aident de R. de Gourmont et* The Return, *une de ses meilleures réussités, où il profite des découvertes de Régnier, il s'écoule 6 mois. Ce dernier poème n'a demandé qu'un quart d'heure de travail*" *(142n)*. Taupin compares the two poems' *vers libre* prosody, 142–44.

26. Qian quotes Giles's version ("O fair white silk, fresh from the weaver's loom, / Clear as the frost, bright as the winter snow— / See! friendship fashions out of thee a fan, / Round as the round moon shines in heaven above, / At home, abroad, a close companion thou, / Stirring at every move the grateful gale. / And yet I fear, ah me! that autumn chills, / Cooling the dying summer's torrid rage, / Will see thee laid neglected on the shelf, / All thought of bygone days, like them bygone") and discusses the formal relations between the original's *wuyan* or pentasyllabic line and the haiku form Pound's version adapts (*Modernism and Orientalism*, 45–46).

27. Ming Xie, "Ezra Pound, Amy Lowell, and the Chinese Example of *Vers Libre,*" *Paideuma* 22, no. 3 (1993): 56.

28. T. S. Eliot, introduction to Ezra Pound's *Selected Poems* (London: Faber and Faber, 1959): "His translations seem to be—and that is the test of excellence—translucencies: we *think* we are closer to the Chinese than when we read, for instance, Legge" (14–15).

29. Ezra Pound, "Taking Leave of a Friend," *Cathay,* in *P,* 141.

30. Marianne Moore, "The Pangolin," in *The Complete Poems of Marianne Moore* (New York: Macmillan/Viking, 1967), 119.

31. Gilles Deleuze and Felix Guattari, *Kafka: Toward a Minor Literature,* trans. Dana Polan (Minneapolis: University of Minnesota Press, 1986), 19; W. S. Merwin, "Losing a Language," in *The Rain in the Trees* (New York: Knopf, 1988), 67. For Yang Lian's poems in English translation see *Non-Person Singular,* trans. Brian

Holton (London: Wellsweep, 1994), *Where the Sea Stands Still,* trans. Brian Holton (Newcastle upon Tyne: Bloodaxe Books, 1999), both bilingual editions; and *Yi,* trans. Mabel Lee (Los Angeles: Green Integer Press, 2002), excerpted in the present volume.

APPENDIX

TITLE POEM OF *Les Médailles d'Argile* BY HENRI DE RÉGNIER (PARIS, 1907).

J'ai feint que des Dieux m'aient parlé;
Celui-là ruisselant d'algues et d'eau,
Cet autre lourd de grappes et de blé,
Cet autre ailé,
Farouche et beau
En sa stature de chair nue,
Et celui-ci toujours voilé,
Cet autre encor
Qui cueille, en chantant, la ciguë
Et la pensée
Et qui noue à son thyrse d'or
Les deux serpents en caducée,
D'autres encor . . .

Alors j'ai dit: Voici de flûtes et des corbeilles,
Mordez aux fruits;
Écoutez chanter les abeilles
Et l'humble bruit
De l'osier vert qu'on tresse et des roseaux qu'on coupe.
J'ai dit encor: Écoute,
Écoute,
Il y a quelqu'un derrière l'écho,
Debout parmi la vie universelle,
Et qui porte l'arc double et le double flambeau,
Et qui est nous
Divinement . . .

Face invisible! je t'ai gravée en médailles
D'argent doux comme l'aube pâle,
D'or ardent comme le soleil,
D'airain sombre comme la nuit;
Il y en a de tout métal,
Qui tintent clair comme la joie,
Qui sonnent lourd comme la gloire,
Comme l'amour, comme la mort;
Et j'ai fait les plus belles de belle argile
Sèche et fragile.

Une à une, vous les comptiez en souriant,
Et vous disiez: Il est habile;
Et vous passiez en souriant.

Aucun de vous n'a donc vu
Que mes mains tremblaient de tendresse,
Que tout le grand songe terrestre
Vivait en moi pour vivre en eux
Que je gravais aux métaux pieux,
Mes Dieux,
Et qu'ils étaient le visage vivant
De ce que nous avons senti des roses,
De l'eau, du vent,
De la forêt et de la mer,
De toutes choses
En notre chair,
Et qu'ils sont nous divinement.

Painting into Poetry:
Pound's Seven Lakes Canto

ZHAOMING QIAN

The story of what Pound's Canto 49, generally known as the Seven Lakes Canto, owes to the "screen book" he received from his parents in 1928[1] has been told and retold. A relic from Japan,[2] the fourteen-fold sourcebook consists of eight ink paintings, eight poems in Chinese, and eight poems in Japanese, mutually representing eight classic views about the shores of the Xiao and Xiang Rivers in central South China. In a 1977 essay Sanehide Kodama points out that the Seven Lakes Canto "significantly pins down the essential quality of the original manuscript poems and paintings."[3] His statement implies that the greater part of the canto is based on exchanges with both verbal and visual representations. Needless to say, all the items of the sourcebook require careful examination. Yet, curiously, few have paid serious attention to the eight painted scenes.

It is so easy to overlook the power of the visual. For decades we have spoken of Pound's translations from the Chinese as reworkings of others' versions, so we take it for granted that Pound relied on a verbal source to paint Chinese scenes in words. True to this assumption, something of that nature was found apropos of the first part of Canto 49.[4] In May 1928, as several Pound letters reveal,[5] a Miss Zeng from the Xiao-Xiang River region, descendent of Confucius's disciple Zeng Xi,[6] offered Pound an oral translation of the eight Chinese poems. Pound copied out these paraphrases in an unmailed letter he wrote to his father on July 30. Is most of Canto 49 made of nothing but Miss Zeng's text?[7] Apparently not. The poems and paintings of Pound's sourcebook are versions of each other doubly or triply representing a traditional Chinese theme in waterscape. "[F]rom the *semantic* point of view," W. J. T. Mitchell contends, "from the standpoint of referring, expressing intentions and producing effects in a viewer/listener, there is no essential difference between texts and images."[8] In Pound's case, his sourcebook's "images" must have impressed him long before Miss Zeng had made its Chinese "texts" readable—or he would not have requested the book in the first place. What's more, when he set out to compose the canto, these "images" continued to interact with the "texts." Some thirty lines of the canto, therefore, must have registered Pound's response to both visual and verbal representations of the eight scenes. Without recognizing Pound's creative response to the painted scenes, the achievement of his Seven Lakes Canto cannot be appreciated properly.

To those familiar with Chinese and Japanese masterpieces of the eight views, the first part of Canto 49 may appear more than verbal representation of eight privately owned ink paintings from Japan. It can be taken as representation of a tradition of ekphrasis, or verbal representation of visual representation, in the Far East. To see this we must dwell a little on the origin of this nine-hundred-year tradition.

In Europe painting and sculpture during the Renaissance relieved themselves of a reputation lower than literature; in China art achieved a position equal to poetry during the Song period.[9] Where Leonardo da Vinci refers to painting as "a poetry that is seen and not heard" and poetry as "painting which is heard and not seen,"[10] the Song spokesman for the poetry-art parallel Su Shi (1037–1101) calls great poems "pictures without forms" and great paintings "unspoken poems."[11] Painting and poetry were able to thrive side by side in Song China partially because the Song emperors, starting with the founder Taizu (r. 960–75), took a great interest in art. The eighth Song emperor, Huizong (r. 1101–25), to give an extreme example, turned government over to his ministers in order to spend more time on artistic activities. His neglect of state affairs eventually led to his capture by the invading troops of the Jin and loss of half of China. It was in this era of political impotence and artistic vigor that the primal works on the eight views were born.

Song Di (ca. 1015–ca. 1080), a Northern Song painter-scholar and a friend of Su Shi, is known to have initiated the theme of the eight views. We owe our knowledge of his lost masterpiece to Su Shi, who recalled watching him "working with facility, forgetting brush" in "Three Poems on Song [Di] Painting Evening Views on the Xiao-Xiang,"[12] and to Shen Kuo (1031–95), another scholar, who entered the subjects into his *Mengxi Jottings (Mengxi bitan)* (1088–93):

Wild Geese Descending to Sandbar *(ping sha yan luo)*;
Sailboats Returning from Distant Shore *(yuan pu fan gui)*;
Mountain Town, Clear with Mist *(shan shi qing lan)*;

River and Sky in Evening Snow *(jiang tian mu xue)*;
Autumn Moon over Lake Dongting *(Dongting qiu yue)*;
Night Rain on the Xiao and Xiang *(Xiao-Xiang ye yu)*;
Evening Bell from Mist-shrouded Temple *(yan si wan zhong)*;
Fishing Village in Twilight Glow *(yu cun luo zhao)*.[13]

From yet another source we have learned when and where Song Di created his masterpiece. In 1063 Song Di was assigned a post in Changsha, Hunan. Shortly after reporting to his post, he traveled by boat to Mt. Tanshanyan, which is situated at a point where the Xiao and Xiang Rivers converge, and returned to paint the eight views on a terrace wall in Changsha.[14] To Song Di the region's appeal must have been from the beautiful scenes as well as from their rich associations. In the third century B.C. China's first great poet, Qu Yuan, was exiled there. The local scenery and shamanist culture inspired him to make the remarkable *Nine Songs*, of which the ninth song, "Shan gui," or "The Mountain Spirit," yielded Pound his imagist "After Ch'u Yuan."

Su Shi's three poems on Song Di's eight views and Shen Kua's listing of the subjects inaugurated a poetry-painting competition destined to cross the boundaries of space, time, and culture. Shortly after the poetic titles of the eight views appeared in *Mengxi Jottings*, a Chan monk-poet called Huihong (1071–1128) was challenged by a fellow monk to compose eight poems on the same theme, following the sequence given by Shen Kua. His set of poems of eight lines of seven characters[15] turned out to outdo the three poems by Su Shi, his mentor and a master of ekphrasis. These poems and Song Di's paintings stimulated more artists and poets to work on the eight scenes. The rivalry soon caught the attention of Emperor Huizong. He is said to have first commissioned his court painters to try their hands at the theme and then himself painted a set of the eight views.[16]

The vogue for making paintings and poems on the eight views culminated in the sets of Southern Song painters Ma Yuan, Wang Hong, Yujian, and Muqi. While Ma Yuan's version has not passed down to us,[17] that of Wang Hong is preserved in the Metropolitan Museum of Art in New York. In a meticulously researched study Alfreda Murck demonstrates that this set translates Huihong's poems back into paintings in a rearranged order.[18] "The present physical sequence of the painting," Murck speculates, "may have resulted when discomfiture with a signature on the sixth painting prompted an owner to have 'Night Rain' mounted at the beginning of the set."[19] Where Wang Hong tried to follow his precursors, the Chan artists Yujian and Muqi endeavored to break from them. Not only did they treat the motif in unorthodox ways but they also improvised a calligraphic style now associated with Chan art. Yujian, moreover, initiated a tradition of adding poems to pictures on the eight views.

Perhaps because most of their significant works have been transferred to Japan, Yujian and Muqi have for centuries enjoyed a greater reputation abroad than in China. Their treatments of the eight views now housed in museums in Tokyo and elsewhere[20] were largely responsible for the Japanese passion for the subject. Among artists in Muromachi Japan who made remarkable copies of the theme were Soami (1472-1525)[21] and Shūkei Sesson (1504-89). Sesson's versions found their way into the British Museum and were displayed in its 1910-12 exhibition of Chinese and Japanese paintings.[22] Soami's *Autumn Moon,* like Sesson's *Wild Geese,* encapsulates the style that influenced postimpressionism. We now know that they owe their "ink splash" technique to Yujian and Muqi.

It is reported that Korean painters and poets began pursuing the theme of the eight views as early as the twelfth century. According to An Hwi-jun, King Myongjong of Koryo Korea (r. 1171-97) commissioned his scholar-officials and a favorite painter to create poems and pictures on the theme. While the Koryo experiments in painting are no longer extant, an early-sixteenth-century Korean artist's eight views on a screen have survived in Itsukushima's Daigan-ji Temple, Japan.[23] This work's physical form—an eight-fold painted screen—anticipates Pound's sourcebook, and its reliance on "ink splashes" calls to mind Yujian.

Pound's awareness of this tradition in China is evidenced by a letter he wrote to his father on May 30, 1928: "Translation of Chinese poems in picture book is at Rapallo. They are poems on a set of scenes in Miss Thseng's part of the country = sort of habit of people to make pictures & poems on that set of scenes."[24] Presumably Miss Zeng addressed the topic in her oral translation. But Pound had, much earlier, learned about the eight views from Laurence Binyon. During his early London years, he attended Binyon's slide lectures (1909), went to his exhibition of Chinese and Japanese paintings at the British Museum (1910-12), and reviewed his book *The Flight of the Dragon* (1911).[25] The series was Binyon's favorite subject. If the slide images Binyon showed during his lectures did not impress Pound, those in the exhibition surely did. The catalog to the exhibition described the eight views as "a traditional se-ries of landscape subjects . . . originally associated with the scenery of Lake Tung-Ting [Dongting] in China."[26] A note to that effect should have been enough to rouse Pound's interest, and in *The Flight of the Dragon* he was to take in more information. The topic is covered in chapter 10, where Song Di is characterized as having advised painters to throw silk over a rugged wall and "fancy travellers wandering among [mountains, streams, and forests]," a strategy favored also by Leonardo. In the eight views, we are then told, "the painter of the Vesper Bell from a Distant Temple would evoke the mellow sound of the evening bell coming over the plain to the traveller's ears."[27]

From *Painting in the Far East* (1908) Pound could have learned more about the tradition. In that earlier work Binyon seeks to explain why gen-eration after generation of Chinese painters and poets should be inter-ested in repeating a commonplace theme. His comment, made after a dis-cussion of Muqi's *Evening Bell,* is revealing: "It is by the new and original treatment—original, because profoundly felt—of matter that is fundamentally familiar, that great art comes into being."[28] For Binyon the success of Muqi's *Evening Bell* offers the West a good lesson. "The sub-ject is essentially the same as that which the poetic genius of Jean François Millet conceived in the twilight of Barbizon, at the hour when the Angelus sounds over the plain from the distant church of Chailly," he writes. But "our foolish and petty misconceptions of originality would cause all the critics to exclaim against any painter who took up the theme again as a trespasser on Millet's property."[29]

To return to Canto 49, it must be stressed that Pound's sourcebook rep-resents a Far Eastern tradition of making pictures and poems side by side on a theme of great masters. In this kind of "mixed arts," to borrow a term from Mitchell, the viewer/reader's attention is split between the two media.[30] What eventually impresses him or her will be the interplay of vi-sual and verbal representation. This should describe Pound's experience of conceiving most of the canto. He had easy access to all parts of the book—eight ink paintings and sixteen poems, half of which he should read with the aid of Miss Zeng's "paraphrases." Moving between the two media, he should have noticed both echoes and discrepancies in representation.

A question may be raised: isn't it possible that Pound had put aside his sourcebook? He could be simply following the "paraphrases" in composing the canto. Let us assume that was the case. Still, Pound would have to return every now and then to the sourcebook with the painted scenes and original poems. He would have to do so because the "paraphrases" were far from comprehensible. Translating a poem from Chinese to English was painstaking enough. When one had to deal with the handwriting of a Japanese artist, the task was doubly strenuous. Here is Pound's typescript for Miss Zeng's version of the opening scene, *Night Rain:*

> Rain, empty river,
> Place for soul to travel
>   (or room to travel)
> Frozen cloud, fire, rain damp twilight.
> One lantern inside boat cover (i.e., sort of
>   shelter, not awning on small boat)
> Throws reflection on bamboo branch,
>   causes tears.[31]

Without substantial aid one simply cannot comprehend what the translator means by "Place for soul to travel / (or room to travel)" or "Throws reflection on bamboo branch, / causes tears." Luckily, Pound had his "picture book" to turn to at his moment of puzzlement. Viewing the painted scene *Night Rain* (fig. 1), he could easily decipher frontal curls as waves stirred up by rain in an empty river, three bold strokes in the middle as small boats amid bent reeds, and blankness across distant hills as chilled cloud. So, "Place for soul to travel" should signify a "voyage" even though no characters in the Chinese poem could verify it; and "reflection on bamboo branch, / causes tears" should imply a poetic reading of nature's response. Consequently lines 2–6 in Canto 49:

> Rain; empty river; a voyage,
> Fire from frozen cloud, heavy rain in the twilight
> Under the cabin roof was one lantern.
> The reeds are heavy; bent;
> and the bamboos speak as if weeping.

> (49/244)

Surprisingly, the lines evoke the same sort of emotion the painted scene and original poem in Chinese combine to evoke. Kodama is not exaggerating when he remarks that Pound's version "is closer to the original Chinese poems than to the paraphrases." For him Pound's success was due to the fact that he "went over the original himself, or had someone re-examine them."[32] This is doubtful. The opening poem in Chinese,

Fig. 1. *Night Rain*, unidentified Japanese artist. (Courtesy Mary de Rache-wiltz, Brunnenburg, Italy. Courtesy Richard Taylor.)

to begin with, is one of the three that are legibly written out in regular script *(kai shu)*.[33] Pound's failure to drop the word "fire," for which there is no matching Chinese character, proves that neither he nor any helper reexamined it. As for how the error could have slipped into the "paraphrases," Kodama's explanation is acceptable: "she [Miss Zeng] might have said 'adhere' for the ideogram meaning 'stick,' which Pound might have heard as 'fire.'"[34] Besides, until 1936, as Kenner has told us, "Pound's forte was haruspication of the single ideogram, not the tracing of sequential connections western syntax specifies."[35] Pound's large debt, therefore, was not to the original poem. His guide had to be the painted scene.

Turning to the *Autumn Moon* scene, we shall find more eloquent evidence that Pound deliberately reexamined the paintings after he acquired the "paraphrases" and before he composed the canto. In mixed arts, in which picture and word are set side by side, their respective elucidating force is at once reinforced and subverted.[36] If in the above example we have focused only on how picture and word illuminate each other, here we are to observe more of their disruptive dynamics. A glance from the draft version of the "Autumn Moon" to the corresponding ink painting (fig. 2) designates that each contains some striking features that disrupt striking features in the other. Thus in the text provided by Miss Zeng the most remarkable details are "evening clouds" *(mu tian xia)*, "Ten thousand ripples" *(wan qing yin bo)*, and "cinnamon flowers" *(gui hua)*.[37] By contrast, the painting presents a high mountain with a cloud across it, a tall pine with an upward point, and no stretch of water with ripples or "cinnamon flowers." Juxtaposed, the visible images of the painting tend to darken those of the paraphrase. Pound evidently examined both the pictorial and verbal representations of the autumn moon, and it was the interaction of the two that yielded lines 7–12 of Canto 49:

> Autumn moon; hills rise about lakes
> against sunset
> Evening is like a curtain of cloud,
> a blurr above ripples; and through it
> sharp long spikes of the cinnamon,
> a cold tune amid reeds.

> (49/244)

Nowhere is Pound more removed from his verbal text than in lines 13–17 of the canto, where he defies what is elaborated in word and freely

Fig. 2. *Autumn Moon,* unidentified Japanese artist. (Courtesy Mary de Rachewiltz, Brunnenburg, Italy. Courtesy Richard Taylor.)

responds to his fancy evoked by visual detail from his sourcebook. Lines
13-14 are said to have come from the paraphrase of "Evening Bell":

Cloud shuts off the hill, hiding the temple
Bell audible only when wind moves toward one,
One can not tell whether the summit is near or far
Sure only that one is in hollow of mountains.[38]

There is Chan illumination in the contrast between what is far off and
what is near at hand. For those who instinctively interpret the bell sound
in wind as a symbol of distance/immediacy, the last two lines of the poem
are superfluous. In turning from the paraphrase to the picture we turn
from verbal redundancy to visual simplicity: a pagoda top and a temple
roof are barely visible behind mountaintops (fig. 3). Many of us will won-
der how we are to hear the temple bell. It is the view of Walter Benjamin
that original works of art "will have aura, or 'speak'" (Benjamin, *Illumi-
nations*). Identifying this potential in van Gogh, J. Hillis Miller explains
that "this power is associated with distance. Van Gogh's painting takes us
'somewhere else [*jäh anderswo*].'"[39] The bell scene Pound held before
him was not a masterpiece, but it was hand painted and could be linked
to Muqi's painting praised by Binyon. The pagoda in ink and light color
and on rice paper could have taken Pound "somewhere else," somewhere
in China, where through the subtle playing of association he envisioned
a temple bell and heard it sound. Lines 13-14, in imitation of an actual
painting's mute language, register his response:

Behind hill the monk's bell
borne on the wind.

(49/244)

The unique pictorial speech of "Evening Bell" brings about more
dynamics in "Sailboats Returning." The sight is rendered thus in the
paraphrase:

Touching green sky at horizon, mists in suggestion of autumn
Sheets of silver reflecting all that one sees
Boats gradually fade, or are lost in turn of the hills,
Only evening sun, and its glory on the water remain.[40]

It is again in the corresponding painted scene that we witness the actual
spectacle at fixation, what Wendy Steiner terms the "frozen moment of
action"[41]—three boats in rapids in broad daylight (fig. 4). The boats de-
lineated as in full sail do not exactly indicate return, however. In Yujian's

Fig. 3. *Evening Bell*, unidentified Japanese artist. (Courtesy Mary de Rachewiltz, Brunnenburg, Italy. Courtesy Richard Taylor.)

Fig. 4. *Sailboats Returning*, unidentified Japanese artist. (Courtesy Mary de Rachewiltz, Brunnenburg, Italy. Courtesy Richard Taylor.)

treatment one catches sight of masts instead.[42] (The word *qiang* or "mast" actually occurs in the third line of the Chinese poem: *gui qiang jian ru lu hua qu* or "Returning masts slowly disappear into reeds.") Pound may well have picked this misleading detail, discarded "green sky," "mists in suggestion of autumn," and "hills" in the paraphrase, and dashed off lines 15–17:

> Sail passed here in April; may return in October
> Boat fades in silver; slowly;
> Sun blaze alone on the river.

> (49/244)

We can pause for a moment now to reflect on the overall design of the sequence. As in the paintings, so in the poems, water-path and shore take turns to occupy the center; ripples, reeds, boats, hills, and clouds that appear and disappear in the previous scenes continue to do so in *Mountain Town*, *Snowy Evening*, *Wild Geese*, and *Fishing Village* (figs. 5–8). Put together, the pictures signal a continuous flow, a journey by boat through seasons. The figure "Under the cabin roof" who hears "the bamboos speak as if weeping" reappears in subsequent scenes to catch glimpses of a "wine flag," "a world . . . covered with jade," and "Wild geese" (49/244), and listen to "the young boys prod stones for shrimp" (245). While the duplication of such a subject is implied in the poems, it is physically presented in the pictorial sequence in the form of a repeated small boat (see figs. 1 and 8).

The preoccupation of multiscened painting with continuity has been examined by various critics. Steiner establishes "repetition of a subject" and "continuity of the road" as two chief strategies of European masters in their attempt to secure pictorial narrativity.[43] For her the latter is a metaphor "shopworn" in the picaresque novel but "in particular pictorial manifestations can be very powerful."[44] Wu Hung describes a continuous long handscroll as a Chinese art medium painted section by section and viewed section by section. "In terms of both painting and viewing," he writes, "a [long] handscroll is literally a moving picture, with shifting moments and loci."[45] Allied to this is a painted screen, an art medium like a long handscroll but with separately zoned scenes. What Pound had was precisely that last format: a fourteen-fold screen with four Chinese scenes on the front and four more on the back, each set between two poems, Chinese to the right and Japanese to the left.[46]

When photographs of the eight pictures are arranged in the original order without interruption of the poems, a multiscened long handscroll emerges.[47] Viewing it from right to left as a Chinese or a Japanese would, the eight separate views appear as a continuous waterscape with a connected outline of hills in the background and a now wide, now narrow water-path in the foreground. The moorings at the left of *Night Rain* join those of *Autumn Moon*. A slope of *Autumn Moon* lengthens into the left of *Evening Bell*. With imposing peaks *Evening Bell* marks a transition in the progression of design. Looking both ways, one recognizes a change in color: from the gray of the views on the right to the green and bright orange of those on the left. The shift in color gradation certainly signals a shift in mood. While in *Night Rain* and *Autumn Moon* the dominant atmosphere is gloom, in *Snowy Evening* and *Wild Geese* it is serenity and leisure, and in *Mountain Town* and *Fishing Village* calm and gaiety. Accordingly, it would be insensible to interpret the water-path here as a "path of life" through hardship. In the Chinese tradition it is more reasonably interpreted as a woeful scholar's retreat into nature, where he attains the Dao and with it bliss.

Now, there is unquestionably a difference between painting the eight views and writing poems about them, a difference between visual presentation of scenes and presentation of them in a figurative sense. In writing these poems in Chinese, moreover, the Japanese artist labors to represent the views in a fixed form of four seven-character lines.[48] Often after presenting a scene he still has space for moralizing or speculating. This of course goes against Pound's imagist credo: "Direct treatment of the thing" and "Don't be viewy" (*LE*, 3,6). Pound is not interested in Chinese or Japanese verse form. He just desires to recapture the essential quality of the eight views. Hence his disregard of all personal reflection for *Evening Bell*. Hence his omissions of all stretched imaginings: "A few country people enjoying their evening drink" for *Mountain Town* and "Fisherman calls his boy, and takes up his wine bottle" for *Fishing Village*.[49] By ignoring such musings he succeeds in producing a version nearer to the "mute speech" of painting, an ideal of modernist ekphrasis.

My last remark reinforces my position that the first part of Pound's Seven Lakes Canto is better understood as ekphrasis of his source-book's painted scenes than as translation of its Chinese poems. Pound

Fig. 5. *Mountain Town*, unidentified Japanese artist. (Courtesy Mary de Rachewiltz, Brunnenburg, Italy. Courtesy Richard Taylor.)

Fig. 6.   *Snowy Evening*, unidentified Japanese artist. (Courtesy Mary de Rachewiltz, Brunnenburg, Italy. Courtesy Richard Taylor.)

Fig. 7. *Wild Geese*, unidentified Japanese artist. (Courtesy Mary de Rache-
wiltz, Brunnenburg, Italy. Courtesy Richard Taylor.)

Fig. 8. *Fishing Village*, unidentified Japanese artist. (Courtesy Mary de Rachewiltz, Brunnenburg, Italy. Courtesy Richard Taylor.)

does make use of the verbal text. But the service it renders is like that of a caption. Without a clue from the text for *Mountain Town*, Pound would-n't have been able to identify in the corresponding picture a "wine flag" sticking out behind a roof, thence giving line 18: "Where wine flag catches the sunset" (49/244). Nor could he have imagined line 28, "Rooks clatter over the fishermen's lanthorns" (244), if not for the text's hint of "birds" stopped around a small boat in the last picture, *Fishing Village.*[50] Despite the text's importance, nonetheless, Pound never seems to have permitted it to influence his direct treatment of the pictures. Indeed, in the canto he mimics the pictorial language so intensely that his lines do not become "audible" unless a source image shows "aura," or breaks muteness. When this occurs first in reference to *Night Rain,* his response, "the bamboos speak as if weeping" (line 6), communicates a feeling of sorrow suggested in the first two painted scenes. Next, when line 12, "Be-hind hill the monk's bell" (244), turns "audible," again it is "audible" like its source picture: its resonance awakens us to a sense of peace and con-tentment that is supported by subsequent silent views such as "wine flag," "a people of leisure," and "Wild geese." When line 30—"the young boys prod stones for shrimp"—"speaks," it echoes the sequence's final note of bliss. Thus, by way of translating the changing tones of the picto-rial composition, the canto signifies its Daoist theme of joyous liberation after withdrawal into nature.

My description of the sourcebook's pictures as having "aura" or power to "speak" may suggest that they are masterpieces. I must point out that the term *aura* has been used here solely for the sake of stressing the representational power of the visual. As for my enthusiasm, it is really for the eight-views tradition in China that has generated numerous mem-orable works of art and poetry in the Far East, of which Pound's screen book is a very late and common example.

It should be clear now why Pound inserts a version of the eight views in the middle of his modernist epic. The subject is a monument of Chi-nese culture, an example of how poets and artists in China (and in Japan) have continuously made an old theme new. All remarkable copies of the eight views have been accepted as such because of their originality. For Pound modernism also demands originality, originality allowing him to interweave texts and make statements about history and politics.

To make Canto 49 modernist Pound must not stop at the eight views.

A quick search through de Mailla's *Histoire générale* yields him lines 31–32: "In seventeen hundred came Tsing to these hill lakes. / A light moves on the south sky line." The reference to the Qing is fitting because it brings Chinese history to its last imperial dynasty. Indeed, it prefigures the conclusion of the Chinese History Cantos—the signing of the Nipchou Treaty with the czar "Year 28th of KANG HI" (59/327), which was a decade before Kangxi's journey to "hill lakes."[51] Kangxi wouldn't have been able to travel to South China by boat without a canal built by an "old king." Pound owed his knowledge of this to Fenollosa, who entered Mori's comment on Emperor Yang of Sui (r. 605–18) into a notebook: "he made a canal from Benrio (Kaifong of Kanan) to Yosingo, and they say that he did this for his own pleasure."[52] Pound simply substitutes "TenShi"[53] for "Kaifong" and proceeds: "This canal goes still to TenShi / though the old king built it for pleasure." (49/245).

Still, Pound has not tracked down the origin of China's ideal system. Two predynastic songs, "Qing yun ge" (Auspicious clouds song) supposedly from legendary emperor Shun and "Ji rang ge" (Clod beating song) supposedly from legendary emperor Yao, are then incorporated into the canto to recall a golden age. Both songs are derived from a notebook in which Fenollosa recorded Mori's lectures on Chinese poetry,[54] and, in fact, the first song "Qing yun ge" is given in Japanese sound, in Kenner's words, a way to remind us that "the Chinese had come to [Pound] by way of Japan."[55]

Pound has certainly added dimensions to his Chinese material. This he does first in lines 33–34: "State by creating riches shd. thereby get into debt? / This is infamy; this is Geryon." And then again in the terminal lines: "Imperial power is? and to us what is it? // The fourth; the dimension of stillness. / And the power over wild beasts" (49/245). These abrupt comments serve to place the eight views in a pre–World War II Euro-American context. Rereading the first part of Canto 49, we begin to see the traveler differently: he becomes a Westerner seeking a way out of political chaos. From the outset this man has a vision of Yao and Shun. The rustlings he hears from the bamboo are the sobs of Yao's daughters, mourning the death of their husband, Shun. Legend says that their tears stained the bamboo all the way, and it also says that they were drowned and metamorphosed into the twin goddesses of the Xiang.[56] Pound might have heard the tale from Miss Zeng. Otherwise he wouldn't have been able to produce a line so approximate to the original in effect. Nor would he have closed his canto with "Qing yun ge" and "Ji rang ge," which echo the opening scene's nostalgia for the lost leaders. But Pound could also have picked the story first from Fenollosa. At one point, Fenollosa had Ariga copy out in Chinese five songs from Qu Yuan's *Nine Songs*. A note to the third song, "Lord of the Xiang" ("Xiang jun"), reads, "The two wives of Shun died on the banks of the river Sho [Xiang]; since that time this river became a good topic of poets. Kutsugen [Qu Yuan] lived near this river and wrote this ode to the god of Sho."[57]

So the two ancient songs are not digressions from representation of the eight views but an integral part of an instance of modernist ekphrasis. What makes ekphrasis modernist, what distinguishes ekphrasis of the twentieth century from its predecessors, according to James Heffernan, are a self-sufficient quality and kinship to the museum. "The ekphrastic poetry of our time," he writes, "represents individual works of art within the context of the museum, which of course includes the words that surround the pictures we see, beginning with picture titles."[58] Pound's Canto 49 is not representation of a museum piece of art. Given its modernist nature, however, it is hardly surprising that it incorporates art-historical commentary, informing us of the making and viewing of his ekphrastic masterpiece.

NOTES

1. The "screen book" from the United States is acknowledged in Ezra Pound to Isabel Pound, March 1, 1928, YCAL, Pound Papers (MSS 43), Box 61, Folder 2695.

2. On Pound's "screen book," see Sanehide Kodama, "The Seven Lakes Canto" (first published under the title "The Eight Scenes of Sho-sho" in *Paideuma* 6, no. 2 [1977]), in his *American Poetry and Japanese Culture* (Hamden: Archon, 1984), 105–20.

3. Kodama, *American Poetry*, 115.

4. For a typescript of an oral translation of the eight Chinese poems, see Ezra Pound to Homer Pound, July 30, YCAL, Pound Papers, Box 61, Folder 2696. The typescript on three separate leaves is transcribed in Hugh Kenner, "More on the Seven Lakes Canto," *Paideuma* 2, no. 1 (1973): 43–44. On the order of the poems, see Richard Taylor, "Canto XLIX, Futurism, and the Fourth Dimension," *Neohelicon* (Budapest) 20, no. 1 (1993): 339–40.

5. Ezra Pound to Isabel Pound, March 1, 1928; Ezra Pound to Homer Pound, May 30, 1928, August 1, 1928, September 1, [1928]; YCAL, Pound Papers, Box 61, Folders 2695–96. See also Ezra Pound to Glenn Hughes, May 17, 1928, YCAL, Pound Papers, Box 23, Folder 1014.

6. A biographical sketch of Zeng Baosun is provided in Angela Jung Palandri, "The 'Seven Lakes Canto' Revisited," *Paideuma* 3, no. 1 (1974): 51–54.

7. See Kenner, "More," 43–44; Taylor, "Canto XLIX," 354–55. See also note 4 above.

8. W. J. T. Mitchell, *Picture Theory* (Chicago: University of Chicago Press, 1994), 160.

9. See Hans H. Frankel, "Poetry and Painting: Chinese and Western Views of Their Convertibility," *Comparative Literature* 9, no. 4 (1957): 289–91.

10. A. Philip McMahon, trans., *Treatise on Painting by Leonardo da Vinci* (Princeton: Princeton University Press, 1956), 1:17.

11. Su Shi: "Tu Fu's writings are pictures without forms, / Han Kan's paintings, unspoken poems." See *Early Chinese Texts on Painting*, ed. Susan Bush and Shih Hsio-yen (Cambridge: Harvard University Press, 1986), 203.

12. For the original poems, see Su Shi, *Dongpo qiji* (Works of Dongpo [Su Shi]) (Taibei: Zhonghua shuju, 1970), 4: *Dongpo xuji, juan* 2: 6.

13. See Shen Kua, *Mengxi bitan jiaozhen* (Mengxi Jottings, with amendations), ed. Yang Jialuo (Taibei: Shijie shuju, 1961), 1:549–50.

14. This account based on "a local history for the [Hunan] province" is taken from Alfreda Murck, "Eight Views on the Hsiao and Hsiang Rivers by Wang Hong," in Wen Fong et al., *Images of the Mind: Selections from the Edward L. Elliott Family and John B. Elliott Collections of Chinese Calligraphy and Painting at the Art Museum, Princeton University* (Princeton: Art Museum, 1984), 216.

15. For a translation of Huihong's eight poems, see ibid., 224–32. For Huihong's original poems, see Huihong, *Shimen wenzi chan* (Shimen Chan words), in *Jingyin wenyuan ge siku quanshu* (Siku complete works) (Taibei: Shangwu, 1986), 1116:239–40.

16. For Huizong's inscription on his own copy of the eight views, see Zhang Cheng, *Hualu guangyi* (Record of Painting, supplement), in *Yishu congbian* (Selected works on art), ed. Yang Jialuo (Taibei: Shijie shuju, 1975), 10:174.

17. Ma Yuan's eight views are mentioned in Zhu Derun, *Cunfuzhai ji* (Confuzhai anthology), in *Peiwenzhai shu hua pu* (Peiwenzhai guide to painting and calligraphy), ed. Wang Yuanqi et al. (Taibei: Xinxing shuju, 1972), *juan* 84:18.

18. Wang Hong's eight views are reproduced in Murck, "Eight Views," 225–34.

19. Ibid., 224.

20. The Idemitsu Museum of Art, Tokyo, owns Yujian's *Mountain Town* and Muqi's *Wild Geese*. The Nezu Institute of Fine Arts, Tokyo, houses Muqi's *Fishing Village*. The Hatakeyama Collection, Tokyo, keeps Muqi's *Evening Bell*. The Tokugawa Museum, Nagoya, preserves Yujian's *Sailboats Returning* and Muqi's *Autumn Moon*.

21. Daitoku-ji, Kyoto, holds Soami's eight views.

22. Nos. 128–34 (last two scenes both numbered 134) in the British Museum 1910–12 exhibition. See Binyon, *Guide to an Exhibition of Chinese and Japanese Paintings* (London: British Museum, 1910), 37–38.

23. An Hwi-jun, "Two Korean Landscape Paintings of the First Half of the 16th

Century," in *Traditional Korean Painting*, ed. Korean National Commission for UNESCO (Arch Cape, Oreg.: Pace International Research, 1983), 22, 24.

24. YCAL, Pound Papers, Box 61, Folder 2695.

25. See Pound's review of *The Flight of the Dragon* in *Blast* 2 (July 1915), reprinted in *P&P*, 2:99. On Pound's friendship with Binyon, see my *Orientalism and Modernism: The Legacy of China in Pound and Williams* (Durham: Duke University Press, 1995), 9–14.

26. Binyon, *Guide*, 37.

27. Binyon, *The Flight of the Dragon* (London: John Murray, 1911), 61.

28. Binyon, *Painting in the Far East* (London: Edward Arnold, 1908), 134.

29. Ibid., 135.

30. Mitchell, *Picture Theory*, 157.

31. See Kenner, "More," 43; Taylor, "Canto XLIX," 354. Whereas Taylor's version incorporates Pound's revisions, Kenner's does not.

32. Kodama, *American Poetry*, 107.

33. The eight Chinese poems are written out in three calligraphic styles: "Night Rain," "Autumn Moon," and "Evening Bell" in regular script *(kai shu);* "Sailboats Returning," "Snowy Evening," and "Wild Geese" in running script *(xing shu);* "Mountain Town" and "Fishing Village" in seal script *(zhuan shu).* The penmanship is characteristically Japanese.

34. Kodama, *American Poetry*, 113.

35. Kenner, "More," 44.

36. See J. Hillis Miller, *Illustration* (Cambridge: Harvard University Press, 1992), 68.

37. See Kenner, "More," 43; Taylor, "Canto XLIX," 354.

38. See Kenner, "More," 44; Taylor, "Canto XLIX," 354.

39. Miller, *Illustration*, 80.

40. Ibid.

41. Wendy Steiner, *Pictures of Romance: Form against Context in Painting and Literature* (Chicago: University of Chicago Press, 1988), 13.

42. In Yujian's masterpiece one witnesses three partially concealed masts in the background. For a reproduction, see Kei Suzuki, *Comprehensive Illustrated Catalog of Chinese Painting* (Tokyo: University of Tokyo Press, 1982), 3:284 (JM 15-008).

43. Steiner, *Pictures of Romance*, 17–22, 36–37.

44. Ibid., 36.

45. Wu Hung, *The Double Screen: Medium and Representation in Chinese Painting* (Chicago: University of Chicago Press, 1996), 59.

46. For a fuller description of Pound's "screen book," see Taylor, "Canto XLIX," 340.

47. I am grateful to Mary de Rachewiltz for providing the slides of the eight paintings and the photographs of the sixteen manuscript poems. The slides were made by Richard Taylor.

48. For transcripts of the poems in Chinese and Japanese accompanied by English versions, see Kodama, *American Poetry*, 108–12.

94

49. See Kenner, "More," 44; Taylor, "Canto XLIX," 355.

50. The "hint" is in the opening lines of the "paraphrase": "Bullrushes have burst into snow-tops / The birds stop to preen their feathers." See Kenner, "More," 44; Taylor, "Canto XLIX," 355.

51. The Nerchinsk Treaty, 1689. In 1684, 1689, 1699, 1703, 1705, and 1707, Kangxi made six "Southern Tours." He saw "hill lakes" not in the Xiao-Xiang region but in Suzhou and Hangzhou in the Yangtze delta. On Kangxi's "Southern Tours," see Jonathan D. Spence, *Ts'ao Yin and the K'ang-hsi Emperor* (New Haven: Yale University Press, 1966), 124–34.

52. The passage (dated September 12, 1901) can be found in Fenollosa, "Mori's Lectures on the History of Chinese Poetry," YCAL, Pound Papers, Box 100, Folder 4226.

53. According to Taylor, "TenShi is taken here for a place name, but is in fact a compounding of two separate Japanese words which mean Son of God" ("Canto XLIX," 344). As the Grand Canal was in the thirteenth century lengthened to Beijing in the North and Hangzhou in the South, it is historically correct to substitute TenShi (the seat of the Son of Heaven) for Kaifeng.

54. For transcripts of the two ancient songs, see Kenner, "More," 45–46.

55. Kenner, *The Pound Era* (Berkeley and Los Angeles: University of California Press, 1971), 222.

56. My account of the tale is based on Yuan Ke, *Zhongguo shenhua chuanshuo* (Chinese mythology) (Beijing: Zhongguo wenyi, 1984), 1:272.

57. Compare Fenollosa, "Early Chinese Poetry: Kutsugen (Ka-Gi): tr. by Ariga," YCAL, Pound Papers, Box 99, Folder 4221: "God lingers in his dwelling place and comes not to us, who can so long stop at the little isle in the middle of the river and wait for you? Please come soon." For a more recent version of the song, see David Hawkes, trans., *The Song of the South: An Ancient Chinese Anthology of Poems by Qu Yuan and Other Poets* (Harmondsworth: Penguin, 1985), 106–7.

58. James Heffernan, *Museum of Words: The Poetics of Ekphrasis from Homer to Ashbery* (Chicago: University of Chicago Press, 1993), 139.

Pound's Quest for Confucian Ideals: The Chinese History Cantos

HONG SUN

It seems odd that Ezra Pound, a modernist poet, should look to Chinese culture for inspiration. His quest-journey to this ancient civilization began when his poetry was coming of age. In 1909, when his mother suggested writing an "epic to the West," Ezra retorted: "What has the West done to deserve it?"[1] After many years of training in the Romance tradition, he was to turn to the East for literary ideals.

The Cantos is a manifesto in which Pound proclaims Confucianism as a "medicine" for the ills of Western civilization. He emphasizes the "Need of Confucius" in explicit terms: "Let me try to get this as clear as possible. A 'need' implies a lack, a sick man has 'need.' Something he has not. Kung [Kong] as medicine?"[2]

What the poet discovers in Confucianism is not merely a few abstruse philosophical formulas. For him truth exists in harmony and order, in the concrete beauty of this world, an elegance revealed by Confucian canons, particularly those in the Confucian classic *Da Xue* (The great learning), in China's long history, and in some of its ideograms. In *The Cantos*, Pound endeavors to present his discovery of this cosmos of truth and beauty.

Pound's role in modern literature is not that of a passive reflector of light from another culture. His concern is above that of conquistadors who shipped back from the Orient gems and gold to decorate their palaces. Pound's mission is that of Prometheus, an active agent not simply carrying forward the light of Chinese philosophy, but rejuvenating Western poetry with its ideals. As he remarks in the *The Cantos*: "our job" is "to build light" (98/704); "to 'see again,' / the verb is 'see,' not 'walk on'" (116/816); we require "A little light, like a rushlight / to lead back to splendour" (116/817). In this sense, Pound is more than a transmitter, he is, in T. S. Eliot's phrase, "the inventor of Chinese poetry for our time."[3]

THE COSMOS AS REVEALED IN *DA XUE*

As a young man, Pound had an ambition to bring freedom and energy into English poetry of the new century. He declared in "Revolt," a poem of 1909:

> I would shake off the lethargy of this our time,
> and give
> For shadows—shapes of power
> For dreams—men.

> (*CEP*, 96)

In a letter of the same year to his mother he spoke of epic in terms of prophecy: "An epic, in the real sense, is the speech of a nation through the mouth of one man." *The Cantos* seems such a prophecy. Yet, later, in a letter of 1924 to Bill Bird, his publisher of *A Draft of XVI Cantos*, he asserted: "it ain't an epic. It's part of a long poem" (*SL*, 189).

By calling *The Cantos* "a long poem," Pound made clear that he was not interested in following the rules of an epic. In a traditional Western epic, form follows the plot, and at the center of the plot is the protagonist. In this sense, *The Cantos* is not an epic, for in it we cannot find any plot or predominant sequence. Although it contains many stories, it is not controlled by a single story line. Pound was aware of the lack of epic quality in *The Cantos*. Critics have called *The Cantos* a "colossal failure," a "gigantic mess," without any "major form."[4] Pound did not believe that there was any need for this "major form": "Form is, indeed, very tiresome when in reading current novels, we observe the thinning residue of pages, 50, 30, and realize that there is now only time (space) for the hero to die a violent death, no other solution being feasible in that number of pages" (*LE*, 396). Some important works, as Pound pointed out, did not have this form either: "Art very possibly *ought* to be the supreme achievement, the 'accomplished'; but there is the other satisfactory effect, that of a man hurling himself at an indomitable chaos, and yanking and hauling as much of it as possible into some sort of order (or beauty), aware of it both as chaos and as potential" (*LE*, 396).

For Pound, order is synonymous with beauty. In his effort to forge this beauty out of chaos, he is unlike other poets who go back only to Homer, trying to evolve an order out of this mythological tradition. Pound pushes his frontier far beyond that point, both in time and space. For him, the

97

frontier is on the other hemisphere, in China, whose civilization is of greater antiquity. Their recorded history goes back to Xia, a dynasty allegedly founded in 2205 B.C. by Da Yu (The Great Yu). This nation has shown unusual power of survival, absorbing all foreign influences without losing its own identity. As Voltaire remarks: "The body of this empire has existed four thousand years, without having undergone any alteration in its laws, customs, language, or even its fashions of apparel. . . . The organization of this empire is in truth the best the world has ever seen."[5]

In this ancient culture Pound sees Confucianism. Confucius never claimed divine revelation. He called himself "a transmitter, and not a maker." As a transmitter, he is said to have collected and edited four ancient Chinese classics: *Shi Jing* (The book of songs), *Shu Jing* (The book of history), *Li Ji* (The book of rites), and *Yi Jing* (The book of changes). These books and *Chun Qiu* (The spring and autumn annals), supposedly written by him, constitute the Five Confucian Canons.

After Confucius died at the age of seventy-two, his disciples put together his sayings in a book called *Lun Yu* (The analects). Later, a record of the sayings of a disciple of Confucius's grandson formed *Mengzi* (The book of Mencius). Zhu Xi, a neo-Confucianist of the Song dynasty, detached from *Li Ji* two sections, *Da Xue* and *Zhong Yong* (The doctrine of the means), which, together with *Lun Yu* and *Mengzi*, form the Four Books of Confucianism.

Of all the Confucian books, *Da Xue* had the strongest impact on Pound. What he viewed as essential in the classic was its emphasis on order. As Hugh Kenner notes, "When the *Ta Hio* [*Da Xue*], *Great Learning* ("Great Digest"), is added [to the Canons], Confucius becomes systematic."[6]

Pound regards *Da Xue* as something to believe in, for it tells us of our duty of "developing and restoring to its primitive clarity our reason."[7] The major principles of *Da Xue* can be summed up by a paraphrase of Pound's translation: The men of ancient times wanting to illustrate illustrious virtue throughout the kingdom first governed their own states well by first establishing order in their own families; wishing to have good order in their families, they first cultivated themselves; and wishing to cultivate themselves, they first rectified their own hearts; wishing to rectify their hearts, they first sought to be sincere in their thoughts; wishing to be sincere in their thoughts, they first extended their knowledge to the utmost. This extension of knowledge is rooted in the investigation of various aspects of life.[8]

What one perceives in this chain of principles is Confucius's persistent search for the origin of social order, a spirit in keeping with Pound's quest for truth. Plants have branches and roots; circumstances have causes and effects. Like Confucius Pound would trace from branches to roots to grasp the essence of matters. The root of social order, as *Da Xue* indicates, lies in men themselves. If the root be in confusion, how can the branches be in good shape? Since "things rooted in disorder and confusion will not, naturally, produce an orderly and ordered result," it is the duty of everyone, noble and humble alike, to create order out of chaos. "From the man in highest dignity, down to the humblest and most obscure, duty is equal: to correct and better one's 'person,' that is the fundamental basis of all progress, of all moral development."[9]

In *Da Xue* Pound finds a system of perfection. He believes that peace and harmony can be maintained in the world so long as we adhere to the order provided by *Da Xue*. Thus, in answer to T. S. Eliot's standing question, "What does Pound believe?" Pound replied in 1934: "I believe in the *Ta Hio* [*Da Xue*]."[10]

This system of *Da Xue* is to provide a profound philosophical basis for Pound's epic, although he might not have been fully aware of its significance at first. He said to James Joyce in a letter of 1917: "I have begun an endless poem, of no known category, Phanapoeia or something or other, all about everything. *Poetry* may print the first three Cantos this spring. I wonder what you will make of it. Probably too sprawling and unmusical to find favor in your ears."[11]

This poem Pound referred to as "Phanapoeia" eventually evolved into *The Cantos*. The modern epic is both singular and plural, both One and Many. But what is the key to the oneness out of the diversity and confusion? What is the structural plan that unifies the seemingly haphazard components of *The Cantos*?

Various scholars have tried to trace such a structural plan to the works of Homer, Ovid, Dante, and other epic poets of the West. David Gordon, by contrast, perceives it in the ten gradations of order in *Da Xue*. These gradations, while in harmony with the qualities of a Western epic, form a much simpler and clearer pattern.[12] Pound wrote explicitly about this order in his "Immediate Need of Confucius" in 1937, after his success with the "5th Decad of Cantos." He emphasized "the Western need of Confucius, and . . . specifically of the first chapter of the *Ta Hio*, which you may treat as a *mantram*,[13] or as a *mantram* reinforced; a *mantram* elaborated so that the meditation may gradually be concentrated into contemplation."[14]

What we see in *The Cantos* is precisely the shape and pattern of *Da Xue*, particularly the first three of its ten Confucian gradations: correcting the self, regulating the family, and governing the state. These gradations give form to Pound's subject matter.

First of all, Pound used self-cultivation, self-discipline, and self-reliance to shape the subject matter for that gradation. In Canto 53 of the Chinese History Cantos, Pound writes:

> Tching prayed on the mountain and
>   wrote MAKE IT NEW
> on his bath tub   新   hsin[1]
>   Day by day make it new.

(53/264–65)

And for the gradation of the family, Pound uses communal activities to shape his material. In the same canto, we find: "Hoang Ti [Huang Di] contrived the making of bricks / and his wife started working the silk worms" (53/262). What Pound has created here is not merely a picture of husband and wife together engaged in productive work, but a much wider scene of the family, including not only its other members but also their involvement in artistic activities:

> He measured the length of Syrinx
>   of the tubes to make tune for song
> Twenty-six (that was) eleven ante Christum
>   had four wives and 25 males of his making.

(53/262)

In a similar way, Pound uses governing as his means of material organization in the gradation of the state. Examples of this category abound in Canto 53:

> Yeou [You] taught men to break branches
> Seu Gin [Sui Ren] set up the stage and taught barter,
>   taught the knotting of cords.
> Fou Hi [Fu Xi] taught men to grow barley
>   2837 ante Christum.

(53/262)

The governing of the primitive people, as we see here, is very much the teaching of basic arts. But in times of deluge emerged another type of governing power: "YU, converter of waters" (53/265). Yet another aspect of this governing is seen in Wu Wang (King Wu):

> Wu Wang entered the city
> gave out grain till the treasures were empty
> by the Nine vases of YU, demobilized army
> sent horses to Hoa-chan [Huashan]
> To the peach groves.
>
> (53/266)

A reversed case of this ideal governing is seen toward the end of the Ming dynasty. As Pound writes in Canto 58: "and south Ming had to fear more from rottenness inside / than from the Manchu north and north east" (58/319). Here again is the Confucian view of governing by keeping order inside oneself.

Indeed, allusions to the Confucian gradations are found not only in the Chinese History Cantos. They recur throughout the entire epic. In Canto 13, for example, we are warned of the danger of the loss of order, starting from its absence at the basic level:

> If a man have not order within him
> He can not spread order about him;
> And if a man have not order within him
> His family will not act with due order;
> And if the prince have not order within him
> He can not put order in his dominions.
>
> (13/59)

In Canto 83 the theme seems focused on social intercourse, from "the queen stitched King Carolus' shirts or whatever" to "in that family group of about 1820" (83/548–49), from "Uncle William" to "Brother Wasp" (548–52). All these allude to activities at the family level.

Canto 84 is full of names of politicians. It begins with three American statesmen, "Senator Bankhead," "Senator Borah" (84/557), and "John Adams" (560). In between these are inserted three rulers of the Shang dynasty, "Wei, Chi [Qi] and Pi-kan [Bigan]" (559), who, in turn, are followed by three modern leaders, Stalin, "Winston P. M.," and Vandenberg (560); (the Russian and British leaders helped to lay the foundation for the United Nations, and Vandenberg served as a U.S. delegate to the U.N. Conference in San Francisco in 1945).[15] In Canto 85 there are I Yin (Yi Yin), chief minister who instructed Cheng Tang's son and successor to the throne, allegedly in 1753 B.C., Wellington (85/563), Alexander, Roosevelt (568), and Tch'eng T'ang (Cheng Tang) (575). These figures in both cantos present the gradation of the governing of the state.[16] However, governing could only rest on the basis of self-improvement and self-understanding: "Perspicax qui excolit se ipsum" (565)," "He is intelligent who perfects himself."[17]

What is particularly noteworthy about this recurrence of *Da Xue*'s gradations is the harmony and smoothness in its proceeding, a quality in agreement with the orderly system that Pound believes in. If *The Cantos* is a giant piano, the gradations of *Da Xue* are its keys. Shuffling his fingers over the keys, Pound produces one of the most fascinating pieces of music of our age. Sometimes he touches the note of family-like geniality, and we hear how it works as a socially unifying force.[18] In Canto 93, for example, we hear Pound's belief that "A man's paradise is his good nature" (93/643); Dante's social instincts, "that men are naturally friendly" (646); and a reference to Pound's own family, "that the child / walk in peace in her basilica" (648). Sometimes, as in Canto 94, we hear the names of political leaders of different ages, Brederode, Rush, Lincoln, John Adams, and the Medici (94/653). Here Tai Wu Tze (Tai Wu Zi) is a name Pound invented, perhaps to stand for Alexander the Great.[19] Further on are Antonius and Constantine the Great, both emperors, and Magnus, king of Norway.[20] All these names, ancient as well as modern, strike the note of the gradation of governing the state. In some parts of this poetic symphony, we hear these notes working in harmony. In Canto 105, for example, while political leaders Talleyrand and Bismarck are mentioned (105/766), more apparent allusions are to the order at the family level, such as Christian Trinity, the pure, motherlike Essentia, and the English royalty's family tree.[21] Another sound of this dual note is heard in Canto 115 of *Drafts & Fragments*: "Wyndham Lewis chose blindness / rather than have his mind stop" (115/814). Here the decision made by Wyndham Lewis embodies self-discipline.[22] But besides this, activities at the family and social levels are alluded to in the same canto by lines about friendship:

> When one's friends hate each other
> how can there be peace in the world?
> Their asperities diverted me in my green time.
>
> (115/814)

For Pound this peace is not remote and unattainable, something belonging only to antiquity. He wants to see it become reality. Therefore, in Canto 116, he uses "Cosmos" as a symbol of harmonious government and calls on the people "To make Cosmos— / To achieve the possible" (116/815). To achieve this, one needs to follow *Da Xue*'s principle: "Those who wished to govern their kingdoms well, began by keeping their own families in order."²³ And Pound sees furthermore a molecular bond connecting the Confucian sequence of self, family, and state. This bond is love: "If love be not in the house there is nothing" (116/816), which statement sums up the entire *Cantos*, as well as the entire Confucian thought: love is "the molecular lock in the Confucian sequence, self, family, state." "To make Cosmos" is not only possible but also simple, for "love in the house" alone can produce harmony in the world.²⁴ Pound compares love to light, for light knows no boundary. Though tiny in appearance, it can brighten the universe: "a little light / in great darkness" (116/815).

During Pound's productive years on *The Cantos*, his other works are also filled with allusions to the same Confucian gradations. For him they represent the sublimity of this world: "We in the West *need* to begin with the first chapter of the *Ta Hio* [*Da Xue*]. . . . There is nothing in this chapter that destroys the best that has been thought in the Occident."²⁵ And he never seems tired of emphasizing the importance of Confucius's teaching for the West and urging people to apply it to Western civilization: "If only for the sake of understanding and valuating our own European past, we have need of the Master Kung [Kong]."²⁶ Like Confucius, Pound sees "the self" as the first priority for the application of the master's doctrine: "You bring order into your surroundings by bringing it first into your self; by knowing the motives of your acts" (*J/M*, 112).

These remarks in prose provide a key to understanding how Pound used the Confucian order as an aesthetic and philosophical pattern for *The Cantos*.

MYTHOLOGY AND HISTORY AS AN ILLUSTRATION OF *DA XUE*

Pound looks upon *Da Xue*'s gradations of order not as rigid dogmas but as profound philosophical principles. In *The Cantos* he aptly uses ancient Chinese mythology and history as illustration for these principles.

His emphasis on mythology and history mirrors a traditional Chinese view: as a Chinese proverb goes, "Past experience, if not forgotten, is a guide for the future."

Pound's adoption of this Confucian standpoint of history also coincides with his turning away from his early idea of the epic as a "beautiful story" to his later definition of it as "a poem including history." This shift reflects Pound's commitment to what he previously referred to as "the modern world." The scope of a traditional epic should be altered and extended to suit modernism. Pound's aim is to create a new model for the new world. In his endeavor to transform the traditional epic, he not only uses *Da Xue*'s gradations as a theme for his epic, but also adds another order, that of history.[27] Confucius sets a fine example by using this order in *Chun Qiu* (Spring and Autumn Annals). It is widely known in China that "by writing *Chun Qiu,* Master Kong terrified all the usurpers and traitors," for in it he at once excoriated the treacherous and eulogized the loyal.[28] In Canto 82, Pound paraphrases what Mencius said about this historical period:

> There are no righteous wars in "The Spring and Autumn"
> that is, perfectly right on one side or the other
> total right on either side of the battle line.

> (82/545)

Living in an era of turmoil, Confucius longed for the good old days of the Zhou dynasty. He admired its founding fathers, King Wen, King Wu, and especially King Wu's brother Duke of Zhou, who established the rites of ancestor worship.[29] Following Confucius's nostalgia for a lost dynasty, Pound wrote in 1918: "I desire to go on with my long poem; and like the Duke of Chang [Zhou], I desire to hear the music of a lost dynasty. (Have managed to hear it, in fact)" (*SL*, 128). Like the duke of Zhou and like Confucius, Pound heard the music of lost dynasties: an order distilled into *Da Xue*'s text by the master. Nowhere in Pound's modern epic is this exemplar of *Da Xue*'s order more evident than in his History Cantos (52–71). But before proceeding to Pound's treatment of Chinese history, I must first clarify the term *history.*

What the term suggests in the Chinese context is not only China's recorded history but its mythological past. Because of this ambiguity, Durant finds it necessary to explain, "China has been called 'the paradise of historians.' For centuries and millennia it has had official historiographers that recorded everything that happened. . . . We cannot trust them further back than 776 B.C., but if you lend them a ready ear they will explain in detail the history of China from 3,000 B.C."[30]

Following Chinese historians, Pound traces China's exemplary figures to its mythological past: "Yeou [You] taught men to break branches" (53/262). This You, a mythological king, is said to have followed the reign of three august powers that had ruled China during the eight thousand years before him. His name, You, or You Chaoshi, means "having nests," implying his having taught people to build nestlike homes and ending vagabond life in China.[31]

Another mythological king named Sui Rensi came after You Chaoshi: "Seu Gin set up the stage and taught barter / taught the knotting of cords" (53/262). As his name suggests, he was the "producer of fire and wood." Two other things are attributed to him: trade and counting by "the knotting of cords."[32]

Then Pound cites Fu Xi, the first of China's five legendary emperors, who is said to have taught hunting, fishing, and keeping stock. His name actually means "to hide or ambush," which is what a hunter has to do. But Pound writes: "Fou Hi [Fu Xi] taught men to grow barley" (53/262). It is not right to attribute to Fu Xi the art of agriculture, which is believed to have been the accomplishment of Shen Nong, or the "divine agriculturist," the second legendary emperor.

Next came Huang Di, the "Yellow Emperor." He was indisputably the most influential of China's legendary rulers. Indeed, all later kings and princes in China claimed themselves his descendants. He not only fought successfully against foreign intruders, especially a fierce tribe led by Chi You, but also made a series of important inventions. He "contrived the making of bricks," and thus the possibility of better housing; "and his wife started working the silk worms," providing the people with clothing. The invention of currency is also attributed to him: "money was in days of Hoang Ti [Huang Di]" (53/262).

Chinese people all over the world consider Huang Di their common ancestor. Every year millions of Chinese gather at Qiao Shan in Huangling County, Shaanxi Province, to worship him. As Pound writes: "his tomb is today in Kiao-Chan [Qiao Shan]" (262). Di Gu, Yao, Shun, and Yu were Huang Di's successors. Di Gu's name means "imperial communication." He was famous for administering justice. His successor was Yao:

> YAO like the sun and rain,
> saw what star is at solstice
> saw what star marks mid summer.

> (53/262)

These lines allude to the calendar Yao and his royal astronomers worked out. It is said that he was such a benevolent emperor that heaven and earth granted favorable weather conditions during his entire reign. Yao named Shun his successor.[33] Yu, or Da Yu, was recommended to Yao by Shun to tame the flood of the Yellow River. He successfully controlled the waters, and Shun had him serve as his vice regent and later offered him his throne.[34]

Yu passed the throne on to his son, thus establishing the Xia dynasty. The Chinese have put up a giant statue of Yu on the bank of the Yellow River in honor of his taming the waters and founding the first Chinese dynasty, even though there is hardly any evidence for either claim. Nonetheless, John Blofeld states in a note to *Yi Jing* (The book of changes): "recent scholarship indicates that the Chinese have been right about such things rather more often than was formerly supposed."[35] Pound also seems to feel that the Chinese are trustworthy in their memory of history. In Canto 53 the prehistoric and historic events are so well linked that the reader cannot tell where mythology ends and where history begins. The event in the following line, however, appears more historical than mythological: "Then an Empress fled with Chao Kang [Shao Kang] in her belly" (53/264).

The empress was Min, wife of Di Xiang. After the emperor was killed by Han Zuo, the usurper, she fled and gave birth to Shao Kang. Shao Kang grew up during the interregnum and came to the throne after Han Zuo was deposed by the people. During his reign (2079–2055 B.C.) Shao Kang restored order in the empire.[36]

Here Pound returns to the mythological emperors and reviews these models for later Chinese rulers: from Fu Xi to Yu. Then he proceeds to the second Chinese dynasty, Shang, founded by Cheng Tang, who reigned 1766–1753 B.C.:

> For years no waters came, no rain fell
> for the Emperor Tching Tang
> grain scarce, prices rising
> so that in 1760 Tching Tang opened the copper mine (ante Christum)

made discs with square holes in the middles
     and gave these to the people
wherewith they might buy grain
              where there was grain.

                                       (53/264)

These lines are about how the king, during a drought, coined money for his people to buy grain. It is interesting to note that his design of "discs with square holes in the middles" remained the shape of Chinese coins for almost four thousand years, down to the end of Qing, the last dynasty in China. Cheng Tang's design of the copper coin was based on the Chinese mythological belief that the heaven is round and the earth is square. Cheng Tang's coin was therefore a prayer to the heaven and earth to bestow good harvests. And he also prayed in other ways:

Tching prayed on the mountain and
     wrote MAKE IT NEW
on his bath tub   新   hsin[1]
     Day by day make it new.

                                  (53/264–65)

These lines allude to the fact that although his people had coins, there was no grain for exchange until heaven and earth accepted Cheng Tang's sacrifices. And he inscribed on his bathtub "MAKE IT NEW." His inscription, like his prayers, testifies to his commitment and devotion to his people.[37]

Unlike Cheng Tang, Zhou Xin, his descendent, was a depraved king: "Uncle Ki [Qi] said: Jewels! / You eat nothing but bears' paws" (53/265). Qi, uncle of this tyrant of Shang or Yin,[38] was put in jail for criticizing the king: "You drink only out of jeweled vases and eat bear's paw and leopard's blood."[39] Zhou Xin's concubine, Da Ji was a notorious partner in tyranny: "In marble tower of Lou Tai [Lu Tai] doors were of jasper / that palace was ten years in the making" (53/265–66).

In this age of turmoil emerged Wen Wang (King Wen), founder of Zhou, who tried to overthrow Zhou Xin. Although he suffered a major setback, he did not stop opposing the last king of Shang. He allegedly recast an ancient document of the legendary emperor Fu Xi and worked out the *Yi Jing* (The book of changes). It was through this classic that he communicated with his people. His son Wu Wang (King Wu) continued his cause and finally defeated the evil king at Mou Ye, ending the Shang

(Yin) dynasty.[40] King Wu's first act as a conqueror, showing his respect for the past, was characteristic of Zhou:

Wu Wang entered the city
gave out grain till the treasures were empty
by the Nine vases of YU, demobilized army.

(53/266)

"The Nine vases" refers to the legendary Nine Tripods, allegedly cast during the reign of Yu. After taming the Yellow River, it is said, Yu collected bronze from all nine states of China and had nine vases cast, each engraved with a different pattern—the mountain spirits and water monsters of a state. These vases were, therefore, ancient documents representing the nine states of China at that time.[41] After Cheng Tang overthrew the Xia dynasty, he had them moved to the Shang capital. Now that Wu Wang had overthrown Shang, he did likewise. When Wu Wang was preparing to return to the capital after conquering Shang, "he took with him the nine vases that the Emperor Yu had cast in bronze which displayed the geographic description of each of the nine provinces of the empire."[42] By paying reverence to the nine vases of the Great Yu, Wu Wang affirmed Zhou's continuity with China's past.[43] This new dynasty's respect for texts, initiated by Wen Wang in working out *Yi Jing*, can also be seen in Zhou Gong (Duke of Zhou) who, in announcing his will,

Called for his hat shaped as a mortar board
        set out the precious stones on his table
saying this is my will and my last will
        Keep peace
Keep the peace, care for the people.
        Ten lines, no more in his testament.

(53/267)

The same juxtaposition of precious documents and precious jewels is seen in Pound's description of the coronation ceremony for Wu Wang's son, Cheng Wang (King Cheng). The ceremony was arranged by Shao Gong (Duke of Shao):

Chao Kong called the historians
        laid out white and violet damask
For the table of jewels, as when Tching-ouang received princes.
On the table of the throne of the West
        laid out the charters
constitutions of ancient kings and two sorts of stone

Hong-pi and Yuen-yen
And on the East table he put the pearls from Mt Hoa-chan.

(53/267)

The same analogy of precious stones as precious documents appearing twice on the same page suggests the importance of a gradation of order—good governing. A ruler's real treasure is not his crown jewels but the documents that guide his governing.[44]

In the rest of the Chinese History Cantos Pound continues this review of Chinese mythology-cum-history, throwing light on *Da Xue*'s order. It is noteworthy that the Confucian perspective history is balanced by an account of the Adams family history, which nurtured a series of early American historical figures, including John Adams. Before becoming the president, he served as delegate to the First Continental Congress (1774); commissioner in France (1777–78); envoy to Great Britain (1785–88); and vice president (1788–96) under George Washington.[45] However, in relating this family history, Pound does not indulge himself in presidential glory. Much like his quest in China's mythological past, he reaches toward the president's less-known ancestors. Canto 62 opens with Thomas Adams, followed by Henry Adams and his son Joseph (62/341). Thomas was one of the grantees of the first charter of the Colony of Massachusetts Bay in 1629, and a relative of Henry.[46] Henry was the founder of the Adams family in America. In 1640 he was granted forty acres of land at Mt. Wollanston, a place later called Braintree.[47] This is how Pound recounts the Adamses' early frontier life and its legacy:

Merry Mount become Braintree, a plantation near Weston's
Capn Wollanston's became Merrymount.
        ten head 40 acres at 3/ (shillings) per acre
who lasted 6 years, brewing commenced by the first Henry
        continues by Joseph Adams, his son
at decease left a malting establishment.

(62/341)

The *Li Ji* in Canto 52 and the legacy of Thomas Adams in Canto 62 represent the social and political norms for both the Chinese and early American cultures. This juxtaposition of what is best in the two cultures provides the reader with a perception of the similarities and differences between them. Both are models of enlightened civic order, but one culture stretches back into a mythological past, whereas the other was born fairly recently. The Adams family was associated with the Revolution that gave birth to a new Republic. This family may be compared to the Chinese dynasties, just as the Confucian moral order runs parallel to the Enlightenment ideals of the Adams family. The juxtaposition of the Chinese and American histories forms an antithesis with the fifty cantos before the Chinese Cantos. Pound believes that China and America present a mode of "constructive effort," of "people struggling upwards," in contrast with the failure of the European culture, the "people dominated by emotion," as seen in the first fifty cantos.[48]

In fact, both the Chinese mythology-cum-history and *Da Xue*'s gradations work as a means for unity and order, not merely in the Chinese History Cantos, but throughout Pound's epic. In "Three Cantos," for example, he wrote:

> Exult with Shang in squatness? The sea monster
> Bulges the squarish bronzes
> (Confucius later taught the world good manners,
> Started with himself, built our perfection.)

(P, 233)

In a word, the use of the two means (Confucian philosophy and history) helps Pound create a poetic order in the chaos of his complex materials. Further, these two means are connected with each other, the mythology-cum-history serving as an illustration for the philosophy and the philosophy guiding the mythology-cum-history. For whatever lessons of China's past Pound relates are a "recurrence of beneficent dynasties by a return to Confucianism," especially its gradations of order as set out in *Da Xue*.[49] And Pound believes that this order could be achieved not only in poetry, but also in a much larger social and artistic context. His confidence is evident in his essay "The Renaissance": "Our opportunity is greater than Leonardo's: we have more aliment, we have not one classic tradition to revivify, we have China and Egypt, and the unknown lands lying upon the roof of the world—Khotan, Kara-shar and Kan-su [Gansu]" (*LE*, 224).

IDEOGRAMS AS EXEMPLARY FIGURES OF *DA XUE*

Pound's adoption of both *Da Xue*'s gradations of order and the Confucian outlook of history doesn't designate him as merely a transmitter, however. He is an inventor in poetry. His use of ideograms as an exemplar is perhaps the most significant invention he brought into poetry in English.

Unlike the order of *Da Xue* and the Chinese mythology-cum-history, which are found almost throughout the epic, these exemplary figures do not appear until the end of Canto 51. In fact, what Pound later came to call "the ideogrammic method" did not become a major structural principle in the poem until the 1920s.[50]

Most readers of *The Cantos* do not know Chinese. Is there a way that they can appreciate the Chinese characters in the poem?[51]

A review of Pound's experience as a learner of the Chinese language might throw light on this question. When taking a six-week vacation in the late summer of 1937, Pound had with him only James Legge's one-volume bilingual edition of the Four Confucian Books. The volume did not have a glossary. Yet Pound was not hindered by the omission. Often he simply glanced from the ideograms to the cribs: "When I disagreed with the crib or was puzzled by it I had only the look of the characters and the radicals to go on from." In this way he went over the text three times, and rose from it with a "better idea of the whole and the unity of the doctrine." And Pound did find unaided reading more beneficial than reading with aid of dictionaries. As he said, "There are categories of the ideograms not indicated as such in the dictionaries, but divided really by the feel of their form, the twisted as evil, the stunted, the radiant. The mountain itself has a 'nature' and that nature is to come forth in trees, though men cut and sheep nibble."[52]

What Pound sees in these natural signs is the realization of an old Western dream of a universal language. In the component of this language, its ideograms, he finds the same Confucian philosophy expressed. If he said that he believed in *Da Xue*, he also believed in the ideograms, which composed the book, and shared the Confucian concern and affection for the visible things in nature. In *The Cantos* Pound reveals to the world his fascinating discovery. At the end of Canto 51, two simple characters 正 名 (*zheng ming*), mark the advent of this new phase of the epic (51/252). These two characters Pound found in *Lun Yu* (The analects):

1. Tze-Lu [Zi lu] said: The Lord of Wei is waiting for you to form a government, what are you going to do first?
2. He said: Settle the names (determine a precise terminology). (*Con*, 249)

Since *zheng ming*, "settling names" or "calling things by their right names," was what Confucius considered the first thing to be done, could

Pound have found a better symbol with which to begin the ideogrammic phase of his modern epic? For him *zheng ming* represents not so much a stylistic as an ethical principle.[53] Although these two characters do not appear in *Da Xue*, this Confucian principle is present as an underlying theme. Pound apparently sees this principle in each of the gradations of order. What cultivating the self, running the family, and governing the state involve, is, in the last analysis, performing one's proper role at each of these levels. This means being honest, first of all, to oneself. As Pound paraphrases, "Finding the precise word for the inarticulate heart's tone means not lying to oneself, as in the case of hating a bad smell or loving a beautiful person, also called respecting one's own nose" (*Con*, 47).

Following *zheng ming*, at the opening of the Chinese History Cantos, Pound gives an ideogram larger in size, 耀 *(yao)*, brilliance (254). The left part of the character, with several strokes radiating from a central point, means "light," and the top of the right "feather." This ideogram, with both its bird's feather and light coming from the sky, is a symbol of *Da Xue*'s teaching about receiving from the sky "the luminous principle of reason."

On the second page of Canto 53 Pound puts, in vertical order, 堯 (Yao), 舜 (Shun), and 禹 (Yu), the names of the three ideal emperors, for they are the standards against which all Chinese monarchs are judged (53/263). And the ideograms 皋 陶 Kao Yao (Gao Yao) on the next page stand for the name of Yu's eminent minister (264). He is said to have introduced law to control crimes.[54] What we have here are visual expressions of the same ideal examined earlier in this essay: emperors and ministers working together to govern the state.

The next ideogram, 新 *(xin)*, was a lucky discovery Pound made in the Morrison dictionary. He found in it Morrison's interesting interpretation of the character: "From *hatchet, to erect,* and *wood*. Fresh, new; to renovate; to renew or improve the state of; to restore or to increase what is good, applied to persons increasing in virtue; and to the daily increase of plants." It is not difficult to see that the ideogram is made up of three parts, on the left a tree with *erect* on top of it, and on the right an axe. Morrison's contribution lies not so much in this analysis as in his understanding of the relativity of these three components. Like Morrison, Pound sees all the actions within this single ideogram: an axe is being raised to cut down a tree.[55]

The interesting discovery led to these lines:

Tching prayed on the mountain and
    wrote MAKE IT NEW
on his bath tub   新   hsin¹
    Day by day make it new   日   jih⁴
cut underbrush,   日   jih⁴
pile the logs   新   hsin¹
keep it growing.

(53/264–65)

Pound's discovery of the ideogram *xin* proved to be significant, as he divined in this single ideogram an expression combining both *Da Xue*'s order and the context of Chinese history. Pound in a letter mentioned the "repeat in history."⁵⁶ Yet what this ideogram reveals is that each repetition is new and, thus, different, for each time the axe is raised, a different tree is cut.

As Dong Zhongshu, a renowned Confucian of the Han dynasty (206 B.C.—220 A.D.) observed, the first three Chinese dynasties, Xia, Shang, and Zhou, present a scheme of three cycles. He cited a remark of Confucius from *Lun Yu*. After considering the three ancient dynasties, Confucius said: "Whatever dynasties may follow the Zhou dynasty, the characteristics they will have during the next one hundred generations can already be recognized now."⁵⁷ Nevertheless, each of the later two cycles was not simply a return to the former one, but a "regenerative and ethical metamorphosis." If this spirit of renewal originated in the Shang dynasty, the pivotal one of the three cycles, it was epitomized by Cheng Tang's inscription on his bath tub: 新日日新 *xin ri ri xin*. These four ideograms mean "make new, day by day, make new." Pound condensed them to "Make it new." "Make it new" later became Pound's motto; the ideograms recur in the rest of *The Cantos*. In Canto 93, for example, he put *ri xin* (daily new) below a shortened version of the lines about Cheng Tang in Canto 53:

    "Renew"
as on the T'ang tub:
          Renew
       jih [*ri*]   日
       hsin [*xin*] 新
       renew

(93/649)

These two ideograms reappear at the end of Canto 94:

To build light

日　jih [*ri*]
新　hsin [*xin*]

(94/662)

In Canto 97, the ideogram *xin* is seen by itself, without *ri:*

New fronds,
novelle piante 新
　　　what ax for clearing?

(97/695)

But in Canto 110, the ideogram resumes its pattern of repeating itself as in Canto 53:

新　hsin¹ [*xin*]
　　　that is, to go forth by day
新　hsin¹ [*xin*]

(110/800)

Here the line "that is, to go forth by day" seems to be moving with momentum into the narrow space between the two *xins*, a good visual reminder of the original text in Canto 53, where Pound does initially put the two ideograms *ris* between the two *xins*. The ideogram *ri* is on the next page, facing these two *xins*, with an explanation why this sign for "sun" means day or daily in the context: "and the sun 日 jih [ri] / new with the day" (110/801).

Therefore, all these different arrangements of the two ideograms *xin* and *ri* are renewed forms of Cheng Tang's inscription, "Make it new." If Cheng Tang, by founding the Shang dynasty, started a pivotal cycle among the three dynasties, Pound uses Canto 53 and particularly the king's admonition in it as the pivot of the whole epic. Canto 53 deserves all the attention that we are giving it not only because of its concentrated reference to *Da Xue*'s order and the Chinese mythology-cum-history context but because of its selective use of Chinese ideograms.

However, a careful reader of Canto 53 may notice that, after citing the text "Make it new," Pound puts down the names of only two dynasties, 夏 (Xia) and 周 (Zhou) (53/265, 268). Why doesn't he show the middle one, Shang? Has he omitted it inadvertently? Most probably not, for the pivotal dynasty with its spirit of renewal is already represented, at its best, by its founder's admonition "Make it new," and, therefore, there is no need to repeat any lesser things about it. Pound repeats, instead, the name of the third dynasty, so that Canto 53 ends with the ideogram 周 (Zhou). And between these two ideograms he puts Confucius's given name, 仲 尼 (Zhongni) (53/272). A good reason for the repetition of Zhou is that there were two Zhou dynasties, the earlier one commonly referred to as Western Zhou, with its capital in Chang'an (now Xi'an), and the succeeding one called Eastern Zhou, with its capital in Luoyang. Confucius's name is most appropriately placed, for Zhou was the dynasty he was born in. As the most sophisticated cycle of the three dynasties, it nurtured his philosophy. An even more important consideration for putting Confucius's name between the two Zhous is that, although the master himself lived in the Eastern Zhou dynasty, his heart went back to the good old days of King Wen's Western Zhou and often lamented the demoralization of his contemporaries.

Pound finds in Morrison's Chinese dictionary another ideogram, 旦 *(dan)*, the sign of the sun above the horizon. He comments: "Magnificent ideogram—phanopoeia."[58] This visual image arouses Pound's imagination and henceforth becomes an important element in his repertoire of ideograms. He uses the character, for example, in Canto 91: "They who are skilled in fire / shall read 旦 tan [*dan*], the dawn" (91/635).

In Canto 97, this ideogram appears three times. Once it is put below *xin* (new), in between two *qins* (akin):

New fronds
novelle piante 新
      what ax for clearing?
親 *ch'in¹* [*qin*] 旦 *tan⁴* [*dan*] 親 *ch'in¹* [*qin*]

                                     (97/695)

By suggesting that *dawn* and *new* are akin to each other, Pound joins the images of the two ideograms and reveals a sense of freedom in both. In a man with an "ax for clearing" and a man at the sunrise of another day, Pound sees the same freedom. For the poet, both are "a man on the threshold of new experience."[59]

When the ideogram *dan* appears again in this canto, it is as if Pound were insisting that his reader share his ecstasy with the image: "that at least a few should perceive this 旦 tan [*dan*]" (97/697).

Some sinologists argue that Pound's method is like "finding iron in irony," but there is good reason for Pound to examine the Chinese ideograms in this natural process. As he writes in Canto 87:

> In nature are signatures
> needing no verbal tradition,
> oak leaf never plane leaf.

(87/593)

It is this natural signature that "enables grass seed to grow grass; the cherry-stone to make cherries."[60] Many people are blind to this signature. And those who notice it see different things. Biologists, for instance, see DNA. Cang Jie divined in it a system of natural signs, the making of a language.[61] Pound discovered the same system, and he interpreted it as Cang Jie allegedly had interpreted it four thousand years earlier. Although some critics challenge Pound's sense of words, he seems to hold on to his conviction: since these ideograms were allegedly discovered amid natural elements, they remain part of nature. They "let no man with an eye forget what energy it is that fills words: the energy of the process in nature."[62]

The energy of nature lies in its process of renewal. Each winter brings back another spring, and each dying has a birth behind it. It is this process in nature that underlies the Chinese motto "Make it new." It is the understanding of nature that enables Pound to gain his orientation toward new beginnings. What he was seeking was not so much a revolution as "a renewal, a revivification of an old tradition." To use his own words, he was seeking "a renaissance."[63] For the poet, "the making of the new always consists of a remaking of the old."[64] Pound's use of the Chinese ideograms in his epic is such a remaking of the old.

In a word, *The Cantos*, though appearing to be hard to comprehend, are not a jumble of exotic words and disjointed phrases. Examine the work in the context of Chinese culture, and readers will see light. With an underlying order provided by the Confucian classic *Da Xue*, and subsidiary illustrations supplied by the mythology-cum-history cycle and the ideograms, Pound's modern epic is a perfectly organized masterpiece.

Pound regards the three heritages he borrows from China not as things static but as things in motion. He sees in *Da Xue*'s system an unceasing spiral of movement upward toward a celestial perfection, starting from the basic order at the personal level. He sees in the succession of dynasties a cycle and recycle of good and bad rulers. And he sees in the ideograms bustling nature in motion. It is this sense of motion that enables him to create, not to copy. Pound grasps the essence of the motto Cheng Tang inscribed on the bathtub, "Make it new." He does not simply quote and make recurring allusion to the inscription; he actually uses it as his creative principle throughout the process of writing *The Cantos*. In his collection of essays *Make It New*, he laments: "Beauty is a brief gasp between one cliché and another."[65] He is never content with clichés, and it is his steadfast faith in, and practice of, this principle that enhances his capacity to call the past to life. His material may be old, but once it is in his hand, he can "Make it new."

NOTES

1. Mary de Rachewiltz, "Pound as Son: Letters Home," *Yale Review* 75 (1986): 324.

2. Pound, "Immediate Need of Confucius," *SP*, 79.

3. Eliot, introduction to *Selected Poems of Ezra Pound* (London: Faber and Faber, 1928), xvi.

4. Richard Sieburth, "The Design of *The Cantos*," *Iowa Review* 15, no. 2 (1985): 12.

5. Quoted in Will Durant, *The Story of Civilization*, part I, *Our Oriental Heritage* (New York: Simon and Schuster, 1954), 639.

6. Hugh Kenner, *The Pound Era* (Berkeley and Los Angeles: University of California Press, 1971), 446.

7. Pound, *Ta Hio, The Great Learning* (Seattle: University of Washington Book Store, 1928), 11.

8. Ibid., 8.

9. Ibid., 9.

10. Kenner, *The Pound Era*, 447.

11. Quoted in Sieburth, "Design of *The Cantos*," 12.

12. David Gordon, "The Great Digest: A Pattern," *Paideuma* 14 (1985): 253.

13. A Sanskrit word referring to a verbal device to assist in meditation.

14. Pound, "Immediate Need of Confucius," *SP*, 77.

15. John Edwards, *Annotated Index to "The Cantos" of Ezra Pound* (Berkeley and Los Angeles: University of California Press, 1956), 235.

16. Gordon, "The Great Digest," 256.

17. Peter Makin, *Pound's Cantos* (Baltimore: Johns Hopkins University Press, 1991), 264.

18. Gordon, "The Great Digest," 256.

19. Carrol Terrell, *A Companion to "The Cantos" of Ezra Pound* (Berkeley and Los Angeles: University of California Press, 1980), 570–71.

20. Ibid., 634–41.

21. Gordon, "The Great Digest," 256–57.

22. Ibid., 257.

23. Pound, *Ta Hio*, 8.

24. Gordon, "The Great Digest," 257.

25. Pound, "Immediate Need of Confucius," *SP*, 77.

26. Ibid., 79.

27. Christine Froula, *To Write Paradise: Style and Error in Pound's Cantos* (New Haven: Yale University Press, 1984), 2.

28. Terrell, *Companion*, 422.

29. James Longenbach, "A Scene of the Past: Pound, Eliot, and Modernist Poetics of History," Ph.D. diss., Princeton University, 1985, 146.

30. Durant, *The Story of Civilization*, 642.

31. Terrell, *Companion*, 203.

32. Ibid.

33. Ibid., 204.

34. Ibid.

35. John Blofeld, *I Ching: A New Translation of the Ancient Chinese Text with Detailed Introduction for Its Practical Use in Divination* (New York: E. P. Dutton, 1965), 23.

36. Terrell, *Companion*, 204.

37. Ibid., 205.

38. Shang was renamed Yin ca. 1401 B.C. when its capital was moved to Yin.

39. Terrell, *Companion*, 205.

40. Philip Furia, *Pound's Cantos Declassified* (University Park: Pennsylvania State University Press, 1984), 78.

41. Edwards, *Annotated Index*, 155.

42. Terrell, *Companion*, 206.

43. Furia, *Pound's Cantos Declassified*, 78.

44. Ibid.

45. Edwards, *Annotated Index*, 2–3.

46. Ibid., 3.

47. Ibid., 2.

48. Sieburth, "Design of *The Cantos*," 26–27.

49. Forrest Read, *'76: One World and the Cantos of Ezra Pound* (Chapel Hill: University of North Carolina Press, 1981), 302.

50. George Kearn, *Guide to Ezra Pound's Selected Cantos* (New Brunswick: Rutgers University Press, 1962), 5.

51. John Cayley, "The Literal Image: Illustrations in *The Cantos*," *Paideuma* 14 (1985): 230.

52. Quoted in Kenner, *The Pound Era*, 448–49.

53. Eva Hesse, *New Approaches to Ezra Pound* (Berkeley and Los Angeles: University of California Press, 1969), 22.

54. Terrell, *Companion*, 204.

55. Kenner, *The Pound Era*, 447–48.

56. Quoted in Ben D. Kimpel and T. C. Duncan Eaves, "'Major Form' in Pound's *Cantos*," *Iowa Review*, 15, no. 2 (1985): 60.

57. Quoted in Wolfgang Bauer, *China and the Research for Happiness* (New York: Seabury, 1976), 6–7.

58. Kenner, *The Pound Era*, 103.

59. Colin McDowell, "As towards a Bridge over Worlds: The Way of Souls in the *Cantos*," *Paideuma* 13 (1984): 199.

60. Kenner, *The Pound Era*, 103.

61. Cang Jie is believed to have lived in 2800 B.C. Mythology has it that one day, as he ascended a mountain overlooking the Luo River, he saw a tortoise rising out of the water. Cang Jie, born with four eyes, caught all the details of the tracings on its back. Inspired by these tracings that "lay bare the permutations of nature," he invented the Chinese character. See Paul Carus, *Chinese Thought: An Exposition of the Main Characteristic Features of the Chinese World-Conception* (Chicago: Open Court, 1907), 2.

62. Kenner, *The Pound Era*, 160.

63. P. E. Firchow, "Ezra Pound's Imagism and the Tradition," *Comparative Literature Studies* 18 (1981): 381.

64. Ibid., 379.

65. "Notes on Elizabethan Classicists," in *Make It New* (New Haven: Yale University Press, 1935), 114.

Ideogram, "Right Naming," and the Authoritarian Streak

PETER MAKIN

Confucian *ch'ing ming*, "right naming" or "rectification of names," on the one hand, and Fenollosan "ideogrammic writing" on the other, are two Pound campaigns that are obviously related: they both come from Chinese sources, in one way or another, and they both arise out of Pound's metaphysic of distinctions. But they are not as closely related as they might seem. One of them, right naming, seems to me in effect un-Poundian, an aberration, something that starts up in about 1935, and reaches a frantic peak in about 1950. In the same period, and apparently in proportion, Pound's interest in the much more Poundian principle of "ideogrammic writing" declines.[1] The interest in right naming rises in step with Pound's need for dogmatic authority; and the interest in ideogrammic writing falls likewise.

I think well-disposed people have not noticed this discrepancy because right naming seems so natural a product of that metaphysic of distinctions, which is itself so attractive.[2]

The right-naming campaign was a campaign for precision in the use of individual words. I am talking here about what Pound meant by his campaign, not what Confucius meant.[3] And the best, in fact the only way to find out what Pound meant by it is to look at Pound's formulations of it, whether in his Confucian translations or elsewhere.

Pound used the right-naming campaign as a weapon against forms of public political deception and hence exploitation. The essential text (*The Analects* 13.3) was paraphrased by Pound in a version published in 1960 thus:

> *Tze-Lu:* The Lord of Wei is waiting for you to form a government, what are you going to do first?
> *Kung:* Settle the names (determine a precise terminology).
> *Tze-Lu:* How's this, you're divagating, why fix 'em?
> *Kung:* You bumkin! Sprout! . . . If words (terminology) are not (is not) precise, they cannot be followed out, or completed in action according to specifications.[4]

The *Guide to Kulchur* (1938) gives a hint as to the application: "The *ch'ing ming* text can mean also that functionaries shd. be called by their proper titles, that is to say a man should not be called controller of currency unless he really controls it. The ch'ing is used continually against ambiguity" (*GK*, 21).

What Pound has in his gunsights here is the point that the U.S. Constitution says Congress shall control the issuance of money "and the value thereof," so that everywhere it is assumed that this legal requirement is being followed; and yet the purchasing power of the dollar is determined (in various ways) by the Federal Reserve Bank, whose directors are a gang of private bankers, or, to put it in a Poundian way, thieves. And this is the point of Pound's later reiteration of the text "name for name, king for king": the sovereignty should lie where the sovereignty is stated to lie: a Congress or a parliament that has given up the enormous power over monetary affairs does not exercise sovereignty.[5] And so on.

To prevent these thieveries, it is necessary to have clarity, precision, explicitness in public language.

Or again: Pound says that there is confusion as to the nature of money. Writers write about it as if it were a container of accumulated value. It then has "rights": it is assumed that if you possess a certain amount of this accumulated-value container, then you have the right not to see it dwindle away, or be taxed away, to nothing, by inflation or by a Gesellite currency tax. But this is wrong, in Pound's view. Money contains no value: that is a fetish. Money is merely a facilitator of the exchange of other things, things that *do* have value. These confusions allow exploitation: they protect speculators in the accumulation of so much of the stuff that, with it, they can manipulate our means of exchange.[6] (For a recent example, one might cite the Southeast Asian recession of the 1990s, which was started by speculators' manipulations of the Thai currency.) Therefore, says Pound, the duty of every writer on such subjects is to make clear and explicit the meanings of his terms: that is, to *define* them, at the start.

This seems a reasonable and indeed important point: in the 1990s as in the 1930s, there seem to be manipulations of the public mind that are carried on by false naming.

To stay within the area of Pound's concerns, let us consider the phrase "injecting public funds into the banking system." This is what the Clinton administration pressed the Japanese government to do, from the moment the bubble collapsed. Few seem to notice that these are in fact mainly funds borrowed from private investors. They are "public" only in the sense that the taxpayer has the great privilege of paying interest on them, and of guaranteeing their return to the profit-making lenders, who of course cannot lose in this transaction. Private funds are being passed to private banks, via "a species of profit sieve,"[7] so that the private banks may in effect be guaranteed by the state against the results of their own past speculation, which is generally admitted to have been remarkably irresponsible. And the public accepts these practices largely because of the nomenclature that hides their nature. Such would be a straightforward Poundian analysis of certain present realities, and their relation to right naming.

The need for an unending critique of the terminology of public life seems obvious. Yet I still claim that, in Pound's hands, the campaign is likely to have done more harm than good.

What was its intended scope?

It is identified—as far as I can see, completely—with the campaign for that "precise definition" which Pound says is part of the medieval European paideuma at its best, with Erigena, Grosseteste, and Richard of St. Victor as the great examples. He runs the two campaigns alternatingly, and sometimes simultaneously, in the same texts.[8]

Here at least it seems reasonable to demand that Pound have understood the verbal precisions of the authors he offered as models. Did he understand their Latin well enough to know when they were being precise, and when vague? It is very hard to check, for there are very few occasions on which Pound quotes a whole Latin sentence and offers a complete translation of it. One such case is in the essay "Immediate Need of Confucius" (1937). There he quotes from Dante's *De Vulgari Eloquentia*, which he ought to know extremely well (it has been his *livre de chevet* since youth), but makes an obscurity of it by mistranslating the key word *quia* as if it meant "because," apparently because he does not distinguish this medieval Latin from classical.[9]

His remarks about what the medieval philosophers say are more usually on the large scale; his quotations, usually of broken phrases, left untranslated. But in the great essay on Cavalcanti appears the phrase "per . . . plura diaphana," from Bishop Grosseteste, and Pound makes such extensive use of this in *The Cantos* that the contexts there seem to allow a check on what he thought it meant.

He seems to have understood these *diaphana* to be things into which light penetrates: including water, air, and glass, but most especially those that have a cloudiness, a veil-like-ness, that allows them to retain a form imparted by the light.[10] But in the Grosseteste passage that was his source, this is a meaning that the word cannot have, because the passage is about the refraction of light. (You cannot observe refraction in cloudy substances.)[11]

A crib would have rescued Pound, had there been one. A dictionary of Scholastic Latin, had he been willing to use one, would have pointed out that *diaphanum* only meant "transparent thing" in that period.[12] The context could have rescued him, had he read it carefully; but by this period he was reading too often by a "quite conscious method of haste," as I have put it elsewhere.[13]

Whether Pound had direct knowledge of the verbal precisions of the medieval philosophers remains, so far, doubtful.

At the least it is clear that he overstates his knowledge of their kind of precision; and this seems to suggest that he overstates the need for that kind.

Let us now consider Pound's precision in his handling of Chinese. This is relevant because it shows further how wobbly was the basis of the campaign for the rectification of names in Pound's own reading. That doesn't prove, in itself, that the campaign was misguided, but it may suggest that it was unnecessary.

The etymological method was Pound's favored way of reading Chinese, as most readers are aware. That is, in a given character he would see one root-element meaning *x*, and another root-element meaning *y*; putting the two etymons together, he would infer that the whole character meant *z*.

Etymological reading is a scattershot method: you may just happen to hit the target, which is the meaning of the word in the text that you are reading. But the probability is not very high.

Almost any word in the dictionary will demonstrate this. There is no reason *in the etymons* why *conscript* should not mean "anthology": don't the root-elements mean "together" and "writing"? There is no reason in the etymons why *refrigerator* should not mean "air conditioner"—but the translator who goes on the assumption that it does will get some funny results. And why shouldn't that common Italian politeness, *Egregio*

Signore, mean "Egregious Sir," as the amused English reader's mind wants it to? Why shouldn't Basil Bunting's favorite word, *concision*—he said Pound's ideogrammic method allowed "a great gain in concision"[14]— mean "circumcision"? The etymons allow that sense, with perfect logic: *con* in one of its common senses, "completely, thoroughly," plus *cidere/ caedere*, "to cut."

If that example seems far-fetched enough to disprove my point, a check in a historical dictionary will show it does the opposite: that word did in fact have that meaning, at least from the Geneva Bible of 1557 onward.

For single etymons, as found in the words they help to constitute, are pretty large grab-bags: they can include a lot of senses. Combining them with others does not greatly narrow the possibilities.

For Pound, the vastness of the possibilities freed his creativity, and the results are often fine. In the *Analects*, Confucius says "the speaking of the man who has virtue is [*jen*]," and all the dictionaries translate this *jen* character as "cautious in speech," "holding back his speech," and so forth. But Pound sees the picture-element for "speech," and the picture-element for "blade": these are the etymons, as he takes it.[15] They set the metaphysic of distinctions to work in his mind; and they allow him to derive the meaning that appears in his translation: "The full man's words *have an edge of definition*" (*Con*, 244; emphasis added).[16]

If Pound wants the word to mean that, very well. The method, in his hands, produces translations that are not merely beautiful and curious, but coherent, at a high level of coherence. But the problem here is the relation of all this to "precision." If we are talking about Pound's own grasp of "precision" in authors' usage of individual words—and that kind of precision was his concern in his campaign for Confucian "right naming"—it is obvious that this method of reading weakens it critically.

There is no special irony in the fact that it weakens it most particularly when he is dealing with the texts of the Confucian tradition. For the method of reading goes much further back in Pound's work: I think he was using it long before he started working in Chinese.

There is the celebrated Provençal phrase *e quel remir*, which Pound takes into *The Cantos* and puts in some important contexts. If we look carefully at Pound's very many attempts at translating the poem in question, I think there can be no doubt at all that he understood this phrase to mean, literally, "and that glowing."[17] Well, Arnaut would have been surprised; there is hardly any doubt that he intended to say, instead, "and that I should gaze on her." How has Pound arrived at his translation? Apparently, he has taken *quel* as if it were Italian, "that," and has taken the *mir* element of *remir* as if it were semantically on the same track of development as in the English word "mirror," thus meaning "reflect"; and *re-* of course means "back" or "again."[18] That is, he has treated the three elements of *quel remir* as three huge semantic pools constituted by everything those three elements have ever meant in the history of the Latin and Latin-derived languages. From those pools he has fished the semantic bits he wanted: for he loved glowings, translucencies, glimmerings, torch-flares on armor, and the rest. The fact that in the Old Provençal language the *mir* element in verbs only ever meant "seeing," and never had to do with reflecting, didn't worry him. The fact that there was then available a Provençal dictionary, Raynouard's, that contained abundant data to make this abundantly clear, was not about to deflect him.[19] It was so good a dictionary that Emil Levy insisted on conceiving his own great dictionary as a multivolume supplement to it; and Pound's own great respect for Levy is recorded in Canto 20. But this didn't deflect Pound either.

Why does this matter? Surely the concept Pound has created in answer to Arnaut's words is still very true to the tone of Arnaut's poem; it is still very precise, in that sense.[20] But it has nothing to do with grasping a precision in Arnaut's use of individual words. And precision in the use of individual terms is what the campaign for the Rectification of Names is all about.

All Pound's discussion of right naming shows that he understood it to mean a stability in the relation between word and concept, to be achieved by explicit defining; and a conscious grasp, by anyone using words, of this relation. And this defining and this conscious grasp of defined or definable meanings concern individual words.

It must be understood that the campaigns for *ch'ing ming* and for precise definition, as they operate together, are a campaign for definition, not only *by* words, but *of* words. That is a critical distinction.

As far as I can tell, Pound was very good at defining particular terms within the field of economics: at least it seems to me that his definitions there clear up some important messes. But I don't see that he was particularly good at defining terms outside that area; a lot of what he calls "defining terms" is not what is usually understood by that at all.[21] And as we have seen, it seems doubtful whether he was good even at understanding particular terms in that great model of the precise use of language that he was always flourishing: the Latin of the medieval philosopher-theologians. But he didn't much need this kind of verbal precision, and we don't much need it, because of the principle of "ideogrammic writing."

At this point, therefore, I must try to describe my view of the Fenollosan/Poundian principle of "ideogrammic writing": putting it as briefly as I can. I shall talk of it only as a method propounded for writing in *non-ideographic* languages: English, for example.[22] That is its most important possible use. It is quite clearly separable from Pound's ideas of its use as a way of reading Chinese characters, which is essentially that scattershot etymological method that I have described.

If we want to know what Pound meant by it as a way of writing in English, the intelligent method is to do what Ron Bush did some years ago in *The Genesis of Ezra Pound's Cantos*, namely to see what examples of Western writing Pound referred to when he used the term.[23] And then we find that "ideogrammic writing" means, precisely, "writing that specifies its meaning by examples." The smallest scale would be something like this, in the Pisan Cantos:

> so that you cd/ crack a flea on eider wan
>   ov her breasts
> sd/ the old Dublin pilot
>   or the precise definition
>
>   (77/489)

The old man—as reported here—described an action: and that described action conveys exactly what the girl's breasts were like. But note: he is part of the situation, and it is the whole situation (as a coherent set of concretenesses) that conveys the information. His devoted gaze is not, vaguely, on the collectivity of her bosom: it is on "eider wan" of her breasts. That concentration of desire tells us something. Also, evidently, he does not think of young female persons as in the remote boudoirs of glamorous novels: the very action that comes to his mind tells us that. Perhaps there is more in his intimate—at least very unformal—Irish tongue. There is a whole mass of information (I doubt if I have exhausted it) in the glimpse-of-concrete-situation we are given; every element of it, whether we bring it to consciousness or not, specifies more precisely the location of the node of this information: makes it a more "precise definition" of the subject. And the precision is evident as soon as we imagine the usual way of trying to convey the subject, which is to name it directly, with some word like *firm* or *resilient* or (quite clearly off the beam in this case) Huxley's *pneumatic*.

The "ideogrammic method" assumes that you cannot directly name the entity, state, or isness that is your prime aim, if it is anything more complicated than a teapot or a steel desk. And it works. I refer to the passage in Canto 83 that goes

> Dryad, thy peace is like water
> There is September sun on the pools
>
> Plura diafana
>   Heliads lift the mist from the young willows
> there is no base seen under Taishan
>   but the brightness of '*udor*   ὕδωϱ
> the poplar tips float in brightness
> only the stockade posts stand

$$(83/550\text{-}51)^{24}$$

The overall condition-of-things and awareness conveyed here is in some way related to that conveyed by Canto 49 (the famous Seven Lakes Canto). But they are different; we apprehend them as different. Nobody is going to confuse them. This seems sufficient proof that the two states, as Pound would have said, have been "defined" precisely. And neither is named by any direct naming: by words like *acceptance* or *quietude* or *the flow* or any other of the flaccid verbal rubbish that populates do-it-yourself handbooks to enlightenment.

Again, both are related to the state conveyed in *Hugh Selwyn Mauberley*, with

> Tawn foreshores
> Washed in the cobalt of oblivions

Related, but quite distinct. Nobody is going to confuse them: the constellations and orderings of things presented are quite enough to distinguish them to the reader's mind.

Ideogrammic writing is a method of indirect naming; and the Fenollosa/Pound theory says, in effect, that direct naming of complex things is lies. It simplifies and lumps. The women's-magazine writer thinks she knows what she means by a big word like *love;* Toni Morrison knows she doesn't, and writes a novel to show what she means: a novel replete with *things*, in a very careful ordering. Middle-range writers, like Lawrence and Hardy, aim at the latter method and are constantly found to have slipped by one subterfuge or another into the former: into demanding our assent to a great proposition named directly in some abstract form and not "justified" by the concrete *ideogrammic* data the writer has assembled.

It is a method of writing that allows you to extend the meanings of words. Some current theory says a writer can't present things: can only present words, that is, the signs that are already part of the language. Ideogrammic theory says that a writer indicates things, somewhat vaguely, by individual words: but it is the implied relations between those indicated things—between the clusters of referential material the writing is taken to offer—that give the precision. And if the concept that the writer attaches to one of those words is somewhat different from that attached to it by any previous writer, the reader will see that too. As Pound says, there is "the word of literary art which presents, defines, suggests the visual image: the word which must rise afresh in each work of art and come down with renewed light."[25] Pound uses the word *awareness* in a sense, I think, not found in any preceding writer; we know this, though he never defines the word. And this is what happens with the phrase *per plura diaphana*: Pound's constructed "ideogrammata" in *The Cantos* give it new meanings that are there, "permanently," subject only to the slow change that afflicts all the words that compose them, but in any case created by crossings of such powerful alignments of concreteness that they are quite independent of what Grosseteste's passage of experimental science had used them for.

These are all arguments for a possible precision in "definition" by the method of ideogrammic writing, which is a definition *by* or even *through* words, using them indirectly to specify (or, as Pound would say, "define") particular states. But it seems to me that Pound hijacks the example of that kind of precision, to argue for the other: the precision of direct naming and the defining of terms.

I return to the 1937 essay, "Immediate Need of Confucius." The greater part of the essay is spent in denouncing modern Western "indistinctness" in thought and in terminology; and in contrasting it with the "dissociation and tidiness" typical of the great medieval writers, in particular of Erigena, Grosseteste, and Dante the Latinist. This paragraph contains an idea that will be familiar to most readers of Pound:

> You can probably date any Western work of art by reference to the ethical estimate of usury prevalent at the time of that work's composition; the greater the composition of tolerance for usury the more blobby and messy the work of art. The kind of thought which distinguishes good from evil, down into the details of commerce, rises into the quality of line in paintings and into the clear definition of the word written. (*SP*, 76)

Note the phrase: "the clear definition *of* the word written." Again, three paragraphs further on: "Catholicism led Europe as long as Erigena, Grosseteste and their fellows struggled for definitions *of* words" (emphasis added).

This "of" is crucial: it seems to me that it constitutes a new and unnecessary demand.

Let us go back for a moment to the other kind of "precise definition." In the Pisan Cantos, from the first page, there is a great deal about it:

> Fear god and the stupidity of the populace,
> but a precise definition
>   transmitted thus Sigismundo
>   thus Duccio, thus Zuan Bellin, or trastevere with La Sposa
>
> (74/445)

This precise defining has nothing to do with words. Words are neither the medium nor the target. When Sigismundo "defined" his awareness—concerning Ixotta, particularly—he didn't do it in words, but in the organization of an architectural whole. One part of the whole was constituted by the "defining" done by Duccio, and *he* defined his awareness of Demeter and Diana, and the rest, in stone: by a certain degree of convexity in a stone of a carefully chosen texture, worked so that it would show a surface of a certain specific smoothness, and so on: nothing to do with words.

Pound, very legitimately I think, uses this sense of *define* a great deal in the Pisan Cantos and elsewhere. When it was put to him that prose sufficed to convey all that was conveyable, he remarked that prose left the thing merely indicated in "elastic" terms, until it was "given rhythmic definition" (*LE*, 71). These are perfectly reasonable uses of the word *define:* and in each case they denote the exact specifying of a set of things, or a state, or an awareness, by the organized elements of your medium: stone, architecture, rhythm.

But what has happened in "The Immediate Need of Confucius"?

Pound is demanding the precise defining *of* the elements of the medium: words.

It is a doubly strange confusion. First, it is obvious that you can, as Pound shows everywhere and especially in the Pisan Cantos, "define" states and awarenesses, in words, without ever defining your words. Second, it twists the logic of Pound's own example in this essay. If antiusury ages produce clear, exact painting, that is art that, through its medium (paint), "defines" states with precision. The parallel for writing ought to be art that, *through its medium* (words), "defines" states with precision. In the analogy, there is no argument for defining *words* at all. You might as well ask the painter to be able to give a systematic account of his paints. (In what medium? Paint?)

The cantos have Vlaminck as "a great brute sweating paint" (74/455), and no doubt every artist must know his or her medium with that sort of intimacy; but it is not necessarily a knowledge that could be made intelligible, in words or diagrams, to some eager art class.

It's a very peculiar slither. I don't think it is typical of Pound, whose thought about art is usually very clear. But I think it may be one early sign of a drift toward word-fetishism, which I shall refer to again later.

Fenollosa's "ideogrammic reading" campaign was begun, and Pound's campaign for "ideogrammic writing" was taken up, as ways of evading the void of verbal abstraction. The Scholastics, Fenollosa said, proceeded by defining things: and this meant, for them, deciding which major category a thing belonged to (*CWC*, 75). The cosmos for Aquinas was a hierarchic set of concepts, each concept including, with precision, below it, a set of subconcepts. The point of all discussion was to mark out exactly the edges of each major category, and thus precisely decide which lower-level concepts its borders enclosed, and which they didn't. As Fenollosa complained, the Scholastics believed things weren't known at all until it was known which part of this great pyramidal brick-stack they belonged in (*CWC*, 76). Their tool was words: each word being "precisely" used in the sense that it was made explicit which concepts it included and what it didn't. And the whole point was mutual exclusion: to have a concept partly in one category and partly in another on the same level was to fail, because it incapacitated the method of discussion: the syllogism.

As Pound says, having little knowledge of the real world, the Scholastics became very exact with these concept-systems and the word-systems that corresponded to them. Pound then tries to persuade us, in his essays on these topics, that we can inherit the verbal exactitude, and include our new, postscience, precision of knowledge about actuality. It seems to me this is very unlikely.[26] As Pound himself notes, scientists don't bother with all this defining of terms; they feel it's not necessary to the further-ance of science. It seems to me more likely in fact to be an obstacle.

A little example, to give the quality of what we are dealing with. In the course of his vast encyclopedia, Aquinas treats of the question whether the soul is transmitted with the father's semen into the womb, or whether it is created after that point. As part of his argument, he notes: "First, no substantial form is susceptible of being more or less. But the addition of a greater perfection makes another species, as the addition of unity makes another species in the realm of numbers."[27] Now, with a lot of thought and a bit of checking, I think I could tell you what each of the key terms here means, with some precision. But the precision comes from their definition by Aquinas: at some point in the great opus or else-where, he will be found to have defined them, and to have refined his definitions, with all the care that Pound could require. And he will have defined them much more in words than by constellations of examples— of things happening, of slices through concrete situations. For he does not have the concrete knowledge such "ideogrammic" definition would require. The definition of the terms is in fact largely in terms of each other,[28] and so there is nothing you could *observe* that would disprove the validity of the terms *perfection* (a concept unknown to biology, for example) or *form* or *species*.

Each of these terms had once, probably, embodied a certain valuable insight into the way things are; and, with a little thought, one can still see what that insight was. At such a stage in the development of the "philos-ophy," there is no danger. The danger comes precisely at the stage of la-bored explicit definition, for there then develops a system (the Aquinist system, for example) whose very coherence imposes. The very elaborate-ness of the interlocking definition makes the outsider feel that unless he understands the whole system—a life's work for professionals—he cannot question the validity of any of its parts. Yet to build a large structure out of such parts, none of which has been checked against concrete data, is to multiply the wobbliness of their relation to reality: so that in the end the whole system is really a parallel world made almost entirely of words.

And the real problem is that a thinker armed with such a system comes to believe he knows something. I suspect that the sixteenth-century Aristotelians felt their own authority, when faced with the interloper Galileo, mainly because they knew he was ignorant—of their system. The same effect seems to possess the followers of Derrida, when faced with some naïve person who has evidence that speech is prior to writing.

The odd thing is that no one was more conscious than Pound of all these objections to "thinking by definitions." Ideogram was only one of the ways he offered for getting round its falsifications. Myth was another: it allowed you, he said, to communicate an awareness without cutting off its ears and nose. Icon was yet a third: to re-erect the statue of Venus at Terracina would be "worth more than any metaphysical argument."

And he went on: "the mosaics in Santa Maria in Trastevere recall a wisdom lost by scholasticism, an understanding denied to Aquinas" (*SP*, 320). Aquinas's hyperverbalism is then linked with the evil of all usury, which Pound says has a secular tendency (supposed to be Semitic) to hide truths under elaborate words.[29] It seems strange that by implication the "precise definer," Aquinas, should in effect end up on both sides of the ancient battle between greed and light.

If I am not mistaken, there is a deep conflict here. Pound wants authority; he wants fixity; he wants to find them manifested in words. And yet he seems to know at the same time that words manifesting them are a kind of death—that they end up as a form of materialism, which is the point at which (I would say) Aquinas and John Locke intersect on a profounder scale of values.

Probably there are places for the explicit defining of terms: the monetary field Pound uses it in is no doubt one. And it seems reasonable to say this, even if one cannot say exactly where explicit definition *of* words should end and intuitive communication *through* words begin.[30]

It is also possible that Pound conceived of a division into two kinds of writing. One kind might be that of the "not taught," the subtler truths, handleable only in poetry, where the method of ideogrammic writing allows an enormous leap in complexity of "content." That might be the realm of Ovid, and of Eleusis. It is possible that in his mind Pound would have divided the cantos in some such way as the Confucian Odes have traditionally been divided: into the songs that show the folkways, and the higher, "statal" odes (as Pound might have called them). The ideogram would then work mainly in the former, and explicitly stabilized terminology in the latter: as when Pound discusses some passage from Alexander Del Mar's monetary histories in *Thrones*. That seems possible; and it also seems possible that such a distinction has value even though (again) the line between the two kinds of passage would be exceedingly difficult to draw.

And it would be a waste of time to dwell on the apparent inconsistencies in Pound's mind as to what definition is. He was working out an insight as he went.

In his English version of *The Analects*, the word *define* becomes very prominent. If one collates the uses of it, one arrives at—I think—some four or five different implicit senses of the word *define:* almost all of them useful, when understood.[31] But there are worrying points. One is that the great majority of these phrases themselves are arrived at by bending the Chinese quite willfully: which shows that Pound is becoming somewhat besotten with the idea of defining. The other is that, so keen is he to brandish this bloody blade, he arrives at using it on one occasion when he means merely "to mention something, with a specific and clear concept in one's head" (*Con*, 117). This, to me, indicates that the genie of this "define" complex of ideas is now controlling Pound's mind more than he it.

It leads him to some dangerous claims. He writes, in 1942, "Without the definition of words knowledge cannot be transmitted from one man to another" (*SP*, 308). I would say that remark implies a very limited conception of knowledge, and one unworthy of the promoter of ideogrammic writing. Again (1944): "thought hinges on the definitions of words" (*SP*, 336). Thank goodness it doesn't, or language and thought would constitute one closed field. He had claimed in *Guide to Kulchur* (1938), when this new campaign was really taking him over, that all renaissances began with a redefinition of terms (*GK*, 58–59); and his harping on the definition of terms in this book so enraged the skeptical, and in some ways much more language-conscious, Bunting, that he wrote in the margin of his copy, "Only a lack of understanding of what language is can make any but saboteur demand 'definition.'"

Pound neglected the value of his own enormous skill in ideogrammic "definition" to make unreasonable claims for the other kind. And he seems to have been unreasonably blind to the limits of his own kind of reading in his authorities for the precise use of words—from Confucius to Grosseteste, Arnaut Daniel, and Cavalcanti. This reading is "ideogrammic" where Pound has enough data to go on; elsewhere it is *either* merely fanciful, *or* brilliantly imaginative, but in neither case has it much to do with the verbal precisions of the original. These are great contradictions; but this was a very emotive nexus for Pound. In the grip of it, the word *define* becomes a flag waved on all possible occasions.

When he made his first prewar formulations about *ch'ing ming*, he was still loyal to the Fenollosan principles of indirect naming, and does not at first seem to have seen that there might be a conflict between the two. But certain passions were aroused by John Adams and right naming: no doubt natural to a man who, like Adams, was generally isolated and mocked. Pound's problem with his economics was that he wasn't being believed, whether by economists, or politicians, or colleagues like Eliot or Yeats or Ford. His assertions about the value of the precise definition of words, and about precision with words in general, are a claim for the authority in the use of words that (he thinks) ought to derive from his life-long exercise of the craft of poetry: for he thinks this authority is transferable to his writings about economics. This is one of the reasons for the fuss in *Thrones* about having a *pen yeh*, a main skill, a craft in which one is rooted: he had his *pen yeh*, and it qualified him to chastise "loose users of words," whether in economics or elsewhere.

Most of what Pound has to say about precise definition provokes valuable thought; and I would not wish to claim any certainty about the defects I seem to see in it, for these are very difficult areas. My only certain objection to Pound's *ch'ing ming* campaign is that the manner of it makes overstated claims about his own knowledge of words and things. In the late cantos there is a great deal of assertive discussion with scholars like Ducange, Nicole, and Liddell about Greek and French terms and their meanings: in a manner that suggests Pound is their equal in this "defining of terms." Cicero, who before the war would not have merited more space than Polonius, is now made a writer worth reading because he said you should define your terms before you start discussing. There are suggestions that "the classics" are being "blacked out" because the classical authors said things like that.[32] In the general assertiveness about the blurring of distinctions and the hiding of historical facts, the overall message seems to be this. Sloppiness in the defining of terms is somewhere near the root of the great economic betrayal. But *this* author—though he ranges from Byzantium to the Exarchate to ancient China and Benton's Washington—knows what he is talking about in each of these areas, and is master of the conceptual systems of each, whether monetary systems or Chinese characters; and his own writing is continuous with the careful and explicit defining of terms by the great lawyers, economists, and lexicographers who have dealt with these areas—such that, had he time, and were he not obstructed by rage at the reader's laziness, he could specify the meanings of each of the terms he uses as clearly as he could those of the words in the American Constitution.

It is quite possible to respect Pound's great contributions to the understanding of many things, and yet suspect a lot of this to be based on hasty readings of shallow texts.

Pound seems even to have taken precise definition *in words* (as distinct from any other sort of precise definition) into the realm of metaphysics. Taken with the foregoing, this seems to me to justify the phrase *word fetishism* that I offered earlier.

In *The Great Digest* and in *The Unwobbling Pivot*, there is an important Chinese character that others translate as "sincerity," but Pound translates as "precise verbal definition." That translation of his seems to me an example of Pound's insistent push toward concern with words. His way of arriving at it is historically arbitrary: it is his old standard, the etymological method. He sees *word* and *lance* and arrives at something like "defined in words with lancelike precision."[33] To judge by Karlgren, who (as far as I can tell) was a sensitive reader of texts (as the really great lexicographers must be), the Chinese tradition has always understood the character to mean a sincerity that does not have to be verbal at all.[34] But Pound's reading also seems to be conceptually arbitrary, that is, as considered in relation to Pound's other deep beliefs. Cannot your actions, your intentions, be sincere, and cannot you know they are, without verbalizing them? Pound, in earlier days, would have said you could. What, he would have said, would be the value of Brancusi's sculpture if Brancusi could have verbalized it? Criticism of one's verbal formulations can no doubt be an extremely valuable therapy in the search for sincerity; but this is another claim altogether.

As he proceeds with the translation of *The Unwobbling Pivot*, and as he encounters the successive uses of that key character, Pound carries the meaning "sincerity" along in parallel with the meaning "precise verbal definition." He comes to chapters 22 and 23, at which point the Rev. Legge had blenched at the presumption of the text; but he boldly proceeds: "Only the most absolute sincerity under heaven can bring the inborn talent to the full and empty the chalice of the nature. [The resultant] understanding of the nature of things can . . . raise man up to be a sort of third partner with heaven and earth. . . . Only the most absolute sincerity under heaven can effect any change [in things, in conditions]" (*Con*, 173–75).[35]

Man, it seems, by sincerity can become more than man: he can "hear the roots speaking together" (47/238); he can foresee; he can be the statesman-as-artist, like Mussolini. I think all these implications may be inferred, and I would not wish to attack them.

But they are not all. This character for "sincerity" (or "precision in one's own terminology") appears in the manuscript for Canto 74, placed at the end of these lines: "in principio verbum / paraclete or the verbum perfectum: / sinceritas" (74/447).[36]

And it is clearly therefore implied in this line:

the paraclete that was present in Yao, the precision

(74/449)[37]

"In the beginning was the Word, and the Word was with God, and the Word was God," it says at the beginning of the Gospel of St. John. This is a mystical statement, and Pound does not have to defend his belief in this mysticism, or explain what it means. But he now adds to it the Chinese character for "sincerity," whose translation by him insistently implies that he thinks the prime or only form of sincerity is in critique of one's verbal manifestations. And he has been running a campaign to persuade his readers that one can't even think properly without verbal self-consciousness. Where does that leave all the other kinds of precision in the universe: the precisions communicated by the dancers, the painters, the musicians; the precisions inherent in the movement of the frogs and grasses?

It seems to me that Pound had from the beginning a love for exact distinguishings that is the source of a lot of his best poetry ("where light shaves grass into emerald" [48/243]). In the 1910s it appears in the terms *fine, fineness*, for example in his work derived from Provence; by the 1940s it has branched out into *demarcation, delineated*, and so on. But his need to find authority for his politics seems to force it all into the area of conscious verbalism; he discovers the term *define*, which conveniently covers the lot. And now all that gets yoked to the star of a mysticism. If I grasped the mysticism of the Logos I would no doubt accept it: but it seems to me I should still not accept these claims about human language.

NOTES

1. I will mention two symptoms of this progression. The *Guide to Kulchur* (1938) seems to be Pound's last serious attempt to expound his ideogrammic theory. In a "Nota" preceding the Italian version of the Confucian *Ta Hsio* (1942; reprinted in Pound, *Opere scelte*, ed. Mary de Rachewiltz [Milan: Mondadori, 1973]), 429-30, he makes a stab at describing a Fenollosan way of reading Chinese characters, but makes no attempt to transfer it to the reading (still less the writing) of English. And even this note is dropped when the Confucian books are brought out after the war in Pound's English versions. The progression with "right naming" is the opposite. Just before and during the war, Pound issues a number of tracts about money, with titles announcing this concern with money. After the war, Pound seems to suggest that their real focus had been the definition of terms: when his disciple Noel Stock reissues them in the collection *Impact* (Chicago: Henry Regnery, 1960), *What Is Money For?* becomes "Integrity of the Word"; *Gold and Work* becomes "The Enemy Is Ignorance"; the section of *A Visiting Card* entitled "System" becomes "Terminology."

2. By the phrase "metaphysic of distinctions" I mean that a clarity that involves the perceiving of distinctions seems to be an ultimate good for Pound. From his earliest days, Pound felt that to see clearly was both in itself a delight and an inexhaustible benefit; so the desired state was that of the Provençal *alba*, or dawn song, when all things are simply clear, simply themselves. But that clarity is a nonconfusion of things. So Pound devotes a long training to discriminating between things that are not easy to distinguish: colors, textures, "pale as the dawn cloud, la luna / thin as Demeter's hair" (74/450-51). The link with Pound's politics seems clear enough. He writes, "in this war were Joe Gould, Bunting and cummings / as against thickness and fatness" (74/452). These writers were "in this war" inasmuch as the purpose of writing is to get things down "distinguishedly," which is what they did; whereas the impulse of the enemy—greed, in art or in economics—is to grab things in haste, hence without distinguishing their isnesses, their characters. I am reminded of Gourmont's dictum, quoted by Pound: "Apprendre pour apprendre est peut-être aussi grossier que manger pour manger" (*LE*, 352). One might imagine him praying—as does an older theology—that the souls of the dead may see God's presence "without confusion": may see the whole of what God is, for He includes everything; and may see Him without muddling any.

3. For discussion of the Confucian meaning of *ch'ing ming*, some references may be found in Makin, *Pound's Cantos* (repr. Baltimore: Johns Hopkins University Press, 1992), 232 n. 12; to which add Fung Yu-Lan, *A History of Chinese Philosophy*,

trans. Derk Bodde (Beijing: Henry Vetch; London: George Allen and Unwin, 1937), 59–62.

4. *Impact*, ed. Noel Stock (Chicago: Henry Regnery, 1960), 72–73.

5. 89/611, where the Chinese characters also mean "king king"; cf. 94/660, 661; see also "Sovereignty [a Note]," *European* 1 (March 1953): 51; reprinted in *P&P*, 8:550.

6. *SP*, 307–8 (*A Visiting Card*, 1942). Cf. esp. *SP*, 290–302 (*What Is Money For?* 1939). As far as I can tell, Pound's main points about the proper definition of money are these. Money should be defined as a measured claim, used as a means of exchange, *only*. It is not a "concentration of energy," or a commodity: therefore it should not be hoardable and tradable as if it were these. Since it is not these, the state does not have to accumulate it (like, say, rice or gold) to spend it on public works, but can issue it against future wealth to be generated. It is not a god, or a growing thing; therefore it has no "right" to interest, for example when it is lent by the purchase of bonds. Since it is not a permanent good, it can be allowed to dwindle away like all the goods it is exchanged for: so it is reasonable to impose a Gesellite tax on the money itself.

7. I transfer this phrase from Pound's discussion of a quite different method of milking the public, in 40/198.

8. Thus for example in the early chapters of the *Guide to Kulchur*; or in *A Visiting Card* (in Italian, 1942), reprinted, *SP*, 306–35.

9. *SP*, 78. In this passage (*De Vulgari Eloquentia*, 2.10), the first two uses of *quia* mean "that": a sense common, for example, in the Roman liturgy.

10. Particularly relevant passages seem to be "Flora Castalia, your petals drift thru the air, / the wind is 1/2 lighted with pollen / diafana" (93/652) and "Plura diafana / Heliads lift the mist from the young willows" (83/550). It also seems highly relevant that Pound translates Cavalcanti's "si formato / chome / Diafan dal lume / d' una schuritade" (*LE*, 164) as "Formed there in manner as *a mist* of light / Upon a dusk" (155) (emphasis added). I would guess that this idea of something misty or veil-like started from Gilson's paraphrase of Grosseteste, quoted with delight by Pound, where it says, of light, "Cette substance extrêmement ténue est aussi l'étoffe dont toutes choses sont faites; elle est la première forme corporelle et ce que certains nomment la corporéité" (*LE*, 160). Pound observes that this paraphrase is more to his Cavalcantian purpose than the original Latin; but he does not seem to have discovered that Gilson in later editions dropped the *étoffe* phrasing, presumably because it had come to seem to him too far from Grosseteste's sense. My suspicion is that Pound fell in love with the "cloth" sense of *étoffe*, for one of the recurrent associations with the *diafana* in the later cantos is veils (Leucothoe's: 95/664, 96/671), and perhaps skirts (the young willows': 83/550). (For further likely associations with Dante's *nuvoletta* and *fil che fa la zona*, see Makin, "Pound's Provence," 39.) The cantos passages all seem to be about moments in which a delicate and female presence takes form in some substance, printed there by light.

11. The relevant fragments quoted by Pound in *LE*, 161, are from Robert Grosseteste, *Die Philosophischen Werke*, ed. Ludwig Baur (Münster: Aschendorffsche,

1912), 73. (The text is *De iride*, and not, as Pound and his commentators often suggest, *De luce*.) Cf. A. C. Crombie, *Robert Grosseteste and the Origins of Experimental Science, 1100–1700* (Oxford: Clarendon Press, 1961), 117–20, which gives a useful summary of the passage. Careful consideration of the whole *De iride* seems to suggest that nothing in it could lead to the metaphysics Pound associates with the phrase *per plura diaphana:* that the phrase itself, misunderstood, simply acted as a trigger for clusters of ideas Pound brought to it.

12. Indeed this modern meaning of *diaphanous*—"veil-like"—is no older than the twentieth century, and is an English meaning. But Pound was working, as usual, from etymology: *dia* plus *phan* gives "through-light," and any sense that could be found in those two vast semantic pools was available to his procedures.

13. Makin, *Pound's Cantos*, 308. But Pound both wanted and did not want the effects of this haste. Of his reading of John Scotus Erigena's Latin, he remarked: "I want corroborations on various points. Often a hurried reading fails to find a 'denegat' ['denies'] at end of passage. A lot of nice ideas start in one's own head that can't be attributed to J.S.E." (*SL*, 332).

14. *Basil Bunting on Poetry*, ed. Peter Makin (Baltimore: Johns Hopkins University Press, 1999), 136.

15. That is, for the purposes of my argument here I accept that they are the etymons; for my argument here only concerns the essentials of Pound's method, and of his "etymological" misconception about words. But it is well known by now that Pound was often in error in identifying pictorial elements of a Chinese character as the etymons of the character: whether because in the given case they had only a phonetic function, or because he used only his own guesswork to decide their pictorial meaning. For discussions of all this, see references below, note 22; also and esp. Makin, "Kennedy, Fenollosa, Pound, and the Chinese Character," *Agenda* 17, nos. 3–4 and 18, no. 1 (1979–80): 22–37.

16. Pound, *Con*, 244. It will be said that Pound was not working from the etymons alone, but from the flow of thought in the context; which would, exactly, save the reader from such misreadings as "a great gain in [circumcision]." But a certain density of information is needed before context can help. In *The Analects*, the total context is often no more than a couple of sentences; and so Pound is totally at the mercy of his "etymology." In other cases, his ignorance of the language or his haste in reading (see below) reduces the contextual data that might help him to little or nothing. A good dictionary, of course, is a condensed cross-reference to other contemporary texts, read (insofar as the dictionary maker is a good one) with sensitivity to the flow of thought in their contexts; but Pound generally rejected that kind of help.

17. See the many drafts in the Beinecke Library, and also, e.g., *Pound's Translations of Arnaut Daniel*, ed. Charlotte Ward (New York: Garland, 1991), e.g. 77, 55, and esp. 36, 99, 111, as well as Pound, *The Spirit of Romance* (London: J. M. Dent, 1910), 28.

18. Hugh Kenner and Massimo Bacigalupo have, in part, traced this process: see full discussion in Makin, "Pound's Provence and the Duecento," *Kansai University Studies in English Language and Literature* 36 (1996): 34–40 and esp. notes 36, 37.

19. M. Raynouard, *Lexique roman* (1836–45; repr. Heidelberg: Carl Winter, n.d.) 4:240–41, cf. 4:238–39 s.v. *mirar*. Cf. further Emil Levy, *Provenzalisches Supplement-Wörterbuch* (1894ff.; repr. Hildesheim: Georg Olms, 1973) 7:219; and (a dictionary Pound sometimes used) Levy, *Petit Dictionnaire Provençal-Français* (1909; repr. Heidelberg: Carl Winter, 1961), 322.

20. See Makin, "Pound's Provence," 35–36.

21. By this I do not mean that Pound's ways of using the words *define* and *definition* are unusable: only that, often, they do not refer to the marking out of a concept in such a way as his campaign for the defining of terms might lead us to expect. See below, note 31. Some good criteria for definition in its usual sense are offered in *SP*, 291 (*What Is Money For?* [1939]): "We will have defined money properly when we have stated what it is in words that can NOT be applied to anything else and when there is nothing about the essential nature of money that is omitted from our definition."

22. It seems to me that the value of this principle as a way of understanding writing in any language is enormous, and has nothing to do with Pound's confusions concerning his original model for the principle, namely the Chinese written character. See Makin, "The Shape of Pound's Dante," in *Dante e Pound*, ed. Maria Luisa Ardizzone (Ravenna: Longo, 1998), 120–24 and notes; and Makin, "Implications of Pound's 'Ideogrammic' Theory," in *Studies in English and American Literature Presented to Professor Akira Yasukawa*, ed. Yoko Wada (Osaka: Kansai University Press, 2002).

23. Ronald Bush, *The Genesis of Ezra Pound's Cantos* (Princeton: Princeton University Press, 1976), 10–14.

24. 83/550–51. See discussion in my *Pound's Cantos*, 248–50.

25. *A Visiting Card*; reprinted *SP*, 321.

26. See e.g. *ABCR*, 19–20; *SP* 76–78 ("Immediate Need of Confucius," 1937); *GK*, 27–28. In *SP*, 78, Pound tries to persuade the reader (quoting Dante) that "the good scholastic . . . recognised the limits of knowledge transmissible by verbal definitions"; but he does not develop this line of thought.

27. St. Thomas Aquinas, *Summa Theologiae* (London: Blackfriars, 1970), 15.151 (*ST* 1a.118, 2).

28. At least it seems true to say that the Scholastic sense of none of the three terms *form*, *perfection*, and *species* can be accepted unless those of the others are accepted: form is what makes matter belong to a given species, and so forth.

29. *SP*, 322: "the theologians who put reason (logic) in place of faith began the slithering process which has ended up with theologians who take no interest in theology whatsoever. [Cf. *GK*, 77: "Aquinas lacked faith."] Tradition *inheres* ("*inerisce*") in the images of the gods, and gets lost in dogmatic definitions." In *SP*, 320 (*A Visiting Card*, 1942), Pound goes out of his way to relate this to a mystery-destroying verbal obscurantism that he considers Semitic, and to link it to protestantism: evidently, for him, it goes straight through into the protestant materialism that created the Bank of England, and all our woe.

30. Pound attempts a division of roles, in *SP*, 321 (quoted above), between "the word of literary art which presents, defines, suggests the visual image" and "the legal

or scientific word which must, at the outset, be defined with the greatest possible precision, and never change its meaning." It seems an extremely difficult distinction to maintain. On the one hand, Pound himself wanted a good deal of his poetry to be "statal"; and on the other, most truly effective writing in law and in philosophy seems more "ideogrammic" than definition-based.

31. One usage of *define* in *The Analects* implies the sense "to give an example of an action or person embodying the quality in question" (thus 240, 253). Another implies the sense "to specify what one means through the composition of the Chinese character itself" (260). By far the commonest implies the sense "to offer one or two distinctions concerning the term, such that the hearer will have a somewhat clearer sense of what it can usefully mean" (thus *Con*, 233, 241, 244, 252, 254, 272). This, I would say, is an extremely valuable activity in anything called "philosophy," because it avoids the specious claim to conceptual exhaustiveness that (as Wittgenstein observes) has traditionally been implied in Western philosophers' use of terms.

It may be that the real model for Pound's thinking about definitions was the triad of distinctions concerning cogitation, meditation, and contemplation he found (through Dante) in Richard of St. Victor; and that his later reading of other theologians added little or nothing. My reasons for suggesting this would be as follows. Richard's triad is always produced as an example of clear definition: notably, in conjunction with the Confucian passage about "right naming" in *Impact*, 73 (which then, having quoted Richard, returns to the topic of the need for correct names as the basis for order in the state). Second, Pound is attracted to making up triads of distinctions for himself: perhaps they have a systematic air that seems "definitive." (See *SP*, 319 [twice], 320, 321.) This making of quite complex distinctions—which are yet not really definitions—then gets extended into the making of lists, wherein a noun is "defined" by one concrete example: thus *GK*, 105, etc. Third, Richard's "definitions" in themselves have an air of definitiveness; yet the terms of which the definitions are made up are almost entirely metaphorical, that is, quasi-concrete; so that they avoid the obvious abstract deadness of proper Scholastic definition—in which all the key terms of the definition itself must be definable—and seem almost nearer to ideogram (see his comments on them in *GK*, 77). So they don't alert Pound to the real dangers of Scholastic thinking. Finally, though he flourishes the names of Aquinas, Erigena, and Grosseteste when he is writing about precise definition, he never (to my knowledge) cites a single instance from them. I suspect that a hasty reading in the massive tomes of the *Patrologia Latina* merely gave Pound the impression that their clarity was of the same nature as Richard's; and their authority was useful to him. Since Pound so rarely offers definitions that amount to what a Scholastic philosopher would have called such; and since he nevertheless so constantly demands definition of terms on the model of those in medieval philosophy, it seems most likely that these ad hoc sets of distinctions, on the model of Richard's, are what he understood thereby.

32. Pound, "Anonymous Contributions to *Strike*," in *Paideuma* 3, no. 3 (1974): 391.

33. Cf. *Con*, 33.

34. Bernhard Karlgren, *Grammata Serica Recensa* (Kungsbacka: Elanders Boktryckeri, 1972), 216–17 (no. 818h).

35. *Con,* 173–75 (last brackets Pound's). Cf. James Legge, *The Chinese Classics* (reprinted Taipei: SMC, 1994), 1.416 note: "What is it but extravagance thus to file man with the supreme Power?"

36. See Massimo Bacigalupo, *The Forméd Trace* (New York: Columbia University Press, 1980), 121, cf. 120 (the *ch'eng* at the end of Canto 77 is a different character).

37. Cf. *SP,* 306 ("A Visiting Card"): "In the beginning was the word, and the word has been betrayed."

Confucius against Confusion: Ezra Pound and the Catholic Chaplain at Pisa

WENDY STALLARD FLORY

For a Confucianist and a Catholic, we get along very well.
— Father Aloysius Vath to Ezra Pound, June 26, 1945

PRESIDENT TRUMAN, WASHINGTON. BEG YOU CABLE ME
MINIMUM TERMS JUST PEACE WITH JAPAN. LET ME
NEGOTIATE VIA JAPANESE EMBASSY RECENTLY ACCREDITED
ITALIAN SOCIAL REPUBLIC, LAGO DI GARDA. FE[N]OL[L]OSA[']S
EXECUTOR AND TRANSLATOR OF CONFUCIUS, CAN WHAT
VIOLENCE CANNOT. CHINA ALSO WILL OBEY VOICE OF
CONFUCIUS. EZRA POUND.

At Genoa in May 1945, as Pound's interrogation by agents of the FBI and of U.S. Counter Intelligence began, his first response—needless to say, not granted—was a request that the above cable be sent. FBI Special Agent Frank L. Amprim, in a memo to J. Edgar Hoover, glossed Pound's message as follows: "The Subject stated that he believed he could negotiate a peace between the United States and Japan, because in November of 1943, at Salo, Italy, he had met two Japanese who were from the Japanese Embassy, and they were surprised to learn that he was familiar with Confucius and [Fenollosa]. He advised further that he would appeal not to the Japanese militarists, but to the ancient culture of Japan." It must have quickly become clear to Pound's interrogators that, aberrant as his sense of reality was and as grandiose his assumptions about his ability to intervene effectively in international diplomacy, he was entirely serious. We see this in the two supplements—"Outline of Historic Bases of Historic Process" and "Further Points" dated "8 May 1945"—that he insisted be added to his sworn statement of May 7. Here he wrote, "If I could bring the slaughter in the Pacific to a sane and speedy end, I should, I believe, have justified my existence" (*L/DP* 73) and also presented himself as qualified, after some instruction in the Georgian dialect, to negotiate with Stalin himself: "Lenin . . . presents a false dilemma when he says the only remedy is the nationalization of the means of production. There are alternate remedies,

143

indicated by C. H. Douglas, by Gesell, and by the Constitution of the U.S. IF applied as its authors intended. That is why I wish,—after due LINGUISTIC preparation to meet Stalin" (*L/DP* 69).

Pound concluded his second supplement by describing his prior experience as adviser to yet another head of state. His account of his counseling of Mussolini presents Pound, not just as transmitting the wisdom of the Confucian texts he has translated, but as himself taking on the role of Confucius:

> 6. As to the sort of advice I gave in Italy, and sent to the Head of the Government, I give one sample. It had to be done as a translation from the Chinese, and is an exact version of the Ta S'eu Cap. 10. v. 16. . . .
>
> To see dishonest men and be incapable of kicking them out; or to fire them and not manage to send them to the furthest frontiers (i.e. the *confino*) is to err.
>
> Poor old Benito erred all right. I was assured he received first edition of this Confucian book, but when his secretary acknowledged the second edition (italian without the chinese text) it was too late. Very much too late. . . .[1]
>
> "To hate what people love is to offend human nature. Calamities will come on him who does so even to doing him physical harm, the wild grass will cover his corpse." Ta S'eu 10/17.[2] (*L/DP* 77)

The concluding quotation is Pound's approximate version of his own translation of a section of the *Da Xue* of Confucius—variously called by Pound *Ta S'eu* or *Ta Hsio* and translated by him as *The Great Digest*—a passage that Pound would repeatedly quote in the future to sum up his renunciation of Mussolini (*Con*, 81). It is worth noting, at this point, how inaccurate it is to suggest that, at the time of the writing of the *Pisan Cantos*, Pound's Confucianism was of a piece with his enthusiasm for Mussolini. By then, Confucius had become, for Pound, the alternative to the Duce— the sage whose words remained so true that after almost twenty-five hundred years they could still be used as explanation of how Mussolini had brought destruction down upon himself and the people of Italy.

By 1945, his reliance on the writings of Confucius had become indispensable to Pound. In the months before his arrest and during his time in the Disciplinary Training Center at Pisa, Confucius became the key reference point for Pound's conception of himself as public activist and private individual, not only intellectually, but, in an even more influential way, psychologically. Canto 13, written in 1924, shows how long Confucius had been important to Pound as one of the most positive models of a right-minded thinker and reformer. By 1945, Pound's Confucius has taken on a strong and intimate symbolic significance as an intrinsic dimension of Pound's own psychological self-conceptualizing. To understand the workings of Pound's mind during his time at Pisa it is essential to have the clearest possible sense of the nature of his Confucianism—and vice versa. Pound had so thoroughly internalized his own "idea" of Confucius that he thought of himself in terms of Confucius and Confucius in terms of himself.

Pound's identification with Confucius had both negative and positive consequences that can be linked to the two poles of the Confucian paradigm of reformist activity—focus upon the governance of the state and attention to psychological "governance" of the self. The sequence of actions that link the rectification of the self and the creation of sound government can be thought of as progress in two directions—from the individual to the state and vice versa. In section 4 and 5 of "Confucius' Text," which opens the *Da Xue,* this is rendered, in Pound's translation, as

> 4. . . . The men of old wanting to clarify and diffuse throughout the empire that light which comes from looking straight into the heart and then acting, first set up good government in their own states; wanting good government in their states, they first established order in their own families; wanting order in the home, they first disciplined themselves; desiring self-discipline, they rectified their own hearts; and wanting to rectify their hearts, they sought precise verbal definitions of their inarticulate thoughts [the tones given off by the heart]. . . .
>
> 5. . . . Having attained this precise verbal definition [*aliter,* this sincerity], they then stabilized their hearts, they disciplined themselves; having attained self-discipline, they set their own houses in order; having order in their own homes, they brought good government to their own states; and when their states were well governed, the empire was brought into equilibrium. (*Con,* 29–33)

This continuum, from individual action to thoroughgoing social change, is an indispensable component of the vision of the reformer. Yet under conditions such as those confronting both Confucius and Pound, which make the desired reform the remotest of possibilities and, finally, completely unrealizable, the "idea" of saving the state can persist only in the realm of the hypothetically potential. Confucius's vision of a "great chain" of enlightened reciprocity stretching from solicitous and respected ruler to thriving and respectful subject identified an ideal rather than any actuality. After 1935, a pronounced symptom of the deterioration of Pound's mental stability is his increasing failure, in his political and economic thinking, to distinguish the symbolic from the actual. By 1945, as the "Sworn Statements" that he gives in Genoa show, he believed himself both qualified and likely to be called to serve as a political and economic authority, acting on behalf of the U.S. government in missions at the highest levels of international, postwar diplomacy.

Pound's literalizing reading of Confucius's idealized mission of "reforming the ruler" aggravated his psychotic dissociation from the actualities of his situation. In marked contrast, Confucius's injunctions about "governance of the self"—control over one's emotions and rectification of one's negative attitudes—contributed materially and decisively to Pound's psychological survival. By the time that he was imprisoned in the DTC at Pisa, his intense focus upon and commitment to the value of Confucius's writings had become the indispensable stabilizing influence that enabled him to keep some measure of control over the angry and manic moods (and their accompanying negative attitudes) that had become increasingly unmanageable as Mussolini dragged Italy ever more deeply into war. Under the extreme stresses of his imprisonment and in the absence of any other help, Pound's faith in the reliability of Confucius's reiterations of the possibilities of mental equilibrium under adversity was his one "stay against confusion"—a defense against even more serious mental disorder.

How seriously one takes the Confucianism of the *Pisan Cantos* very much depends upon one's assumptions about the spirit in which Pound was writing, and any outside evidence that helps to clarify what his moods and attitudes were is particularly valuable. I have written on other dimensions of Pound's Confucianism in *Ezra Pound and "The Cantos"* and in *The American Ezra Pound*.[3] What I will add here takes as its reference point a very particular Confucian moment that occurred during Pound's time in the DTC—the occasion when he wrote a Confucian commentary or "manifesto" for the Catholic priest whom he had chosen to walk with him when the camp doctors allowed him to have twice-daily exercise releases from the cage.

When first imprisoned in the DTC, Pound was held incommunicado in his specially reinforced "cage." When he was finally given the choice of one person to whom he would be allowed to speak each day, he picked the camp's Catholic chaplain. The chaplain wondered why Pound, who was not a Catholic, had chosen a priest, rather than one of the two Protestant ministers. When he asked Pound, "Why did you pick on me?" Pound said, "What can the other guys tell me. You can tell me something," and, the priest recalled, "He asked me a lot about the Catholic religion," and "several times he quoted Thomas Aquinas." "I suppose that he was more interested in the Catholic religion than in the Episcopalian or something."[4] On June 26, 1945, at a time when he was still being held in one of the "death cells," Pound wrote in pencil, on cheap paper, a two-page instructional commentary for the priest. In the *Pisan Cantos*, this priest is identified only as the "R.C. chaplain." In 1981, I was contacted by Father Aloysius H. Vath, who identified himself as this same chaplain and who asked if I would be interested in talking to him. At our meeting, he described Pound's first month at the DTC. He also gave me the two pages of commentary that Pound had written for him while still in the cage.

In the detention camp, Pound was surrounded by the beauty of the Italian landscape and of the "cielo di Pisa," yet looked out at this from within the barbed-wire confines of an artificial world that was its antithesis—a strange "inferno-like" version of America's worst—the dropouts of the war effort—both delinquent soldiers and many who had been hard-core criminals before they were given the option of going to jail or joining the army. For those convicted of only *military* crimes such as going AWOL or sleeping on guard duty, there was some possibility of rescue. If they submitted to the grueling discipline of daily fourteen-hour drilling and inspections they could be reinstated: their offense would be removed from their record and they could obtain an honorable discharge. More serious crimes, such as murder, rape, and grand larceny were punished by repatriation to a penitentiary or by execution at the Aversa camp, outside Naples. No executions took place at the Pisa DTC, although one officer reports that some soldiers were fatally wounded in escape attempts.

Father Vath recalled Pound's arrival at the camp:

> I came in one night around eight or nine o'clock in the evening, and I was going into the compound, and they were working on one of those death cells. On the way out, I said to the officer of the guard, "What's going on in there?" "Military secret." I said, "Wait a minute. I'm chaplain here. You remember me?" "I'm sorry, I can't tell you." I thought, "Well, I don't care." So I went back and went to bed.

And the next morning I went back around seven. I used to go in and say a private mass for myself. This is during the week. On Sunday, I had a public mass for the prisoners, and one of the prisoners used to be a server for me. At about seven-thirty or eight the prisoner came in to serve for my mass, and he knew all about it. He didn't know Pound, but he said, "Hey, there's big goings-on. We got a State Department prisoner." And he told me all about it. Well, for several days, Pound was kept incommunicado, and a couple of the doctors—we were all good friends—got worried because, they said, he seemed to be an important prisoner, and if something happens, they were afraid the guy'd blow his top because he couldn't speak to anybody, and if something happens, they would blame it on the medical men. So they created some kind of fuss. They told Pound that he could speak to one person, and then he said, "Do you have an RC chaplain?" And they said, "Yes." "Well," he said, "I'll talk to *him*."

So every day, morning and afternoon, I think it was for about an hour, we'd walk around the prison compound. And we'd talk. And there was always a soldier behind us [Corporal Casey]. He couldn't hear us, but he was there in case Pound tried to attack me or I don't know what.

Father Vath's comments showed his annoyance at the officials' overreaction in their treatment of Pound. About the reinforced cage he said, quite heatedly, "You'd think they were going to get a big gorilla or something." "I mean, he couldn't have broken out of this room." He was also angry to learn from his family that his chaplain's privilege of sending uncensored mail had been suspended. He said, "If I'd have known they were censoring my mail I'd have put in some of the darndest things that you ever heard. True or not," "any kind of screwy information." "Of course," he added, "I'd have probably been put in a cage too."

Father Vath expressed frustration at not having known anything about Pound at that time. "I know we never studied about him in the seminary. That's for sure," he said. Had he known, he would have taken notes of their conversations. He did recall Pound's comment about the black prisoner, charged with murder, in the cell next to his: "I remember . . . one day we were walking and he says, 'Y'know that dark gentleman in the room next to me,' or something like that. 'He's come a long way in this life with a vocabulary of fifteen words and one is the compound adjective *god-damn*.' I mean, that's the way he spoke. He was very interesting and funny." "I remember he was so witty. He also talked about having written an article or book, something about, all wars for the last three or four centuries were started by the Bank of England or something. I remember he'd bring in the Bank of England and I said, 'Well, were you on the

board of directors of a big bank or something?' and he said no, that he
was nothing. He blamed it on the money men." In response to questions
of mine, Father Vath said, "I don't remember that he talked about Jews
and so forth; he just sort of said 'money men.'" "I don't remember him
saying anything antisemitic."

Father Vath recalled:

> I remember kidding him about our conversations. I said, "For a Confucianist
> and a Catholic, we get along very well." Because he used to, every once in a
> while, write this and that about the Catholic religion. He'd say this and that.
> He'd say, "Now this I agree with, but this I don't." But he seemed to be very
> Confucius-minded. He was very interested in Confession; in the Catholic act
> of contrition, act of sorrow, that was in his [field prayer book]. He quoted that
> so often and he was interested in that. The version they had then was "Oh, my
> God, I am heartily sorry for having offended thee. I detest all my sins and [in
> the end] I promise to do better." Something like that. . . . That's from the act
> of contrition in the mass, the Confiteor, the beginning of the mass: "Through
> my fault, through my fault, through my most grievous fault."

Pound's two-page, handwritten commentary for Father Vath is both
thoroughly anomalous and very revealing about the strange combination
of earnestness and extremity that was Pound's state of mind at that time.
It certainly shows that, in describing himself as a Confucian, he is being
entirely serious. When he can focus undistractedly on his work with the
Confucian texts and the Chinese language, he is able to preserve his men-
tal balance and sense of proportion. When his attention turns, in any
sense, to politics and economics—or even when he begins to think about
change and action—his obsessions and lack of contact with reality imme-
diately become apparent. The writing of these suggested initiatives for
the priest is enough of a movement in the direction of action to bring
Pound's irrationality quickly to the fore.

In a way that supports Father Vath's point, Pound begins with a refer-
ence to "Directions for Confession," the first instruction of which is "Say
the *Confiteor*." Here Pound is developing his larger point, about the
compatibility of Confucianism and Catholicism, by noting the impor-
tance of the discipline of self-examination in both. By referring to the
"spirits of the parents" as "intercessors," Pound seems to be trying to an-
ticipate the inevitable objection that the Chinese tradition of ancestor-
worship is unreconcilable with Catholic belief and practice. He is prob-
ably taking as his point of reference the "direction for confession" that

asks one to consider, "Have I dishonored or neglected my parents?" Pound's next emphasis is Catholic missionary activity in China, and he suggests the strategy of incorporating in a Chinese version of the Catholic prayer book Chinese characters that have particular Confucian significance. He also suggests that, by teaching the Confucian Classics, the *Ta S'eu (Da Xue)* and the *Ciung Yung (Zhong Yong)*, with their focus on "equity," Catholic priests would be able to attract Protestants to convert to Catholicism. (It is not clear whether the "protestant sectaries" he refers to here are people in China or in the United States.) Then, with the kind of sweeping extrapolation that has become so typical of his thinking about government, he quotes Mencius to support the idea that there is nothing to prevent a pope from being an ideal world-ruler in the mold of the ancient Chinese emperors of legendary virtue. When he ends with the idea of a priest "accepting" Confucius in some way that will leave his status as a Catholic priest unchanged, the question arises of what "accepting Confucius" could possibly mean in this case. The only way to find any "logic" in this is to see it as Pound's unconscious expression of his personal desire that this particular priest be able to "accept"—in the sense of "being able to understand"—Pound's own commitment to a Confucian ideal and to see it as a "reasonable" position.

> "The confucian, qua Confucian, is
> <u>constantly</u> in the state of mind
>
> indicated in the "Directions for
>   confession"—   p. 34
>   Prayer bk for
>   Army & navy.
> (i.e. before confession)

> spirits of the parents being the first
> or immediate intercessors.   This
> incites to ~~holi~~ sainthood <u>in</u>
> the family.
>   not jumping at once to
> seek intercession on part of a
>   "distant" saint or angel (spirit)
> not "belonging" to the supplicant.
> =

> Also use of using ideograms of Confucian
>   school in chinese version of

prayer book. if not already
    so used.
[page 2]
          Ta S'eu
1. Confucius.   &   as <u>laic</u> instruction
      Ciung Yung
  by inducted conduct leading the
catechumen to consider equity—
would bring in many serious protestant sectaries.
2. Mencius continuing the confucian school, says
quite specificly . .
                If a wise & just
sovreign should arise—
                [no reason
why this sovreign should not be a sovreign
pontif]
           all would flock to him
                =
The ideal emperor (or emperors Yaou & Shun)
governing by character not by force—;
by example of their own conduct.) . united
          "all within the four seas".)
           --
any priest accepting Confucius would
be <u>obliged</u> as confucian to go on ~~saying~~
preserving the form of the mass.

Pound's "all would flock to him" is an echo of the prophet's vision of
world peace, in Micah 4, in which the "people [of "many nations"] shall
flow unto" the "house of the Lord [that] shall be established in the top of
the mountains," and "strong nations . . . shall beat their swords into plow-
shares, and their spears into pruninghooks: nation shall not lift up a
sword against nation, neither shall they learn war any more. . . . For all
people will walk every one in the name of his god."

The "Prayer bk for Army & Navy" to which Pound refers in his com-
mentary is also mentioned on the second page of *The Pisan Cantos*,
where we find: "'I have not done unnecessary manual labour' / says the
R. C. chaplain's field book / (preparation before confession)" (74/446).
He is referring to his reading of this book when he writes, in Canto 77,

learned what the Mass meant,
        how one shd/ perform it.

                                    (487)

On the same page he gives the Chinese characters for "To sacrifice to a spirit not one's own is flattery (sycophancy)," the same point that he makes in his written comment to Father Vath about the importance of "not jumping at once to / seek intercession on part of a / 'distant' saint or angel (spirit) / not 'belonging' to the supplicant." Pound's prayer book was the pocket-size (5" × 3.25") *Catholic Prayer Book for Army and Navy,* edited by John J. Burke, CSP, published in New York by the Paulist Press with a 1917 copyright in a special edition for National Catholic Community Service and for distribution by the USO. Father Vath gave him this prayer book, and, as he recommended in the commentary he wrote for the priest, Pound has included "ideograms of [the] Confucian school" in its margins.[5] These marginal ideograms are very revealing of Pound's thinking at this time, especially when they are seen in conjunction with the Confucian passages in *The Pisan Cantos,* with Pound's own translations of the Confucian Classics, now collected in *Confucius,* and with Father Vath's recollections of his conversations with Pound in the DTC. An often-reproduced and (until Omar Pound and Robert Spoo's 1999 edition of the 1945–46 letters of Dorothy and Ezra) misidentified photograph shows Pound at the typewriter, in 1945, working on his Confucian translations. (This photograph was taken, not in the dispensary at the DTC, but before this, in the Counter Intelligence Corps Headquarters in Genoa.) Here he is shown working from the James Legge edition of the *Confucian Classics* (lying open on his desk) that he had brought with him from Rapallo. It is easy to identify as one of Legge's editions because of its format, with the Chinese characters on the top half of the page and the English translation and editorial notes below. This particular reprinting, published with the title *The Four Books* by the Commercial Press of Shanghai in 1900, 1923, or 1943 (the title page of Pound's copy is missing), was shortened by the omission of its glossary ("Index of Chinese Characters and Phrases"). In the absence of this enormously useful glossary that includes both characters and citations for the passages in which they appear, Pound had to rely on his *Chinese-English Dictionary,* a 1933 Commercial Press publication, edited by Zhang Tiemin. My references to Legge will be to the unabridged reprint of the 1893 first volume of *The Chinese Classics* that is readily available in paperback—the 1971 Dover edition.

The Chinese characters that Pound has written in the margins of his

Catholic prayer book provide traces of an immersion in the Chinese of the Confucian texts that, given Pound's precarious mental state at that time, would have been, psychologically, "lifesaving." The process that I relied on for identifying Pound's marginal characters and their Confucian sources was close enough to Pound's own way of working to provide some counterpart to his own experience of exploration of and immersion in these texts. Having, like Pound, received no instruction in the Chinese language, I taught myself to identify the characters that Pound had written down, by learning to find them in Legge's glossary. I had developed this procedure when I was working on Cantos 75 and 76, which are largely composed of characters from the *Shu Jing,* so I knew how it leads to an involvement with the form of the Chinese characters and with their contexts that is deeply engrossing. Pound, beginning with a passage in Legge's translation, identified the corresponding characters, some by recognition and others by using his dictionary. As I had to begin with Pound's characters and then to identify the passage in the Chinese texts to which they referred, my first task was to find the character in Legge's glossary by identifying its main radical and then to check all the passages he listed in which it appeared until I found the right one. I then needed to use a dictionary, not to *find* the characters, but to be able to identify them most accurately for my reader. I worked with the dictionary that Pound himself used in his later work with Chinese and whose system of identifying characters is used in Carroll Terrell's *Companion to "The Cantos of Ezra Pound."* This is the monumental work of linguistic scholarship, *Mathews' Chinese-English Dictionary,* compiled by R. H. Mathews in 1931 for the China Inland Mission and published in 1943 by Harvard University Press in the revised edition that I used and that Pound owned when he was in St. Elizabeths. Where Legge organizes his glossary according to the radicals of the characters, Mathews organizes his characters according to their sounds and their tones, which are indicated by superscript numbers. The rendering of the sounds of Chinese in English spelling (before the use of Pinyin, the official standardized system adopted by the People's Republic of China in 1979) was bound to be only approximate. Some of Mathews's spellings differ a little from Legge's, yet Mathews uses a system that makes it possible to identify a character with a precision that makes his dictionary very satisfying to use. He provides all 7,773 characters with their own number.

One effect of working closely with the characters, as they appear to a non-Chinese speaker, is the impact that their form makes on an eye that sees them completely as "shape." In the absence of the Chinese-speaker's response that sees meaning first and form (for its own sake) very much less, the beauty of the characters' shapes, arranged in the lists of "dictionary format," is particularly striking. Working independently with the characters, by trial and error, provides several satisfactions—that of learning to recognize the shapes of the radicals in their standard and modified forms, that of being able to single out the main radical in a character so that it can be found in the glossary, and the aesthetic pleasure provided by the form of the brushstrokes and of the proliferation of their arrangements in new characters. I give the "Mathews number" for the characters that I refer to here, both as the most direct and definitive means of identification and to point the reader toward this fascinating context within which to encounter them.

To be caught up in the processes of hunting through Confucian text and English translation to check which of Legge's citations is Pound's referent and of reading the historical, cultural information presented in Legge's footnotes, is to be drawn deeply into a Confucian ambience that is philosophical, cultural, and ethical as well as linguistic. This serves as a reminder of the nature of Pound's immersion in his Confucian studies and of how valuable a refuge his work with these texts and their language provided—how necessary a temporary escape from the conditions of his imprisonment and distraction from what was far more distressing, his fears about his eventual fate as a prisoner under indictment for treason.

The complexity involved in bridging the two languages, in the context of earlier Chinese-to-English translation, is mirrored even in the decision about which names to use for the three Confucian books to which Pound's marginal characters refer. I will call these the *Analects, The Great Learning,* and *Chung Yung,* even though this is to mix together various "provenances." The English spelling of *Lun Yu* has not varied from Legge's version down to modern Pinyin orthography, yet this book is most widely referred to by English-speakers as the *Analects. Da Xue* (in Pinyin) is spelled *Ta Hsio* by Legge and by Pound in *Confucius,* and *Ta Hsüeh* by Mathews. Pound uses *Ta S'eu* when referring to his own translation of it into Italian. I have chosen to refer to it by Legge's phrase, *The Great Learning,* which is more straightforwardly descriptive than Pound's *The*

Great Digest. Pound, Mathews, and Legge use the form *Chung Yung* (*Zhong Yong* in Pinyin), and I will use this in preference to Pound's *The Unwobbling Pivot.* This is despite the fact that Pound's translation is actually less quirky than it seems: Mathews's definition of the title's meaning is "without inclination to either side and admitting of no change." (Legge chose the now dated-sounding translation, *The Doctrine of the Mean.*)

The purpose served by Confucius's writings for Pound when he is in the "cage" and throughout his time in the DTC is similar, in many ways, to the purposes that a prayer book serves. He finds in them what he most needs at this time of psychological confusion and fear for his life—reassurance of some enduring principle of order that he can continue to believe in. Where the Catholic liturgy invokes the Trinity and the Blessed Virgin Mary, the Confucian writings speak of the legendary emperors in their capacity as paragons of virtuous conduct whose example is taken as evidence of the existence of a beneficent force animating and ordering the universe. In the DTC, Pound's most pressing concern is not the reform of governments, but self-governance. When, by means of his marginal characters, he pairs Confucian and Catholic commentaries on self-examination and self-knowledge, he does so not because he considers himself proficient in these exercises, but because he is aware of how great his need for them is.

Some of Pound's marginal notations in his prayer book are of single characters, and, of these, some are readily recognizable to readers of Pound's poetry as the pivotal ones that appear in *The Cantos* and that he includes in the "Terminology" section at the beginning of his *Confucius.* The first two marginal characters are 成 *ch'eng²* "to perfect" (M379) and 言 *yen²* "word[s]" (M7334). Standing together, they form one character 誠 *ch'eng²* "sincere" or "sincerity" (M381) for which Pound provides the "precise definition of the word. . . . The righthand half of this compound means: to perfect, bring to focus" (*Con*, 20). The passage in the prayer book with which this is coupled is "O God of strength, to Whom belongeth all that is **perfect, implant in our hearts** the love of Thy name . . . that Thou mayest **nourish in us what is good**" (14) (emphasis mine). Pound has included *ch'eng²* also beside the opening lines of "The Divine Praises": "Blessed be God. / Blessed be His holy Name" (41). The characters for *word* and for *sincerity* are written in beside "In the beginning was the **Word,** and the Word was with God, and the Word was God"

(30). Beside the passage that follows—"All things were made by Him, and without Him was made nothing that was made: in Him was life, and the life was the light of men: and the light shineth in the darkness, and the darkness did not comprehend it"—Pound has written, as a gloss on "light," the character 明 *ming²* (M4534), which shows, as his "Terminology" definition notes, "The sun and moon, the total light process, the radiation, reception and reflection of light; hence, the intelligence. Bright, brightness, shining" (20). Pound has also written, in the top margin, *omnia quae sunt sunt lumina*, Johannes Scotus Erigena's "All things that are are lights" and, in the left margin, "this light" with an underlining of "light" in the text (30).

Pound writes *ming²* beside "God of God, **Light of Light**" in the Nicene Creed also (16) and again, followed by the character 示 *shih⁴* (M5788) "to manifest" under "Prayers to the Holy Spirit" beside "We beseech Thee, O Lord, that the **Paraclete** Who proceedeth from Thee may **enlighten our minds** and lead us . . . into all truth" (44). Pound also adds *ming²* beside "O Jesus, Son of the living God, **brightness of eternal light**" in the "Prayer for Purity" (54). By "To Thee, O Lord, have I lifted up my soul. In Thee, O my God, I put my trust," which opens the "Offertory" stage of the Mass during which the elements are consecrated, Pound has written 志 *chih⁴* (M971), which is defined in "Terminology" as "The will, the direction of the will, *directio voluntatis*, the officer [radical] standing over the heart [radical]" (*Con*, 22). Beside the prayer "After Confession," he has added three characters. 中 *chung¹* (M1504), "the middle," points to "O God, Who knowest that through human frailty we cannot **stand firm** in the dangers that surround us." 正 *cheng⁴* (M351) "upright, true" and *chih⁴* (971) "the will, the aim" are a gloss on "secure mind" in the continuation of this prayer, which asks that "we may be able to overcome whatsoever things we suffer on account of our sins and that cleansed from all our offenses, we may serve Thee **with a secure mind**" (35–36).

Sections of the ritual of the consecration of the wine are "highlighted" with five characters. 帝 *ti⁴* (M6204) "God," 生 *sheng¹* (M5738) "to produce or create," and 新 *hsin¹* (M2737) "new, renew" are written beside "O **God**, Who, in **creating** human nature, didst wonderfully dignify it, and hast still more wonderfully **renewed** it." 配 *p'ei⁴* (M5019) "to appear before, worthy, fit" accompanies "We offer unto Thee, O Lord, the chalice of salvation, beseeching Thy clemency that, in the sight of Thy divine Majesty, **it may ascend** with the odor of sweetness." It is also written beside the words for the elevation of the Host, "taking also this excellent chalice into His holy and venerable hands" (22). *Shih*⁴ (M5788) "to manifest" glosses "**Come, O Sanctifier, Almighty, Eternal God, and bless this Sacrifice set forth to Thy holy Name**" (18). 生 *sheng*¹ and 新 *hsin*¹ appear together again by the passage in "Memento for the Dead," "By whom, O Lord, Thou dost always **create**, sanctify, **quicken** [and] bless" (24). 新 *hsin*¹ is one of the most recognizable of the characters that Pound uses, because, together with 日 *jih*⁴ᐟ⁵ (M3124) "the sun, a day, daily," it constitutes the "Make it new" phrase—*hsin jih jih hsin*—in *The Great Learning*, which Pound translates, "AS THE SUN MAKES IT NEW / DAY BY DAY MAKE IT NEW / YET AGAIN MAKE IT NEW (*Con*, 36). Pound writes the last three characters of this phrase by the ending of the prayer "Before Confession," "Send forth Thy Holy Spirit, and our hearts shall be **regenerated**; and Thou shalt **renew** the face of the earth," and he has underlined "renew." By the "Prayer after Holy Communion" he has written "jih jih" beside "**Day by day** we magnify Thee" (38).

Father Vath's comment about Pound's particular interest in the rite of Confession is borne out by the number of his marginal characters in this section of the prayer book. At the top of the page of "Prayers for Confession" is 仁 *jen*² (M3099), which Pound defines in his "Terminology" as "Humanitas, humanity, in the full sense of the word, 'manhood.' The man and his full contents" (22). Mathews's definition is, "Perfect virtue, free from selfishness, the ideal of Confucius. The inner love for man that prompts to just deeds. Benevolence, charity, humanity, love." Above the "renewal" characters, *jih, jih, hsin,* are the characters for the exemplary ancient emperors 堯 Yao² (M7295) and 舜 Shun⁴ (M5936), which, together with 人 *jen*², allude to *The Great Learning* IX, 4, "Yao and Shun led the empire by their humanity and the people followed" (*C*, 61). In a *Criterion* essay of July 1938, "Mang Tsze [Mencius]," Pound had written, "The 'Christian virtues' are THERE in the emperors who had responsibility in their hearts and willed the good of the people" (*SP*, 90). Pound registers this concept by writing in the characters 亦 *yi*⁴ᐟ⁵ (M3021) "also" and 人 *jen*² (M3097) "man" beside "O God, Whose only-begotten Son hath appeared to the world in the substance of our flesh, grant, we beseech Thee, that as we confess Him to be outwardly **like to ourselves**, so through Him we may deserve to be inwardly reformed to his likeness" (32). One of the instructions for self-examination before Confession that follow is "Have I indulged in fortune-telling or any other superstition?" and Pound finds a counterpart to this in Confucius's statement, in *Chung Yung* XI, 1: "To live in obscurity and yet practice wonders, in order to be mentioned with honour in future ages:—this is what I do not do" (391). Pound renders this, "To seek mysteries in the obscure, poking into magic and committing eccentricities in order to be talked about later, this I do not" (113–15). The characters here are 行 *hsing²* (M2754) "practice," 怪 *kwai⁴* (M3536) "extraordinary things," 弗 *fu²·⁵* (M1981) "not," and 爲 *wei²* (M7059) "do."

Pound is also reminded of what Confucius said about the role of the great emperors as models, by the ending of the prayers after Communion: "O God, Who makest the faithful to be of one mind: **grant that Thy people may love what Thou commandest and desire what Thou promisest:** that amid the uncertainties of this world we may place our affections where there are true joys" (39). The six characters that he writes in are from *The Great Learning*, III, 5, which says of the ancient emperors, "*Future* princes deem worthy what they deemed worthy, and love what they loved. The common people delight in what delighted them, and are benefited by their beneficial arrangements" (Legge, 364). In writing down the characters for "love what they loved," Pound has substituted 新 *hsin¹* "to renew" for 親 *ch'in¹* (M1107) "to love." This may be a simple mistake in that both characters have the same left-hand radical, yet he does incorporate something of the "make it new" paradigm into his translation of this passage: "hold in attentive affection the growing and ordered things which they held in affection" (*Con*, 45). The repeated character for "delight" is 樂 *lo⁴·⁵* (M4129), which Legge calls *ao*.

In the prayers for after Communion, Pound focuses on "I am resolved **to watch over myself with the greatest diligence,**" writing in the five characters for the passage from *The Great Learning*, VI, 1, for "[the superior man] must be watchful over himself when he is alone." Pound's more idiosyncratic translation reads, "has to look his heart in the eye even when he is alone" (*Con*, 47). This reflects his "Terminology" definition of 慎 *shen⁴* (M5734), "To act with care; be cautious," as "The eye (at the right) looking straight into the heart." That by this he means self-awareness is clear from his definition of the character that follows it in the list,

德 *te*$^{2.5}$ (M6162) "virtue"—"the action resultant from this straight gaze into the heart. The 'know thyself' carried into action. Said action also serving to clarify the self knowledge" (*Con*, 21).

Pound has written the characters from *The Great Learning* VI, 4— 德 *te*$^{2.5}$, 潤 *jun*^{4} (M3178), 身 *shen*^{1} (M5718) "Virtue adorns the person"—beside the passage that ends the prayer before Communion, "enrich me with all Thy good. My soul desires ardently to receive Thee." Pound's translation of these characters, "you enrich and irrigate the character by the process of looking straight into the heart and acting on the results" (*Con*, 51), incorporates both his "specialized" definition of *te* and the additional meanings of *jun* (with its "water" radical) beyond "to adorn." These are "to soak, moisten, enrich" (37).

A reference to "assisting angels," in the prayer of preparation to receive Holy Communion, causes Pound to recall one of the most explicit Confucian references to spiritual beings. Legge translates this passage from *Chung Yung* XVI as follows:

"1. The Master said, How abundantly do spiritual beings display the powers that belong to them! 2. We look for them, but do not see them; we listen to, but do not hear them; yet they enter into all things, and there is nothing without them. 3. They cause all the people in the kingdom to fast and purify themselves, and array themselves in their richest dresses, in order to attend at their sacrifices. Then, like overflowing water, they seem to be over the heads, and on the right and left *of their worshippers*." (397-98)

Pound writes in, beside "in the invisible presence of assisting angels," the eleven characters that end this passage and that he translates, "they seem to move above (the heads of the officiants) as water wool-white in a torrent, and to stand on their right hand and left hand" (*Con*, 131).

Pound chose to end his translation of *Chung Yung* at chapter XXVI, verse 10, a passage that had great resonance for him and contained three characters to which he attributed a particularly "luminous" significance"— 德 *te*$^{2.5}$ "virtue," 顯 *hsien*^{3} (M2692) "to be manifest" or "illustrious" (Pound's "the tensile light"), and 純 *shun*^{2} (M5930), the last of which is included in the four-character sequence that he writes into his prayer book. Its radical (120) is *szu*^{1} (M5570) "silk," and Legge gives as the meaning of *shun*^{2} "(1) 'silken, made of silk,' (2) 'Harmonious,' (3) 'Singleness'" and translates the sequence as "Singleness likewise is unceasing." In this verse of the *Chung Yung*, the subject is the undeviating nature of the principle of harmonious order that governs and informs the operation of all the processes of "Heaven and Earth" and is mirrored in the conduct of the exemplary ruler Wan [Wen]. This "singleness" is also called *ch'eng²* "sincerity," the "way of Heaven," and in his introductory note to his translation, Pound gives his definition of "the Confucian metaphysics" as "Only the most absolute sincerity under heaven can effect any change" (95). Where Legge translates verse 10 simply as, "It is said in the Book of Poetry, 'The ordinances of Heaven, how profound they are and unceasing! . . .' And again, 'How illustrious was it, the singleness of the virtue of King Wan!'" Pound embellishes his version with imagery of silk and sunlight—"*As silky light, King Wen's virtue / Coming down with the sunlight, / what purity! / He looks in his heart / And does.*" / —*Shi King*, IV, 1, 2, I. "Here the sense is: In this way was Wen perfect." Pound's counterpart to Legge's "Singleness likewise is unceasing" is closer in spirit to Mathews's definitions of *shun²*—"Pure. Simple. Of one colour; unmixed; sincere"—and is considerably more "mystical" than Legge's wording. Pound's version reads, "The *unmixed* functions [in time and in space] without bourne. // This unmixed is the tensile light, the / Immaculata. There is no end / to its action" (*Con*, 187). Pound links *shun²* "pure" ("unmixed"), with its "silk" radical, to *hsien³*, which also contains the character for "silk," hence the "silky light" and "tensile light" of Wen's "illustrious manifesting" of the eternal principle of "singleness" or "sincerity." The choice of "Immaculata" here is particularly deliberate.

Pound specifically aligns this principle of "singleness," "unmixedness," or "purity"—upon which all people can place their absolute reliance—with the Christian "Immaculata," the Blessed Virgin Mary. He does this when he chooses to write in *shun* beside two prayers to the Virgin. The first is "Hail, holy Queen, Mother of Mercy; our life, our sweetness, and our hope . . . Turn then, most gracious advocate, thine eyes of mercy towards us. . . . O clement, O loving, O sweet Virgin Mary" (31). The second is "The Litany of the Blessed Virgin," which begins, "We fly to thy patronage, O holy Mother of God. Despise not our petitions in our necessities: but deliver us from all dangers." Pound has written *shun* beside the section that reads, "Holy Virgin of virgins, / Mother of Christ, / Mother of divine grace, / Mother most pure, / Mother most chaste, / Mother inviolate, / Mother undefiled" (49). In Canto 74, when Pound refers to the "Light tensile immaculata," he does so partly in the context of his prayer book (by quoting "Linus, Cletus, Clement / whose prayers" from "The Memento of the Living"), but with even more emphasis on the Confucian emperor-sages. Beside the character *hsien*[3] he writes,

> plowed in the sacred field and unwound the silk worms early
> in tensile
> in the light of light is the *virtù*
> "sunt lumina" said Erigena Scotus 顯
> as of Shun on Mt Taishan
> and in the hall of the forebears
> as from the beginning of wonders
> the paraclete that was present in Yao, the precision
> in Shun the compassionate
> in Yu the guider of waters.
>
> (449)

In Canto 81, however, Pound's full attention is on the Blessed Virgin Mary as the "Immaculata" in lines that constitute a sincere confession. He quotes "Introibo" from the beginning of the mass ("I will go unto the altar of the Lord") and, before giving the names of saints from "Memento of the Dead," he quotes from the final prayer in his book, "For All in Trouble." This begins, "Most Blessed Virgin, in your life of glory, remember the sorrows of earth. / Look with kindness on those who suffer, who struggle against difficulties, who drink unceasingly the bitterness of this life" (63). Finally, in a truly penitent state, "drowning," far too belatedly, in the tears that he has brought upon himself, he confesses to a lifelong habit of hard-heartedness.

> Immaculata, Introibo
> for those who drink of the bitterness
> Perpetua, Agatha, Anastasia
> saeculorum
> repos donnez à çils
> senza termine funge   Immaculata Regina
> Les larmes que j'ai creées m'inondent
> Tard, très tard je t'ai connue, la Tristesse,
> I have been hard as youth sixty years.
>
> (80/533)

Pound's contact with the priest, his study of the Catholic prayer book, and his reflections upon the ethical and spiritual dimension of the Confucian writings seen comparatively, as counterparts to the ethics and spirituality encoded in the Catholic liturgy, amount to a "Pisan Confucianism" that makes untenable the view that it was the authoritarianism of Confucian thought that attracted Pound. To work closely with the Confucian writings in the idiosyncratic way of the autodidact that I have undertaken here, is, perhaps, to come as close as possible to Pound's own negotiations with them. It is also to see vividly how the hierarchized social arrangements that were the inevitable reference points for Confucius in his own day are incidental rather than integral to the vision of enlightened thought, attitude, and action that he was able to hold in his mind and communicate, independently of the grim historical actuality that was "the world as he knew it" and despite all that he understood of the destructive and self-sabotaging impulses of the human mind. It is no coincidence that Confucius is still known and that the perceptiveness of his insights can still be appreciated, two and a half millennia after his death.

NOTES

1. Pound is referring here to his Chinese/Italian edition of *The Great Learning: Confucio. Ta S'eu, Dai Gaku* (Rapallo: Studio Integrale, 1942) and his Italian-only translation of it: *Testamento di Confucio* (Venice: Casa Editrice, 1944).

2. *Ezra and Dorothy Pound: Letters in Captivity, 1945–1946*, ed. Omar Pound and Robert Spoo (New York: Oxford University Press, 1999), 51, 73, 69, 77.

3. See Flory, *Ezra Pound and "The Cantos": A Record of Struggle* (New Haven: Yale University Press, 1980), 154–69, 184, 87; and *The American Ezra Pound* (New Haven: Yale University Press, 1989), 173–84.

4. Father Vath's comments are from an unpublished, taped interview that I conducted with him in 1981. Father Vath was born on November 10, 1909, ordained on May 18, 1940, and died on May 28, 1992. He served as Chaplain in the U.S. Army from June 1943 to October 1946. He was thirty-five years old when he met Pound in 1945.

5. I am indebted to Mary de Rachewiltz for telling me about the existence of this prayer book with its marginal ideograms and for sending me copies of the pages on which they appear.

Confucius Erased: The Missing Ideograms *in* The Pisan Cantos

RONALD BUSH

Because most of the Chinese characters that Ezra Pound inscribed onto his own typescript of *The Pisan Cantos* did not survive into the published text, the imprint of Confucius on the poem has remained blurred. This is so despite our knowledge that Pound composed *The Pisan Cantos* in the same months he was Englishing *The Great Digest* and *The Unwobbling Pivot* and despite the efforts of a number of commendable commentaries on Pound and Confucius. To supplement and correct these last—notably Achilles Fang's unpublished 1958 Harvard dissertation, Carroll Terrell's commentary in *A Companion to "The Cantos" of Ezra Pound*, and Mary Paterson Cheadle's *Ezra Pound's Confucian Translations*—what follows reexamines Pound's missing ideograms.[1] Its larger aim is to continue the work of a previous essay in which I argued that Pound's published opening verses and closing canto were last-minute additions to his working draft, altering the sequence he had in mind (74 to 83), which began and ended by telescoping a *stilnovisti* vision of the beloved's eyes with a representation of human compassion derived from Confucius.[2] With the compositional history of *The Pisan Cantos* laid bare, the importance of Confucius—not just of the two volumes whose translations Pound finished at Pisa, but of *The Analects* and *Mencius* as well, will, I hope, start to become legible in a way that the accidents of textual transmission and publication have obscured.

THE CASE OF THE MISSING CHARACTERS

A word first about the reasons for and history of the textual gap. Almost all of *The Pisan Cantos'* fifty-odd sets of missing or garbled characters (spread throughout all eleven cantos) are excerpts that Pound copied out from the small volume of *The Four Books* (the Confucian Classics) he had been allowed to carry to Pisa. This was a dual language text edited without acknowledgment by James Legge and referred to in Canto 80 as "old Legge."[3] Most of the excerpts are from the *Analects*, with a fair smattering from *Mencius* and a surprising few from *The Great Digest* or *The Unwobbling Pivot.* Pound transferred all but a handful of these excerpts from his manuscript to the typescript he produced at Pisa.[4] (This essay with a few exceptions supplies only those transferred onto the typescript.)

After Pound finished his typescript, the characters were orphaned not once but several times. As Omar Pound and Robert Spoo document in their edition of Ezra and Dorothy Pound's letters, Pound in the course of his composition sent four separate fragments of his typescript to Dorothy, so that Mary might retype them. Dorothy then was to draw the Chinese characters properly. This she did with remarkable accuracy, considering that she did not have recourse to the Legge text, only to the Pounds' cherished multivolume edition of the Reverend Robert Morrison's Chinese dictionary.[5] She was forced to locate the ideograms in Morrison's schematic chart of radicals, a not inconsiderable task. At first she wrote, "I thought I should have quite forgotten how to look up the dictionary." Later, explaining her success, she would add: "I have enjoyed working on the Ch[inese] so much! I have found all of them: thank goodness you marked the dictionary!"[6]

However, Dorothy's typescripts and carbons, though dutifully sent to James Laughlin and T. S. Eliot in the expectation that they would be used in the New Directions and Faber and Faber editions, were abandoned, and now rest in the Beinecke, Houghton, and Butler Libraries at Yale, Harvard, and Columbia, forgotten testimony to Pound's Pisan intentions. For reasons both deliberate and accidental the first New Directions text was produced without them. On October 30, 1945, still in the camp, Pound had written to his daughter Mary that his plan was to use "my own [characters], or a regular Chinese font for the volume" (private collection). In any case, when Pound was suddenly transported to Washington, D.C., in November 1945, he brought with him to America two mixed copies not of Dorothy's but of his own original typescript and carbons, and it was from these that New Directions worked. As James Laughlin wrote T. S. Eliot on December 23, 1945, shortly after an early meeting in Washington with the recently returned Pound: "We discussed at length the writings that he has entrusted to me and he showed me exactly what to do with them. . . . he wished me to have fresh copies made of the Cantos and he will go over them finally before they are sent to you to be printed. I am going to hurry all I can with this but the work can only be done by persons who know his style intimately because of the condition of the manuscripts. They are very rough and messy. This means, I guess, that [Laughlin's assistant, Hubert] Creekmore and I will have to do the work ourselves. We will rush it as fast as we can. We will print them here too" (Lilly Library, Indiana).

And so Creekmore retyped the text again, this time with no attempt to reproduce the Chinese characters—Pound, it was agreed, would supply them at a later stage. But the usual mix of bad luck and accident intruded, over a period much longer than the one Laughlin had anticipated. Pound had requested that Laughlin do the Confucian translations first, and Laughlin complied.[7] It soon became apparent, though, that other issues were involved in the delay. Though Pound began to suspect it was just Laughlin spending too much time on the ski slopes and too little in the office, his friend and publisher obviously had more serious things on his mind.[8] As Laughlin wrote Dorothy about collecting even the preceding cantos, he believed it would be better to wait until "things quiet down a little" lest the offensive bits trigger new cries for Pound's blood.[9] Also, it seemed prudent to parcel out individual cantos, partly to earn a little much-needed cash, partly to give Pound a chance to proofread the serial publications.[10]

One reason Laughlin deemed the extra money useful had to do with the Chinese characters. In the December 23, 1945, letter to Eliot, Laughlin had concluded: "There are a great many Chinese characters to go in as marginal glosses. Would you care to share the expense of getting these drawn with me?" Eliot agreed to share the production expenses, but both the expense and the trouble associated with getting the ideograms printed haunted the serial and volume publication of the text.[11] By July 31, 1946, after Pound had been told that the ideograms were holding things up, Dorothy wrote to Laughlin that "yesterday E said to photograph his pencilled-in ideograms if it would hurry up the printing of the last cant[o]s. It would at least add an interest anyway."[12] Then in August 1946, when the *Rocky Mountain Review* was in the process of publishing Canto 77, Pound inspected an edition of *Cantos LII—LXXI* and noticed that one of the Chinese characters from Canto 53 was "printed *upside down*."[13] The immediate upshot was that Dorothy herself felt compelled to do something, most immediately about the characters for Canto 77.

The most ominous record in the archive is in a letter from Pound to Laughlin on August 1, 1946: "With all China Town in S. Fr[anc]isco, MUST be some chink who can WRITE with brush—am puttin' all ids. *I can remember* in proof."[14]

A short-term fix was arranged for Canto 77. Dorothy discovered in the Library of Congress "A. W. Hammel—a very nice man, head of Chinese Dept who knows Ezra"—and in a letter of August 8, 1946, wrote Laughlin that she had arranged to have "the ideograms written out in official script" by him and checked by Pound—"a really lovely piece of work. But please be sure of getting these printed *right side up*."[15] The larger and more disturbing reality was that Pound was getting impatient, forgetful, and alarmingly willing to settle for getting the ideograms "I can remember" set in print. Laughlin apparently could not have been more pleased. In a letter to Dorothy of August 12, 1946 (at the Beinecke), though he knew the answer, he plaintively asked, "will there be chinkese to go in all of the new cantos"—clearly a sign he wished there weren't. Soon afterward these pressures grew even stronger. Instructing Laughlin (February 21 [?] 1947) about the magazine publication of Canto 83 in the *Yale Poetry Review*, Pound bitterly complained that there were no ideograms in the proofs and insisted that at least "one ideogram" be included—adding that if Laughlin would "send me a copy of the original typescript [which included eleven ideograms] I will do the ideograms." Then in exasperation, "There may have been more but the text don't need 'em."[16]

But, though Pound was obviously working without his original typescript, "the text" did need 'em, as Pound intermittently recalled. He was still insisting on their restoration even *after* New Directions at long last published *The Pisan Cantos* on July 30, 1948, and he pleaded in his letter accompanying a copy of corrected American proofs to Eliot at Faber and Faber that there were still "IDEOGRAMS, sent herewith those that J[ames] L[aughlin] may not have had."[17] The problem was, by that time Pound had forgotten exactly how many there were and insisted (as with Canto 83) merely on the few he recalled (or thought he recalled). By that point, however, some of the characters he insisted on (as for example the Ming ideogram against "in the light of light" in Canto 74) corresponded neither to the ideograms printed in the New Directions text (now 74/449) nor to any ideogram in the Pisan typescript.

The fact that Pound did read proof for the little magazine versions and the New Directions text of *The Pisan Cantos,* albeit under the difficulties just described, means that the editor of any future "corrected" edition of the text needs to think twice about restoring the ideograms to an authorized text. However, that does not mean that the omitted characters are irrelevant. Whatever the editorial model that governs an edited text, the ideograms retain their critical interest.

THE MISSING CHARACTERS: A THEMATIC OVERVIEW

Some of *The Pisan Cantos'* missing characters reinforce the implications of the English text. Others provide interesting and unavailable counterpoint. But the broad pattern of the ideograms deepens the implications of a genetic study of Pound's revisions and argues that a sense of the sequence (74 to 83) was in his mind from the beginning of composition.

A number of the ideograms of course are simply confirmations of the expected. The great majority of them embody recurrent refrains, and some of these refrains are entirely familiar. So we find that Pound inserted Chinese characters to draw attention to and sharpen the meanings of themes like verbal sincerity, the educated man, making it new, and the affirmation that resounds at the end of *The Unwobbling Pivot*—in Pound's translation, "the *unmixed* functions [in time and space] without bourne. This unmixed is the tensile light, the Immaculata. There is no end to its action" (*Con,* 187).

One surprise, however, is how relatively unrepresented are the larger philosophical assertions of *The Unwobbling Pivot* and *The Great Digest,* and how extensive are Pound's invocations of *The Analects* and to a lesser extent *Mencius.* Mary Cheadle reminds us that Pound read the *Analects* as early as the late teens, and in the twenties compiled a brief digest of its major concerns (115–16). She also notes that Pound's lengthy article (now in *SP*) about *Mencius* first appeared in 1938, that Pound was working on a translation of *Mencius* when he was arrested in 1945, and that Pound wrote in an unpublished essay in 1943 that the *Mencius* was "the most modern book I know" (116). Even so, she adds, "the events of 1945 forced a drastic revision of Pound's Confucianism. *Mencius,* which like *The Unwobbling Pivot* contains a Confucian metaphysics . . . was no longer at the center of his belief. . . . *The Analects* was. . . . The *Analects* gathers the shards of Confucianism left from the shattering of Pound's totalitarian 'vision' and arranges them not neatly but nearly into a mosaic of Confucian ethics." *The Analects,* she usefully points out, "is pluralistic in respect to the number of voices represented" and the number of perspectives entertained (116–17). And though Cheadle would specify the appropriateness of *The Analects* to "Pound at St. Elizabeths" during the last phase of his translation of the text, the Pisan material makes it very clear that the attractiveness of *The Analects'* heterogeneity and modesty was fully established at the Disciplinary Training Center.

Against Cheadle, the following will suggest that critical passages at the beginning and the end of *The Pisan Cantos* come from *Mencius.* But it will make clear her perceptiveness in stressing the importance in 1945 of *The Analects* for everything in between. It is above all in the variegated moods and voices of *The Analects* that Pound finds expression for both sides of some of his most fundamental artistic and emotional ambivalences. About the true nature of literature, he reminds himself recurrently on one hand of a need "to communicate and then stop, that is the / law of discourse" (80/514, etc., from *Analects* XV.40) and on the other of the delights of "pleasure in counterpoint" (79/505, etc., from *Analects* III.33). About the pressure of time passing, so obvious to a man of near sixty facing a potential death penalty, the *Analects* allows him to sound both the poignancy of the theme, in "day comes after day" (77/487, etc. from *Analects* IX.16), and to soften it, with the association of "HUDOR et Pax" (water and peace, 83/548, etc., associated by an ideogram with *Analects* VI.xxi, "the wise find pleasure in water"). About his loss of position, esteem, and even self, he will balance the Odyssean desperation of "I am noman, my name is noman" (74/446, etc.) with an ideogram announcing Confucian resolution (*Analects* IV.xiv), "A man should say, I am not concerned that I have no place, I am concerned how I may fit myself for one. I am not concerned that I am not known, I seek to be worthy to be known."

Ultimately, the Confucian comfort Pound gathers in *The Pisan Cantos* culminates in a generalized philosophical support, but even this, the ideograms tell us, derives as much from a constellation of passages from *The Analects* and *Mencius* as from *The Unwobbling Pivot's* triumphant assertion of "the process." This is the subject of a long essay in itself, but an illustrative example may suffice. From a line early in the sequence, "fills up every hollow" (74/453), Pound heightens and interweaves the numerous allusions to the comfort of mist and water in *The Analects* with allusions in the ideograms to a crucial group of verses, *Mencius* II.i.2.13–17. Without the missing ideograms, though, this premeditation is nearly invisible. Thus Fang, for example (see 4:134), reads this as an allusion to a related but much less substantial passage in *Mencius* IV.ii.18.1–2 ("a spring of water . . . fills up every hole, and then advances, flowing on to the four seas"), and Terrell agrees (373). But Pound's now-omitted ideograms point us instead to *Mencius* II.1.2, verses

> 13. This is the passion-nature:—It is exceedingly great, and exceedingly strong. Being nourished by rectitude, and sustaining no injury, it fills up all between heaven and earth.
>
> 14. This is the passion-nature:—It is the mate and assistant of righteousness and reason. Without it, *man* is in a state of starvation.
>
> 15. It is produced by the accumulation of righteous deeds; it is not to be obtained by incidental acts of righteousness. If the mind does not feel complacency in the conduct, *the nature* becomes starved. I therefore said, "Kâo has never understood righteousness, because he makes it something external."

It is these verses that Pound uses finally to celebrate his survival at 83/551: "this breath wholly covers the mountains. / . . . overstanding the earth it fills the nine fields / to heaven." They speak of a force of nature that goes beyond mere mutability and of a purpose in suffering that permeates the wind and the rain. The verses complete *The Pisan Cantos'* water imagery in a passage that, beyond anything in *The Great Digest* or *The Unwobbling Pivot,* fuses feeling and statement. That Pound as early as 74/453 had these verses in mind says a great deal about his understanding of what he was about to write. We know this (and know about his elaborate intertextual study of *The Analects* and *Mencius*) definitively because of the characters on his typescript.

THE MISSING CHARACTERS IDENTIFIED AND GLOSSED

In many cases Pound's first typescript and its carbons differ slightly from the published English text. What follows does not attempt to replicate the earlier text except to reinsert those Chinese characters that were omitted or altered in transmission. In all but a handful of cases, the characters are reproduced from the Confucian text supplied by Legge from which Pound was quoting. (For the exceptions a copy of the ideograms Pound drew himself has been provided.) Passages are identified as to canto and page number as in the conventions of this collection. They are followed by

Legge's translation of the passage Pound alludes to, Pound's translations in *Confucius (Con)*, and in some cases brief commentary.[18]

POUND'S MISSING CHARACTERS

74/445

誠

but a precise definition

Legge, *Confucius* (*Doctrine of the Mean* [DM] XXII), 415: "It is only he who is possessed of the most complete **sincerity** that can exist under heaven, who can give its full development to his nature" (boldface added to indicate the English equivalent of Pound's ideogram).

Pound, *Con*, 173: "Only the most absolute sincerity under heaven can bring the inborn talent to the full and empty the chalice of the nature."

74/446

惟
義
所
在

言
不
必
信
行
不
必
果

not words whereto to be faithful
nor deeds that they be resolute
only that bird-hearted equity make timber
and lay hold of the earth

Legge, *Mencius* (IV.ii.11), 321–22: "Mencius said, 'The great man **does not think before-hand of his words that they may be sincere, nor of his actions that they may be resolute;**—he simply *speaks and does* what is right.'"

Fang (4:133–34) is caustic: "Pound's etymosinological translation . . . cannot be reconciled with the Chinese language. The first ideogram *wei* is analysed into its two components *hsin* (heart) and *chui* (bird). . . . As for 'make timber,' Pound probably read axe *(chin)* out of the adverb of the place *so*. . . . The last word in Pound's version, 'earth,' corresponds to the component *t'u* (earth) of the verb *tsai* (to be); but Pound has not bothered to explain the other, sound-giving component. . . . If Pound were not so serious about all this, his translation could be considered a hoax." Terrell in the *Companion* (365) cites a mistaken but related reference to *Analects* IV.x, but offers a plausible defense: "Pound's intent is probably to evoke the intelligence of nature in process. Neither birds nor trees think: they express themselves naturally and the right follows."

74/446

but Wanjina is, shall we say, Ouan Jin　　文
　　　　　　　　　　　　　　　　　　　人

74/447

文　Ouan Jin spoke and thereby created the named
人　　　　　　　　　　　　　thereby making clutter

Cheadle, 260: "Ouan Jin is the 'complete man' . . . [or] the man with an education." This is part Confucius, part Pound's wordplay (but with a Confucian basis). The characters for "complete man" can be found in Legge, *Confucius* (*Analects* [A] XIV.xiii.1), 279. Pound then found the character for "literature" in the previous column, and fused them to approximate the Australian figure of Wanjina.

74/447

　　　　　　　　　in principio verbum

誠

paraclete or the verbum perfectum: sinceritas

As per 74/445. Legge, *Confucius* (DM XXII), 415: "complete **sincerity**."

74/449

　　　　　　　　in tensile

As opposed to the first New Directions and Faber texts, Pound's Pisan typescript (TS) carries no ideogram here.

74/449

Light tensile immaculata　　　純
　　　the sun's cord unspotted

Legge, *Confucius* (DM XXVI.10), 421: "It is said in the Book of Poetry, 'The ordinances of Heaven, how profound are they and unceasing!' The meaning is, that it is thus that Heaven is Heaven. *And again,* 'How illustrious was it, the **singleness** of the virtue of king Wan!' indicating that it was thus that king Wan was what he was. **Singleness** likewise is unceasing."

Pound, *Con*, 187:

10. The *Book of the Odes* says:
The decree of heaven
　　takes the bird in its net.
Fair as the grain white-bearded
There is no end to its beauty.

The hidden meaning of these lines is:
thus heaven is heaven [or this is the heavenly nature, co-involgent].

> *As silky light, King Wen's virtue*
> *Coming down with the sunlight,*
> > *what purity!*
> *He looks in his heart*
> *And does.*
>
> > > —*Shi King*, IV, i, 2, i.

Here the sense is: In this way was Wen perfect.

The *unmixed* functions [in time and in space] without bourne.

This unmixed is the tensile light, the Immaculata. Thre is no end to its action.

74/451

莫

a man on whom the sun has gone down

A refrain: repeating the ideogram that appears in 74/450. The Confucian figure of an "unknown" man who is not worried by it but seeks through honorable means to be knowable softens the harshness of the near desperate Homeric "No Man" Odysseus.

Legge, *Confucius* (A IV.xiv), 169: "The Master said, '*A Man should say,* I am not concerned that I have no place, I am concerned how I may fit myself for one. I am not concerned that I am **not** known, I seek to be worthy to be known.'"

Pound, *Con*, 207: "He said: Not worried at being out of a job, but about being fit for one; not worried about being unknown but about doing something knowable."

74/455

Kuanon, this stone bringeth sleep;
> offered the wine bowl

> > 配
> > grass nowhere out of place

Legge, *Mencius* (II.1.ii.14), 190: "This is the passion-nature:—It is the **mate and assistant** of righteousness and reason. Without it, *man* is in a state of starvation."

The ideogram—*p'ei* (mate)—stands at the center of three verses that describe the way that the "passion-nature" (as Pound puts it at 74/453) "fills up every hollow" between heaven and earth. Pound is playing on variations of it here to relate it in his text not only to the idea of being "mated" to the order of things ("nowhere out of place") but also (since the left part of the ideogram has to do with wine) to the "wine bowl."

74/459

and for three months did not know the taste of his food
in Chi 齊 heard Shun's music 韶
the sharp song with sun under its radiance
圖

Legge, *Confucius* (A VII.xiii), 199: "When the Master was in **Ch'î,** he heard the **Shâo,** and for three months did not know the taste of flesh. 'I did not **think,**' he said, 'that music could have been made so excellent as this.'"

Pound, *Con,* 220: "In Ch'i he heard the 'Shao' sung, and for three months did not know the taste of his meat; said: didn't figure the performance of music had attained to that summit."

74/460

Yu has nothing pinned on Jehovah
sent and named Shun who to the
autumnal heavens *sha-o*   盡
美
with the sun under its melody   韶

The first two ideograms here are from Legge, *Confucius* (A VIII.xxi), 215, which lavishly praise Yü. It was Shun who made the Shâo music that Confucius hears in *Analects* VII.xiii, and Pound's third ideogram here repeats the one given on 74/459. For the first two ideograms see Legge, *Confucius,* 215, and for the third *Confucius,* 199.

74/462

Yaou chose Shun to longevity   壽
[TS: Shun chose Yaou, to longevity]

Legge, *Confucius* (A VI.xxi), 192: "The Master said, 'The wise find pleasure in water; the virtuous find pleasure in hills. The wise are active; the virtuous are tranquil. The wise are joyful; the virtuous are **long-lived.**'"

Legge comments: "The wise or knowing are active and restless, like the waters of a stream, ceaselessly flowing and advancing. The virtuous are tranquil and firm, like the stable mountains."

Pound, *Con*, 217: "He said: the wise delight in water, the humane delight in the hills. The knowing are active; the humane, tranquil; the knowing get the pleasure, and the humane get long life."

Analects VI.xxi is a key Poundian text that looks forward to Canto 83. It also supplies an important nuance—the pleasure of activity—to the water of Cantos 74–83.

> 74/462
>> who seized the extremities and the opposites
>> holding true course between them   舜
>> shielding men from their errors
>> cleaving to the good they had found
>> holding empire as if not in a mortar with it
>>   nor dazzled thereby

Legge, *Confucius* (DM VI), 388: "The Master said, 'There was **Shun**:— He indeed was greatly wise! **Shun** loved to question *others,* and to study their words, though they might be shallow. He concealed what was bad *in them,* and displayed what was good. He took hold of their two extremes, *determined* the Mean, and employed it in *his government of* the people. It was by this that he was **Shun!**'"

Pound, *Con*, 107: "Kung said: Shun, for example, understood; he was a great and uprising knower. He liked to ask questions of people, and to listen to their simple answers. He passed over the malice and winnowed out the good. He observed their discordant motives and followed the middle line between these inharmonic extremes in governing the people, thus he deserved his name. [That is the significance of the ideogram *Shun* the hand which grasps, the cover that shields the discordant extremes.] *Further examination of the 136th radical might find a root for 'the discordant opposites,' in the signs of the waning and new-horned moon.*"

Fang (4:102) is dubious about Pound's translations.

74/465

> and it is (in parenthesis) doubtless
> > easier to teach them to roar like gorillas
> than to scan φαίνεταί μοι
> > > inferior gorillas
> of course, lacking the wind sack
> > and although Siki was quite observable
> > > we have not yet calculated the sum gorilla + bayonet

朽
木
不
可
雕

Legge, *Confucius* (A V.ix.1), 176: "Tsâi Yü being asleep during the day-time, the Master said, '**Rotten wood cannot be carved;** a wall of dirty earth will not receive the trowel. This Yü!—what is the use of my reproving him?'"

Pound, *Con*, 210: "Tsai Yu was sleeping in day-time. Confucius said: Rotten wood cannot be carved; a wall of dung won't hold plaster, what's the use of reproving him?"

74/465

> and there was a good man named Burr
> > descendant of Aaron during the other war
> who was amused by the British
> > but he didn't last long AND
> Corporal Casey tells me that Stalin
> > le bonhomme Staline
> > has no sense of humour (dear Koba!)

不
幸
短
命

Legge, *Confucius* (A VI.ii), 185: "Confucius replied to him, 'There was Yen Hui; he loved to learn. He did not transfer his anger; he did not repeat a fault. **Unfortunately, his appointed time was short** and he died; and now there is not *such another.* I have not yet heard of any one who loves to learn *as he did.*'"

Pound, *Con*, 214: "Confucius replied: There was Yen Hui who loved to study, he didn't shift a grudge or double an error [L. repeat a fault]. Not lucky, short life, died and the pattern is lost, I don't hear of anyone who likes study."

I have here reproduced Pound's handwritten ideograms.

74/466
Beauty is difficult. . . . the plain ground

                           precedes the colours

繪
事
後
素

Legge, *Confucius* (A III.viii.2), 157: "The Master said, 'The business of laying on the colours follows (the preparation of) the plain ground.'"

Pound, *Con*, 202: "He said: the broidery is done after the simple weaving."

74/466
and that certain images be formed in the mind
                  to remain there
                        formato locho
            Arachne mi porta fortuna

                            經
                            綸

Legge, *Confucius* (DM XXXII.1), 429: "It is only the individual possessed of the most entire sincerity that can exist under heaven, who can **adjust the great invariable relations of mankind,** establish the great fundamental virtues of humanity, and know the transforming and nurturing operations of Heaven and Earth;—shall this individual have any being or anything beyond himself on which he depends?"

Pound has scribbled "warp? woof" under the two characters in his manuscript, and repeats them on 80/514.

74/468
    難
in the winter season

The present woeful times. See Legge, *Confucius* (A VI.xiv), 190: "The Master said, 'Without the specious speech of the litanist T'o, and the beauty of *the prince* Châo of Sung, it is **difficult** to escape in the present age.'"

Pound, *Con*, 216: "He said: if you haven't the smooth tongue of T'o the prayer-master, or Sung Chao's beauty, it's hard to get away with it in this generation."

74/469

How soft the wind under Taishan
    where the sea is remembered
out of hell, the pit

達

上

Legge, *Confucius* (A XIV.xxiv), 285: "The Master said, 'The **progress** of the superior man is **upwards**; the progress of the mean man is downwards.'"

Pound, *Con*, 258: "He said: A proper man progresses upward (far), a mean man progresses downward (far)."

76/473

by Babylonian wall (memorat Cheever)
    out of his bas relief, for that line
we recall him
    and who's dead, and who isn't

偏
其
反

Legge, *Confucius* (A IX.xxx.1), 226: "How the flowers of the aspen-plum **flutter and turn!** Do I not think of you? But your house is distant."

Pound, *Con*, 233: "The flowers of the prunus japonica deflect and turn, do I not think of you dwelling afar?"

It should be noted that the very next section, *Analects* IX.xxx.2, involves Pound's refrain "How is it far" and is alluded to in the English and the Chinese characters published at 76/479.

76/479

O white-chested martin, God damn it,
    as no one else will carry a message,
say to La Cara: amo.

Her bed-posts are of sapphire
    for this stone giveth sleep.

    and in spite of hoi barbaroi
    pervenche and a sort of dwarf morning-glory
    that knots in the grass, and a sort of buttercup

I can find no sequence in *Confucius* or *Mencius* corresponding to these characters, and have reproduced Pound's script. The third character, connoting "a witch," can be found in Legge, *Confucius* (A XIII.xxii), 272.

77/485
As Arcturus passes over my smoke-hole
    the excess electric illumination   明

The *ming* ideogram (sun and moon), as in Legge, *Confucius* (GL I.i), 356. Used wittily here with "illumination."

77/485
and Mt Taishan is faint as the wraith of my first friend
who comes talking ceramics;   思
       mist glaze over mountain   也
                              何
   "How is it far, if you think of it?"   遠

Legge, *Confucius* (A IX.xxx.2), 226: "The Master said, '**It is the want of thought about it. How is it distant?**'"

Pound, *Con*, 233: "He said: It is not the thought, how can there be distance in that?"

This is the verse that follows the one alluded to at 76/473. In the typescript Pound gives four characters rather than the two finally published.

77/486
           just watchin' the water,
                 逝

Legge, *Confucius* (A IX.xvi), 222: "The Master standing by a stream, said, '**It passes on** just like this, not ceasing day or night!'"

Pound, *Con*, 231: "Standing on a river-bank he said: it is what passes like that, indeed, not stopping day, night."

The first instance of a refrain also associated with the Greek phrase *panta hrei* (see e.g. 80/532) and ultimately softened by the association with the passion-nature that fills all, and with the serenity of the rain altars.

77/486
nothing counts save the quality of the affection
                  意
mouth, is the sun that is god's mouth

Legge, *Confucius* (GL.4), 358: "The ancients who wished to illustrate illustrious virtue throughout the kingdom, first ordered well their own

States. . . . Wishing to rectify their hearts, they first sought to be sincere in their **thoughts**."

Pound, *Con*, 29–31: "The men of old wanting to clarify and diffuse throughout the empire that light which comes from looking straight into the heart and then acting, first set up good government. . . . and wanting to rectify their hearts, they sought precise verbal definitions of their inarticulate thoughts [the tones given off by the heart]."

The published version gives a different ideogram. Pound, without his first typescript, apparently forgot which English phrase it was meant to gloss.

77/486
"To his native mountain"　信　明

Pound here (perhaps his own collocation) aligns *ming* (illumination) with *hsin* (sincerity). For *hsin*, see Legge, *Confucius* (A I.viii.2), 141: "Hold faithfulness and sincerity as first principles." Pound, at *Con*, 22, defines *hsin* as "fidelity to the given word. The man here standing by his word."

77/487
day comes after day　夜

The last character in Legge, *Confucius* (A IX.xvi), 222 (as 77/486)—that is, a repetition of the *panta hrei* (all things pass) motif.

77/488
Le Paradis n'est pas artificiel

莫
不
善
於
莫

Legge, *Mencius* (III.1.iii.7), 241-2: "Lung said, 'For regulating the lands, there is no better system than that of mutual aid, and **none which is not better than** that of taxing. By the tax system, the regular amount was fixed by taking the average of several years. In good years, when the grain lies about in abundance, much might be taken without this being oppressive, and the actual exaction would be small. But in bad years, the produce being not sufficient to repay the manuring of the fields, this system still requires the taking of the full amount. When the parent of the people causes the people to wear looks of distress, and, after the whole year's toil, yet not to be able to nourish their parents, so that they proceed to borrowing to increase their means, till the old people and children are found lying in the ditches and water-channels:—where, *in such a case*, is his parental relation to the people?'"

For Pound's direct invocation of this passage in English, see 78/500 and his "Mang Tsze" essay in *SP*, 94.

77/489
sd/ the old Dublin pilot

誠   or the precise definition

As per 74/445.

77/490
       lacking that treasure of honesty
which is the treasure of states　　　義

One of the characters from the sequence of *Mencius* (IV.ii.11), 322, at 74/446.

77/492
above which, the lotus, white nenuphar
Kuanon, the mythologies

和
不
如
樂

I find no sequence in Confucius or Mencius that precisely corresponds to this one. The first, third, and fourth of Pound's characters can be found in Legge, *Confucius* (DM XV.2), 396: "It is said in the Book of Poetry, 'Happy union with wife and children, is **like** the music of lutes and harps. When there is concord among brethren, the **harmony** is **delightful** and enduring.'"

77/494
for Wanjina has lost his mouth　　文
　　　　　　　　　　　　　　　人

As 74/447.

78/499
    "each one in the name"

君
子

in whom are the voices, keeping hand on the reins

180

Characters for "the superior man." The phrase appears numerous times in *Confucius* and has a number of possible English equivalents. Pound may have in mind a passage like *Analects* I.ii.2 (*Confucius*, 138–39): "**The superior man** bends his attention to what is radical. That being established, all practical courses naturally grow up. Filial piety and fraternal submission!—are they not the root of all benevolent actions?" In *Con*, 195, Pound translates "the superior man" as "the real gentleman."

Cheadle notes that in *Analects* XX.ii.1 Pound translates the phrase (*Con*, 287) as "the proper man (*here*, man-in-authority)" and that the Chinese *jun-zi* is rendered by Morrison's dictionary as "a wise and virtuous man . . . rulers or teachers" (Cheadle, 121). (For an extended discussion of the importance of these figures to the texts of Confucius, see Cheadle, 121–24.)

78/500
nothing worse than fixed charge   常
    several years' average
Mencius III, i. T'ang Wan Kung
         Chapter 3 and verse 7

The *Mencius* verse is about taxes, as per 77/488. The character (meaning "often") here reproduced (see *Mencius*, 241) occurs later in the verse than the ones at 77/488.

78/501
as under the rain altars

Legge, *Confucius* (A XII.xxi.1), 260: "Fan Ch'ih rambling with the Master under *the trees* **about the rain** altars, said, 'I venture to ask how to exalt virtue, to correct cherished evil, and to discover delusions.'"

Pound, *Con*, 247: "Fan Ch'ih walking with him below the rain altars (or to celebration of the rain sacrifice pantomime) said: Venture to ask how to lift one's conscience in action; to correct the hidden tare, and separate one's errors?"

This is the first appearance of a refrain (associated with *Analects* VI.xxi—"the wise find pleasure in water") that will eventually soften and transfigure the melancholy of *panta hrei* and of *Analects* IX.16.

78/501
Two with him in the whole house against the constriction of
                                                        Bacchus
moved to repeal that god-damned amendment
            Number XVIII   酒
                                             無
                                             量

Legge, *Confucius* (A X.viii.4), 232: "It was only **in wine** that he laid down **no limit** for himself, but he did not allow himself to be confused by it."

Pound, Con, 235: "only in matter of wine was no blue nose (set no limit) but didn't get fuddled."

It is typical of Pound that he cites one of the few (perhaps the only) occurrences of the "wine" character that does not speak of limiting one's consumption.

78/503
In the spring and autumn
                                    春
                                    秋

        In "The Spring and Autumn"
                there
                are
                no   無
            righteous   義
              wars   戰

Legge, *Mencius* (VII.2.ii.1), 478: "Mencius said, '**In the "Spring and Autumn" there are *no* righteous wars.** Instances indeed there are of one better than another.'"

As Terrell (422) notes, the title, "Spring and Autumn," refers to the last of the Five Classics, the *Chun Qin*, or *Spring and Autumn Annals*. Pound mentions the work in "Mang Tsze," *SP*, 87. Zhaoming Qian informs me that the phrase can also refer to the historical period (770–476 B.C.) in which Confucius lived.

79/505
some minds take pleasure in counterpoint
樂
                pleasure in counterpoint

182

Legge, *Confucius* (A III.xxiii), 163: "The Master instructing the Grand music-master of Lü said, 'How to play **music** may be known. At the commencement of the piece, all the parts should sound together. As it proceeds, they should be in harmony, *while* severally distinct and flowing without a break, and thus on to the conclusion.'"

Pound, *Con*, 205: "Talking with the superintendent of music in Lu, he said: One can understand this music; a rousing start in unison, then the parts follow pure, clear one from another, (brilliant) explicit to the conclusion."

79/506

in

discourse

辭　　　　　what matters is 達

to get it across e poi basta

Legge, *Confucius* (A XV.xl), 305: "The Master said, 'In language it is simply required that it **convey the meaning.**'"

Pound, *Con*, 269: "He said: Problem of style? Get the meaning across and then STOP."

The "bird" who drew the characters for Dorothy renders the ideograms in a way slightly different from the way they appear in Legge. Hence I reproduce the Legge here. The verse will become a recurrent refrain in the Pisans, and is contrasted to the principle of "pleasure in counterpoint" just alluded to. (They are the contrasting poles of Pound's art.)

79/507

what's the name of that bastard? D'Arezzo, Gui D'Arezzo

notation　於
　　　　　止
　　　　　知
　　　　　其
　　　　　所　3 on 3
　　　　　止　鳥 chiacchierona 黃 the yellow bird
止　to rest

Legge, *Confucius* (GL.c.III.2), 362: "In the Book of Poetry, it is said, 'The twittering **yellow bird rests** on a corner of the mound.' The Master

183

said, 'When it rests, it knows where to rest. Is it possible that a man should not be equal to this bird?'"

Pound, *Con*, 39:

> The *Book of Poems* says:
> *The twittering yellow bird,*
> *The bright silky warbler*
> *Talkative as a cricket*
> *Comes to rest in the hollow corner*
>   *of the hill.*
>
>   —*Shi King*, II, 8, 6, 2.

Kung said: comes to its rest, alights, knows what its rest is, what its ease is. Is man, for all his wit, less wise than this bird of the yellow plumage that he should not know his resting place or fix the point of his aim?

The published version offers three of Legge's ideograms, but not the sequence of six Pound indicated on his typescript.

79/507

畿
千
里
惟
民   "half dead at the top"
所   My dear William B.Y. your 1/2 was too moderate
止

From the verse right before the one just cited. Legge, *Confucius* (GL.c.III.1), 362: "In the Book of Poetry, it is said, 'The royal domain of a thousand lî is where the people rest.'"

Pound, *Con*, 39:

> The *Book of Poems* says:
> *The royal domain is of 1ooo li*
> *Thither the people would fly to its rest*
> *[would hew out its resting place].*
>
>   —*Shi King*, IV, 3, 3, 4.

The implication here is that society (the people) never rests, being, in Yeats's analysis, half-dead at the top.

184

80/514
inexorable 　至
　　　　　　誠

       this is from heaven

Legge, *Confucius* (DM XXII), 415: "It is only he who is possessed of **the most complete sincerity** that can exist under heaven, who can give its full development to his nature."

Pound, *Con*, 173: "Only the most absolute sincerity under heaven can bring the inborn talent to the full and empty the chalice of the nature."

80/514
the warp 　　　經
and the woof 　綸

As 74/466 (*Confucius*, 429).

80/514
To communicate and then stop, that is the 　已
    law of discourse 　　　　　　　　　　　矣

A continuation of the Chinese characters in *Analects* XV.xl (*Confucius*, 305) begun on 79/506. Pound's manuscript contains four characters, beginning with the second character on 79/506. His typescript contains only two.

80/519-20
to bring your g.r. to the nutriment 　　　　　辭
    gentle reader　to the gist of the discourse

Another inscription of the Chinese characters in *Analects* XV.xl (*Confucius*, 305). Cf. 79/506 and 80/514.

80/520
to sort out the animals

唯天下至誠爲能盡爲能化

As per 80/514, but Pound fuses the first eight and the last three characters in Legge, *Confucius* (DM XXII–XXIII), 415–16 and 417. "It is only **he who is possessed of the most complete sincerity that can exist under heaven, who can give its full development to his nature . . . who can transform.**" "To sort out the animals" here refers to the middle of DM XXII: "he can give their full development to the natures of animals and things."

80/521
wan 文 caritas ΧΑΡΙΤΕΣ

One of the characters from "Ouan Jin." See 74/446.

80/527
but old William was right in contending
        that the crumbling of a fine house
profits no one
   (Celtic or otherwise)   誰
nor under Gesell would it happen   能

Legge, *Confucius* (A VI.xv), 190: "The Master said, '**Who can** go out but by the door? How is it that men will not walk according to these ways?'"

Pound, *Con*, 216: "He said: The way out is via the door, how is it that no one will use this method."

Pound's MS contained six characters from this verse, but his TS offers only the two above.

80/532
books, arms, men, as with Sigismundo

Legge, *Confucius* (A XVI.viii.1), 313: "Confucius said, 'There are three things of which the superior man stands in awe. He stands in awe of the ordinances of Heaven. He stands in awe of great men. He stands in awe of **the words of sages.**'"

Pound, *Con*, 271: "Kung-tze said: The proper man has three awes; he stands in awe of the decrees of destiny [*heaven's mouth and seal*], he stands in awe of great men, and of the words of the sages."

80/532
[Attached to the Greek for *panta hrei*]

逝
者
如
斯

This refrain invokes *Analects* IX.xvi and the passing of things like a stream (*Confucius*, 222), as per 77/486 and 77/487, etc. Pound includes four characters here instead of the earlier one or two.

(On Pound's MS, but not his TS, there are below this on 80/532 five characters from *Confucius*, 260, from the passage in *Analects* XXI.i concerning the rain altars, as per 78/501.)

80/533
I have been hard as youth sixty years

定

This character occurs on Pound's MS but not his TS; however, it is interesting enough to include here. It comes from Legge, *Confucius* (A XVI.vii), 312: "Confucius said, 'There are three things which the superior man guards against. In youth, when the physical powers are not yet **settled,** he guards against lust. When he is strong, and the physical powers are full of vigour, he guards against quarrelsomeness. When he is old, and the animal powers are decayed, he guards against covetousness.'" (Pound in *Con*, 271, translates the first error as "taking root in luxurious appearances.")

82/544
even I can remember 吾
猶
及

Legge, *Confucius* (A XV.xxv), 301: "The Master said, 'Even in my *early* days, a historiographer would leave a blank in his text, and he who had a horse would lend him to another to ride. Now, alas! there are no such things.'"

Pound, *Con*, 267: "Even I reach back to a time when historians left blanks (for what they didn't know), and when a man would lend a horse for another to ride; a forgotten era, lost."

Pound had used this verse much earlier in 13/60.

83/548
Gemisto stemmed all from Neptune   知
     hence the Rimini bas reliefs   者
                                  樂
                                  水

On Pound's MS but not his TS. Legge, *Confucius* (A VI.21), 192: "The Master said, '**The wise find pleasure in water**; the virtuous find pleasure in hills.'" (As per 74/462.)

83/549
樂
水   the sage
delighteth in water

See 83/548. The ideograms, now accompanying an English version of the verse from *Analects* VI.21, occur in Pound's MS but not his TS.

83/549
[Greek for *panta hrei*]   逝

Another allusion to *Analects* IX.xvi (as per 77/487,etc.).

83/551
this breath wholly covers the mountains
                 it shines and divides   剛
it nourishes by its rectitude
does no injury
overstanding the earth it fills the nine fields
                       to heaven   塞

Boon companion to equity
   it joins with the process   配
      lacking it, there is inanition

When the equities are gathered together   集
as birds alighting
it springeth up vital

If deeds be not ensheaved and garnered in the heart
there is inanition
  (have I perchance a debt to a man named Clower)

that he eat of the barley corn   氣
and move with the seed's breath

The five characters represent the culminating instance of the theme of the all-pervading breath of Heaven: *Mencius* II.i.2.13–15, 190, which was introduced briefly at 74/453:

13. This is the passion-nature:—It is exceedingly great, and exceedingly **strong**. Being nourished by rectitude, and sustaining no injury, it **fills up** all between heaven and earth.

14. This is the **passion-nature:**—It is the **mate and assistant** of righteousness and reason. Without it, *man* is in a state of starvation.

15. It is produced by the **accumulation** of righteous deeds; it is not to be obtained by incidental acts of righteousness. If the mind does not feel complacency in the conduct, *the nature* becomes starved. I therefore said, "Kâo has never understood righteousness, because he makes it something external."

83/551-52
"Non combaattere" said Giovanna
    meaning, as before stated, don't work so hard
    don't   助
                                                    苗
                                                    長
        as it stands in the Kung-Sun Chow.

Pound's ideograms are slightly different from the ones printed at 83/552, although both sequences come from *Mencius* (II.1.ii.16), 190–91, which reads in part: "Let not the mind forget its work, but let there be **no assisting the growth** *of that nature.*"

83/553
out of Madame La Vespa's bottle
                                    日
                                    新
mint springs up again

Pound's characters here are the second half of "Make it New," from *Confucius* (GL.c.II.i), 361.

84/559
                jên²
                    仁

The ideogram, as published on 82/545.

84/560
        there is our norm of spirit   忠

Legge, *Confucius* (GL.c.X.18), 378, where it is translated "entire self-devotion." Pound translates the verse (*Con,* 81): "Thus the true man has his great mode of action which must be from the plumb center of his heart, maintaining his given word."

84/560
whereto we may pay our
　　　homage　祭

Legge, *Confucius* (A III.xii.1), 159: "He **sacrificed** *to the dead,* as if they were present. He **sacrificed** to the spirits as if the spirits were present."

Pound, *Con,* 203: "He sacrificed as if he had taken root-hold in the earth, he sacrificed to the circumvolent spirits as if they took root."

A fitting final ideogram to the sequence. For comment, see Cheadle, 128.

NOTES

1. See Achilles Fang, "Materials for the Study of Pound's Cantos," 1958 (The thesis is in four volumes, and references to Confucius are contained in volume 4); Carroll F. Terrell, *A Companion to "The Cantos" of Ezra Pound* (Berkeley and Los Angeles: University of California Press, rvd. ed. 1993); and Mary Paterson Cheadle, *Ezra Pound's Confucian Translations* (Ann Arbor: University of Michigan Press, 1997).

2. See Ronald Bush, "'Quiet, Not Scornful'? The Composition of *The Pisan Cantos,*" in *A Poem Containing History: Textual Studies in "The Cantos,"* ed. Lawrence Rainey (Ann Arbor: University of Michigan Press, 1997), 169–213, especially 189.

3. See *Ezra Pound and Dorothy Pound: Letters in Captivity, 1945–1946,* ed. Omar Pound and Robert Spoo (Oxford: Oxford University Press, 1999), 102. The Legge is now at Hamilton College, as is the small Chinese dictionary Pound used to work through the characters for his new translation and composition. The Chinese dictionary was published by "The Commercial Press, Limited, Shanghai, China [1933]." Inside the front cover (besides a number of Pound's notes) there is an inscription: "To my friend Ezra Pound, From Lyons, Milan January 1938."

4. Pound's Pisan MS is at the Beinecke, and part of the three copies of his Pisan TS is also there, though other parts are at the Houghton and Butler, and a few pages are scattered. (For a fuller account, see Ronald Bush, "Remaking Canto 74," *Paideuma,* forthcoming.)

5. Robert Morrison, *A Dictionary of the Chinese Language in Three Parts. Part the First, Containing Chinese and English, Arranged According to the Radicals; Part the Second, Chinese and English Arranged Alphabetically; and Part the Third, English and Chinese* (Macao: Printed at the Honorable East India Company's Press, 1815). Pound's copy is kept in the Hamilton College Library.

6. *L/DP*, 139, 219.

7. As early as November 15, 1945, Dorothy wrote Laughlin that "EP I know wants more than anything to have the Confucius out—two small vols. To go into one—nearly redone. Ta Hio and Chung Yung in English. The MSS has gone to Shakespeare and Parkyn as part of defence" (YCAL, Laughlin photocopy).

8. Pound wrote to Laughlin along with some corrections on February 12, 1947: "course of you spend 2 / 4s yr. Time slidin' down an ice cream cone" (YCAL, Laughlin photocopy).

9. September 17, 1945. See David M. Gordon, ed., *Ezra Pound and James Laughlin: Selected Letters* (New York: Norton, 1994), 138. The original, at the Lilly Library in Indiana, is more graphic, foreseeing that leftists might "burn down the place." Laughlin was more forthcoming still to Olga Rudge in January 1948, near the end of the long delay in *The Pisan Cantos* production. He admitted then that his most important goal "for the moment . . . is not to give the newspapers anything which they can write about. For a long time I didn't even want to publish the Confucius or the new [Pisan] Cantos for fear they would get a hold of them, but finally we decided that his literary reputation could not be let die out during the long time it might take to get him released" (YCAL 53, Olga Rudge Papers, Box 52, Folder 1413).

10. Some time in 1946 Laughlin wrote to Dorothy Pound: "Magazines lining up well on the Cantos. I think we'll place each onem and get a couple of hundred bucks anyway" (YCAL, Laughlin photocopy).

11. For Eliot's agreement, see his letter to Pound of January 7, 1948, where he laments Laughlin's delay, and refers to the lack of ideograms: "I have received uncorrected galley proofs of THE PISAN CANTOS (good title) from the printers in the U.S.A. They contain no ideograms, and in any case I don't want to set up here from any but the FINAL proof. I have been in communication with Laughlin who is in Switzerland but I don't think much can be accomplished until he gets back to New York and does his job. He has promised to lend us the blocks, we sharing the expenses of the work done in America. I hope he will bring this business to an end quickly" (YCAL 53, Olga Rudge Papers, Box 5, Folder 125). Eliot then goes on to explain why he won't use the proofs to print from even when he gets them ("we have so far followed the policy of setting up each volume of Cantos in uniform type, to facilitate putting them all together when finished; so our typography will be different from Laughlin's."

12. YCAL, Laughlin photocopy.

13. Letter from Dorothy Pound to Laughlin August 7, 1946 (YCAL, Laughlin photocopy).

14. Letters in YCAL, Laughlin photocopy.

15. Letters of July 14 and August 8, 1946, YCAL, Laughlin photocopy. Laughlin responded, August 12, 1946: "thanks for sending a long the ideograms for the Canto 77, drawn by the bird in the Library. I personally do not find his script as beautiful as the printed kind in the book [the bilingual *Confucius*], but they are nice just the same, and this is probably the easiest way to handle getting the ones that will be needed for the different cantos."

16. YCAL, Laughlin photocopy.

17. Page included with the proofs, which were sent back to New Directions, then stolen and sold to the Grammercy Book Shop and then to the Butler Library at Columbia.

18. I quote from the Dover reprints of the texts in *The Four Books: Confucius: Confucian Analects, The Great Learning and The Doctrine of the Mean, Chinese Text; Translation with Exegetical Notes and Dictionary of All Characters. By James Legge* (New York: Dover, 1971) (abbreviated as *Confucius*); and *The Works of Mencius. Translated with Critical and Exegetical Notes, Prolegomena, and Copious Indexes. By James Legge* (New York: Dover, 1970) (abbreviated as *Mencius*).

"Enigma" at the Heart of Paradise: Buddhism, Kuanon, and the Feminine Ideogram in The Cantos

BRITTON GILDERSLEEVE

Scholars have dealt with elements of the mystic within *The Cantos*. Almost all seem to privilege Western mythologies even when treating Eastern materials. This is especially evident in their analyses of Kuanon (Guanyin), who figures in a number of cantos. Given the Eleusinian agendas of many of the critics who focus on mystic components of *The Cantos*, it is no surprise that Kuanon is neglected. She cannot be seen simply as a Chinese version of Koré, as Akiko Miyake argues Isis works for the later Egyptians.[1] Nor does she function as a traditional mother goddess, on the order of Demeter, although there are aspects of maternity tied in with her traditional depictions, and her maternal element is critical in Pound's schema. Instead, she appears to embody for Pound what she has embodied for centuries to Buddhists worldwide: the most salient spiritual aspect of Buddhism—compassion. But this, too, is a reductive reading of a complex figure: for Pound, Kuanon—in addition to her traditional functions within the Buddhist pantheon—is a female figure who eludes easy delineation, one who draws upon a legacy of androgyny and Orientalist perspectives to become daughter, mother, wife, and lover in a feminine ideogram that ultimately partakes of both Eleusinian and Eastern mysticism. Juxtaposing various elements of the feminine, Kuanon is the enigma at the heart of Pound's flawed journey-quest toward mystic union with the divine; she is his Beatrice, his Circe, his Ariadne, and his Aphrodite, the ideogram of the feminine divine with which he seeks to join.

In general Pound is no fan of Buddhism. When he mentions it in *The Cantos*, it is almost always with negative inflection. Often he links it with Daoism—"bonzes" and "taozers" (55/291)—slyly deprecating the mystic associations he sees the two religions sharing.[2] He speaks of the "Bhud mess" (54/282), "hochangs" (54/287), "Bhud-foés" (98/707), and "Bhud rot" (99/717) through much of *The Cantos*. Understandably, this has led to

Fig. 1. *Standing Guanyin,* after Wu Daozi, eighth-century Chinese artist.
(Courtesy Freer Gallery of Art, Smithsonian Institution, Washington, D.C.)

the reading that *The Cantos*—and Pound—are anti-Buddhist. But as with many readings of Pound that initially seem reasonable, this one is a bit facile. It is not the ultimate spiritual objectives of Buddhism that Pound satirizes in *The Cantos;* rather, it is both the abuses of power to which no systematized religion is immune, and perhaps more critically, Buddhism's goal of nonattachment to everyday affairs. Given Pound's "constant concern for good government,"[3] Buddhism's emphasis on the transience and unimportance of the temporal and worldly—in contrast to Confucianism's focus on the sociopolitical matrix—is, for him, unacceptable.

Strategically, Pound often associates Buddhism with the feminine, in a manner that highlights what he sees in the institutionalized forms as corruption and a lack of virility. He couples Buddhism with maternity and infantilism, with decadence and corruption, with emasculation in both the literal and figurative senses of the term. This negative feminization of Buddhism differs from his handling of the Buddha himself: a reference in Canto 38 to the Buddha, where Pound recounts having been asked by "Schlossmann" to remain "in Vienna / As stool-pigeon against the Anschluss / Because the Ausstrians needed a Buddha" (38/189), implies that Schlossmann believes Pound could—if he wanted to—"awaken" the Austrians to the reality of their union with Hitler ("Buddha" means "Awakened One").[4] The inference is that the Buddha does have the power to awaken, that his name is deserved. This implicit valorization of the Buddha as "awakened"—as a legitimate religious figure, even if used as a source for a pun—is in contrast with the subsequent mention of Buddhism in Canto 54, certainly negative, if only very subtly feminized: "And now was seepage of bhuddists" (280). The term "seepage," with its connotations of sewage, "taints" the purer body of Confucianism with Buddhism. "Seepage" may refer, as well, to the seepage of blood, the "unclean" monthly menses during which so many cultures—from ancient to present-day—have segregated women.

Pound moves on to a retelling of the legends surrounding the Buddha's birth. He begins with the impregnation of Siddhartha's "virgin" mother "Nana" (54/283), not Mahamaya, or Maya, as she is more commonly known:[5]

Et les Indiens disent que Boudha
in the form of a white buck elephant
slid into Queen Nana's bosom, she virgin,

and after nine months ingestion
   emerged on the dexter side

                (283)

In contrast to Pound's construction, Nobel nominee Thich Nhat Hanh's life of the Buddha presents the legend in its more traditional form, where Maya dreams of the white elephant holding "a brilliant pink lotus flower in its trunk," and placing it in her body, after which "the elephant, too, entered her effortlessly."[6] No mention is made of any virginal status on the part of Maya, a condition that would be highly unlikely for an already crowned queen. Pound's retelling also treats as reality what is traditionally seen as dream. In all readily available versions of the Buddha's birth, the white elephant figures as part of a dream had by Maya heralding the Buddha's birth: "When he was nine years old, Siddhartha was told about the dream his mother had before giving birth to him. A magnificent white elephant with six tusks descended from the heavens . . . approached her [Maya] . . . and placed the flower within the queen's body."[7] Positing a virginal Maya creates an interesting analogue with the Immaculate Conception, a parallel Pound highlights when he makes the "white buck elephant" a form of the Buddha, an element not present in the traditional legend. In effect, the Buddha's birth mirrors the Immaculate Conception, with the white elephant substituting for the Holy Ghost, and "Nana" for Mary. This is the first among several linkings of Buddhism and Christianity.

  In another association of Buddhism with the female, Pound juggles "Hou-chi the she empress" with the destruction of the forty-six-tablet "Stone Classics"[8] and the "goddam bhuddists" (54/284). Here Pound makes one of his more overt references to the historic conflict between Buddhism and Confucianism, using the destruction of the Confucian tablets to build a Buddhist temple as a metaphor for Buddhism's destruction of Confucianism's superior ethical system. He puns on the old French term for Buddhist—*foé, foéist*—linking these "foes" with the empress Hou-chi, "an unscrupulous but able woman . . . [who] perpetrated the most horrible crimes but also, as a devout Buddhist, did much to further the Buddhist cause in N[orth] China."[9] In case the relationship is not clear, Pound's next line mentions "OU TI," who "went into cloister / Empire rotted by hochang" (54/284), a prince "who had allowed himself to become infatuated with the sect of Foé . . . and entered their order."[10]

Pound's choice of the word "cloister" over monastery is critical: "cloister" carries connotations of nuns as well as monks, and may be applied to life in either monastery or convent; it also implies a kind of androgynous, even neuter domestic space, while "monastery" is used almost exclusively for the residences of monks. Once again, Pound lays a feminine subtext beneath a discussion of Buddhist practitioners.

In entry after entry Pound links institutionalized Buddhism to negative females and/or feminine traits, either explicitly or through juxtaposition. He notes of Empress Ou-heou that "the hochang [Buddhist priests] ran the old empress / the old bitch ruled by prescription and hochangs / who told her she was the daughter of Buddha" (54/287), then juxtaposes "bonzes" and eunuchs—"chased out the bonzes from temples / 46 thousand temples / chased out the eunuchs" (55/291)—and lists in quick succession "Hochang, eunuchs, and taozers / empresses' relatives" (55/302). As Leon Surette notes, Pound often associates "eunuchs, Taoists and Buddhists" even when his original source—in this specific case, de Moyriac de Mailla—mentions only Buddhists.[11] The joined references tangle the feminine and/or the neuter(ed) with Buddhism, with its use of "superstitious signs . . . [drawn] from different natural occurrences,"[12] in a way that is clearly directed toward Buddhism in its structured, organized incarnation.

In other ways, however, Pound sees Eastern religions as superior to Christianity. In a 1957 letter to Ryozo Iwasaki, Pound concedes that he has "never heard of either Bhudists [*sic*] or Taoists using religion as a pretext for slaughter. Nor," he continues, "is it Confucian."[13] It is one of the rare times when Pound speaks positively of Buddhism the religion, conjoining it with his beloved Confucianism. Usually, as Jean-Michel Rabaté affirms, Buddhism represents for Pound a kind of "mystic decadence":[14] "When everything goes wrong, they [Buddhists] are not far away," Rabaté notes dryly.[15] Leon Surette agrees, explaining that "the alien Buddhists and native Chinese Taoists catch all of the virulence Pound was later to direct at the Jews and money conspirators in his radio broadcasts. They represent the 'secret corruptions, the personal lusts, avarices, etc. that,' Pound tells us in *Guide to Kulchur*, 'scoundrels keep hidden.'"[16] This supports the reading that what Pound objects most to in Buddhism—and Daoism—are corrupt institutionalizations.

In addition, Pound sees parallels between Buddhism and Christianity that are incompatible with his own political agenda. In a 1936 letter to Katue Kitasano, Pound contends that "neither Zen nor Christianity can serve toward international understanding . . . in the way the *Ta Hio* of Kung fu Tseu can . . . [as] a basis of ethics & of national action, (patriotic) which does not produce international discord."[17] What Pound sees as the biggest—and mutual—flaw of Christianity and Buddhism, then, is that neither religion concerns itself with the temporal—with governmental ethics—in the ways he sees Confucianism functioning.[18] As Roland Barthes argues, Buddhism resembles for "the Occident" an orientalized Christianity, with "nuns . . . monks . . . and . . . the faithful."[19] This neatly summarizes much of Pound's attitude toward Buddhism. Unlike his views of either Buddhism or Christianity, however, Pound sees Confucianism as predicated on right behavior in social context, in contrast to Buddhism's major element of nonattachment, which Pound quite probably saw—as many Westerners do—as detachment. For these reasons, he views Confucianism as more logical and useful for his own project: to critique the spiritual excesses he sees in Christianity and Christian states. "The ethic of Confucius and Mencius," Pound notes, may be used "to better advantage" with "Occidentals than may Buddhism," while Confucianism better "serves as a road map through the forests of Christian theology."[20] There are inherent theological oppositions between Christianity and Buddhism that make it difficult to use Buddhism as a critique in the way that he uses Confucianism, Pound argues. Buddhism's law addresses compassion and the way to enlightenment, not the Confucian protocols of leadership and system of civil government. It is Buddhism's compassion that is embodied in the figure of Kuanon, Buddhist saint of compassion and mercy.

At least as early as 1909 Pound was captivated by oriental art and its cultural context. His friendship with the Far Eastern art expert Laurence Binyon would have exposed him to the considerable knowledge Binyon mined for his 1909 lectures on oriental and European art.[21] By the time of Pound's 1913 meeting with Mary Fenollosa, he was familiar with the subject of oriental art, and ready to gain full benefit from Ernest Fenollosa's work.

In his earliest readings of Fenollosa, Pound would have been aware of the translator-scholar's Buddhist context for his own Chinese and Japanese explorations. In *Epochs of Chinese and Japanese Art*, Fenollosa frequently discusses Buddhism—the Chinese Chan or the Japanese Zen sects—and its influences on Chinese and Japanese art and culture. A letter from Pound to his father, dated December 5, 1913,[22] recommends the reading of Fenollosa's *Epochs* as a way for his father to familiarize himself with "what his [Fenollosa's] work means,"[23] establishing Pound's own familiarity with the book's contents. In the two-volume work, Fenollosa not only analyzes numerous artistic representations of the Buddhist figure Kuanon (Guanyin),[24] but also includes several black-and-white plates of the deity, ranging from the "Corean" Kuanon at Horuji[25] to the Chinese Mokkei (Muqi) Kuanon in Japan.[26] While Pound seems to have been unaware of Fenollosa's status as a Zen devotee,[27] he cannot have been ignorant of Fenollosa's admiration and respect for Buddhism, which Fenollosa explicitly compares to Christianity when discussing the bodhisattva vows[28] in which he himself was confirmed. Indeed, Fenollosa maintains in *Epochs* that Buddhism underlies much, if not most, of Chinese art. He argues that "a very large part of the finest thought and standards of living that have gone into Chinese life, and the finest part of what has issued therefrom in literature and art, is strongly tinged with Buddhism," adding that "[t]o write the history of the Chinese soul without seriously considering Buddhism, would be like writing the history of Europe under the hypothesis that Christianity was a foreign and alien faith whose re-rooting in Western soil had been sporadic, disturbing, and on the whole deletrious."[29] To read Fenollosa, in other words, is to clarify the connection he establishes between Buddhism and its significant role in Chinese art, literature, and philosophy.

That Pound does not share Fenollosa's deep-set admiration for Buddhism as a religion does not militate against his having read *Epochs*; Pound often disagrees politically with close friends, and patches together what he sees as the relevant—or most useful—pieces of others' philosophies. It is not simply Pound's familiarity with and implied acceptance of Buddhism that is in question, but the force of Fenollosa's feelings for Buddhism, specifically Kuanon.[30] Fenollosa's high regard for Kuanon—whom he describes as having "the face of a sweet, loving spirit, pathetic and tender, with eyes closed in inner contemplation"[31]—is evident throughout the *Epochs*, infusing the many pages he devotes to analyzing paintings and sculptures of the Buddhist saint of "providence, sustenance, and salvation from physical evil."[32] This extensive and positive portrayal of Buddhism in general, and Kuanon in particular, vividly counterpoints Pound's ambivalence to Buddhism throughout *The Cantos,* foregrounding instead his more favorable depictions of the figure of Kuanon.

In her debut in *Three Cantos,* "Kwannon / Footing a boat that's but one lotus petal"[33] has yet to become the "Kuanon of all delights" (74/448) who appears in *The Cantos* several decades later. Carroll Terrell argues that in Canto 74 Kuanon is connected with Daoism: "The wind is part of the process / The rain is part of the process" (74/455).[34] It seems more likely, however, that these references are not to Daoism per se, but to "the elements of water and ether, which Kwannon symbolizes,"[35] as Fenollosa explains. Fenollosa adds that "Kwannon is especially the Mother of Water,"[36] which would account for Pound's use of rain in reference to her. However, Pound is fond of getting double play from an allusion, reference, or metaphor. That the wind and rain work for both Kuanon and Daoism is good poetry; it also repeats associative links established earlier among Buddhism, Daoism, and the feminine.

Kuanon is not only a figure of Buddhism, associated with water and air; she also is a figure of androgyny, whose origins Fenollosa traces from the Indian male Avalokitesvara to the ultimately female Chinese and Japanese figures Guanyin or Kuanon. Fenollosa makes careful mention of the male and female representations of Kuanon in Tang and Song art, explaining that "a great Bodhisattwa [*sic*] is in its own nature indeterminate as to sex, having risen above the distinction, or rather embodying in itself the united spiritual graces of both sexes. It is a matter of accident which one it may assume upon incarnation."[37] Martin Palmer and Jay Ramsay trace the Chinese bodhisattva's origins to Avalokitesvara, who "can take on any form in order to reach a person in need of salvation. He can appear as ... male or female, depending upon the needs of the time, the person and the place."[38] The earliest Chinese representations of Kuanon (Guanyin)—from the fifth century to the mideighth—are of a man, according to Palmer and Ramsay.[39] However, they note that by the end of the eighth century, Kuanon was "beginning to be regularly" depicted as female.[40]

In Pound's work Kuanon is clearly female, despite her androgynous origins, and he consistently refers to her by the feminine pronoun. In her first appearance in the completed *Cantos,* in Canto 74, Pound links

Kuanon to "Mt Taishan" (74/448). Taishan, a holy mountain in China, is the ancient site of sacrifices,[41] but Pound also uses the name for a mountain he could see from the U.S. Army Disciplinary Training Center, where he was detained outside Pisa.

Kuanon next emerges from lines visualizing the rebirth of Aphrodite from the sea and the restoration of her shrine at Terracina (74/455). Both references blur lines between East and West, with the Aphrodite passage blurring sectarian boundaries between Daoist and Buddhist belief systems—"The wind is part of the process / The rain is part of the process"—and the Eleusinian mysteries—"in coitu inluminatio" (74/455), as well. Kuanon's is the name mentioned, but she is explicitly linked with other divine female figures: Aphrodite, the Pleiades, even Demeter in the Greek phrase that Terrell translates as "Nether earth, Mother."[42] Pound's insertion of this line is provocative: Fenollosa describes the Mokkei (Muqi) Kuanon as emblematic "in the all-comprehensive Zen symbolism . . . of the great human and sub-human category of 'motherhood.'"[43] Elaborating, he recounts the "seven centuries" of prayer by the Chinese and Japanese to "the divine motherhood" that "millions of European believers" see incarnate in "the Holy Virgin, Mother of Christ."[44] This returns provocatively to the Buddhist-Christian connection implicit in Pound's earlier recount of the Buddha's birth, in Canto 54.

Throughout *The Cantos* there is a collapsing of boundaries, categories, and concepts consistent with Pound's ideogrammic method: things flow into and from one another. Aphrodite is placed on her pedestal again, through the aegis of the wind and rain; the Pleiades bloom in her mirror, and Kuanon becomes the earth mother, with whom it is possible to join in "coitu inluminatio." As Bob Perelman explains, Pound's ideogram is defined primarily by its marriage of specifics and nonlogic, "a generalization formed by joining particulars in a nonlogical, nonsequential way."[45] Pound himself defines it as "the examination and juxtaposition of particular specimens—e.g. particular works, passages of literature."[46] Thus the sequencing of several female figures is a means of suggesting the polyvalence of the feminine divine, which may carry more than one icon and feature more than one role (although all of them will be predictable). It is the slippage between these specifics, and the "nonlogic" by which they are arrayed, that does much of the poem's work. Indeed, *The Cantos* is a text begging for poststructural reading of the slippage between various objects, incidents, images, and events and their lack of chronological (or other) ordering.

Is Pound always in control of such slippage? Is any writer? In the next passage where Kuanon appears, he names her "enigma" (74/463), and certainly the name is well deserved. Pound first invokes the daughter ("KOPH"), then mentions the Sirens twice, and follows with the Graces, before finally introducing Kuanon. Leon Surette reads this passage as Aphrodite appearing to Pound, which is in keeping with Surette's own Eleusinian project.[47] However, Pound sketches a figure that bears a marked resemblance to a copy of an older, Godoshi (Wu Daozi) school painting of Kuanon included in *Epochs*, a painting that Fenollosa de-scribes in minute detail. Both the painting and Fenollosa's description of it are congruent with certain aspects of Pound's lines: Pound mentions "the mast held by the left hand" (74/463), while Fenollosa remarks, "In his raised hand he [Kuanon] sways the wisp of willow."[48] Pound brings Kuanon to shore "a la marina" (74/463), placing a large, white-colored shell on the sea's waves, which are "By no means . . . orderly" (74/463). Neither is the "leaping foamy water"—white and oddly shell-shaped—on which Kuanon descends through space in the Godoshi (Wu Daozi) copy (fig. 1).[49] There is, as well, further reference to the air that we have already seen associated with Kuanon: the passage "in this air as of Kuanon" (74/463) rhymes with the earlier passage—"the air was made open / for Kuanon of all delights" (74/448). Kuanon's masculinity in the Fenollosa description—a condition already discussed—would not deter Pound from using the visual elements of the tableau described.

Ronald Bush's analysis of the drafts of Italian Cantos 74 and 75— which predate the holograph first manuscript of the *Pisan Cantos*—cor-roborates the identification of Kuanon instead of, and/or in addition to, Aphrodite. As Bush demonstrates, "Pound borrowed freely from his ear-lier Italian verses" for the later-published Canto 74;[50] in his earliest draft of the Italian Canto 75, Pound conjures Kuanon with

> Ave Maris Stella, sounded in my ear
> through the evening air
> and with a branch of   . I saw her
> as Kuanon, with willow branch/ saw the eternal sweetness
> created: of pity the mother, protectress of the sea
> succor in shipwreck[51]

There is a strong correlation between these lines and the lines of Pisan Canto 74, with its "in this air" and its references to the sea—"marina" and "seawaves." However, there is also a strong evocation of Fenollosa's discussion of the "great white Kwannon,"[52] involving numerous parallels: "For Kwannon is especially the Mother of Waters, the Providence who guards the travelers upon ships. . . . [I]n the all-comprehensive Zen symbolism, we may say that she here typifies . . . the great human and subhuman category of 'motherhood.'"[53] In his description of the painting, Fenollosa mentions "a sprig of willow" that is associated with Kwannon and the "ether" that she symbolizes.[54] In the draft of Italian Canto 75, which Bush translates, there is mention of both willow and shipwreck, as well as "protectress of the seas" and motherhood. Other critics—notably Akiko Miyake—also connect Fenollosa's representations of Kuanon to Pound's work, although Miyake sees the connection as more operative in *Three Cantos*, foregrounding the later cantos.[55]

None of these critics, however, seems willing to engage Kuanon on Eastern ground; all defer to other, more Western allusions, conflating Kuanon with Aphrodite, Isis, Venus, and others, often to the elision of Kuanon. Wendy Stallard Flory, for instance, sees Venus in the passage from Canto 74, arguing that "instead of the Goddess of Mercy herself, we have only 'this air as of Kuanon,'"[56] while Miyake sees an early subtextual appearance of Isis in the appearance of the lotus in the ur-cantos, despite the lotus' historic identification with Buddhism, and Kuanon's association with Buddhist history and doctrine. As Charles Eliot notes in *Japanese Buddhism*, Kuanon "is undoubtedly one of the deities most widely honoured in Japan,"[57] and she frequently is shown holding a lotus in her left hand, encouraging the lotus's growth with her right, a posture symbolizing her support for human beings on their path to enlightenment.[58] In *The Three Pillars of Zen*, Buddhist scholar Philip Kapleau cites Rinzai Zen master Bassui Tokusho—born in 1327, at the wane of the Kamakura period—as chastising a Buddhist abbess: "Upon your enlightenment the lotus will blossom in a roaring fire and endure throughout eternity. Man is inherently no different from the lotus."[59] Later, Kapleau explains that the lotus, "which grows in mud yet is undefiled by it," is the symbol in Buddhism of the pure and perfect.[60] It is the symbol of "the Buddha-nature which is intrinsic to all,"[61] giving its name to the posture used to sit *zazen* meditation. From the earliest histories of Buddhism the lotus is widely associated with both the Buddha and his teachings. To insist, as Miyake does, that the lotus petal is a symbol that "indicates Queen Isis"[62] seems to overlook the obvious for the obscure. Certainly Miyake is correct in seeing Isis where Pound uses her more explicitly, in the Isis/Kuanon cantos, for instance. However, associations such as the above demonstrate not the subtextual presence of Isis, but the strong desire of Miyake to locate her presence, despite substantive evidence otherwise. It is this privileging of Western contexts that pervades the little criticism of Kuanon; her fate thus far has been subsumed by the more familiar Western female deities invoked.

The term Pound uses in reference to Kuanon—"enigma"—is fitting not only in reference to the cultural and textual puzzle she presents for critics, but also—as Hélène Cixous argues—for Pound, the male writer, for whom the female is "[n]ight to his day . . . . [b]lack to his white . . . . the repressed that ensures the system's functioning. . . . she, who is distance and postponement, will keep alive the enigma."[63] The collapsing of boundaries that occurs in the passage where Kuanon blooms from the seed of Aphrodite, then appears to merge with the earth mother, presages the passage where Kuanon materializes out of a reference to the daughter, and to daughter figures. Turning once again to Cixous, "the *body* of what is strange must not disappear, but its force must be conquered and returned to the master. Both the appropriate and the inappropriate must exist."[64] When Pound refers to Kuanon only by attribute—compassion—not even by name—"have compassion, / Picarda, / compassion / By the wing'd head, / by the caduceus, / compassion; / By the horns of Isis-Luna, / compassion" (93/648)—he is claiming her "force," having done away with her physical "body" altogether. He is attempting to "conquer" her strangeness, taking her malleable female form and remaking it, making it "behave." Kuanon will be mother—part of her traditional context—when he needs her. But she will be daughter as well, another traditional role for the female. Most significantly, however, she will be enigma, function of the female, but also at the heart of Buddhist doctrine.

In discussing language and clarity, Trinh Minh-ha says that "[t]he language of Taoism and Zen . . . which is perfectly accessible but rife with paradox does not qualify as 'clear' (paradox is 'illogical' and 'nonsensical' to many Westerners), for its intent lies outside the realm of persuasion."[65] There is an uncanny echo in this passage of Perelman's definition of the nonlogic and specificity of the ideogram. By attributing to Kuanon various female roles, logical or non-, Pound makes of her an ideogram for the female. She becomes a kind of icon, a signifier of sorts, a communication beyond the strictly spoken. In the tradition of her Buddhist begetting, she is—as Trinh says of the language of Buddhism—often accessible, but rarely logical. She is outside/beyond the realm of logic and persuasion, combining elements of the mystic with the feminine: Eastern mysticism gone female, as it were. Trinh, citing Cixous, highlights the appropriateness of such a conflation: "Woman, as Cixous defines her, is a whole—whole composed of parts that are wholes'—through which language is born over and over again. (The One is the All and the All is the One; and yet the One remains the One and the All. Not two, not one either. This is what Zen has been repeating for centuries.)"[66] In the way Pound uses Kuanon, often blurring into other female deities, later being conflated entirely with Isis, she is one of the "parts that are whole" that defines the "whole" female divine. It is this conceptualization of paradox—the "enigma"—that Kuanon personifies. She is Zen koan, is the female that confounds the male. And yet she is not so easily essentialized: she has her roots in male and female, is more than one, is less than two. Pound uses her but does not always control her.

Kuanon is notably Asian. As Cixous notes of another female Eastern figure, Cleopatra, "She had to be from the Orient to be so lofty, so free, so much the mistress of herself. . . . She had to be foreign. The 'great women' who pass through history or the historical imagination of the western side of the world come, can come only from an elsewhere."[67] Although so much of *The Cantos* is drawn from Greek and Roman mythologies, Pound is perhaps too familiar with Greek, with Roman, mythologies for them to offer the same kind of seduction as do Fenollosa's China and Japan. Speaking of "Flaubert's encounter with an Egyptian courtesan," Edward Said argues that it becomes almost paradigmatic of the relationship between Western male and Eastern female: "she never spoke of herself, she never represented her emotions, presence or history. *He* spoke for and represented her."[68] This rather neatly describes the relationship between the Eastern female figure of Kuanon and the Western male figure of Pound: he "represents" her, despite his inability to contain her, to explain her. "In the Orient," Cixous argues in a parallel passage, "the Impossible is born; she who is incomprehensible, who exceeds the imagination, who rewards the most powerful desire of the most powerful of men, she who has all, and who is more than all, no existence can contain her, no man has been able to equal her in radiance."[69] Pound's desire through *The Cantos* is for paradise, "to make a paradiso / terrestre . . . to write Paradise" (Notes for 117 et seq./822), and it is Isis and Kuanon, in the conjoining of Eastern and Western myth, who lift him up in Canto 90, and who sustain him through the hell ("Erebus") of Pisa and its aftermath, in his journey toward his paradise.

This joining of East and West is significant, as Pound consistently seeks cultural fusion within *The Cantos:* Confucius is juxtaposed with John Adams; Kuanon with Isis. The two goddesses appear together more than once, even though Kuanon's "appearance" at one point must be inferred from the repetition of her major attribute—compassion. It is Kuanon's compassion, invoked through the female figures of Isis and the moon, that leaves Pound feeling pity—"J'ai eu pitié des autres. / Pas assez! Pas assez!" (93/648)—however inadequate. So that the lifting up begun in Canto 90—"m'elevasti / from the dulled air and the dust, / m'elevasti / by the great flight, / m'elevasti, / Isis Kuanon / from the cusp of the moon, / m'elevasti" (626)—can ascend even higher in Canto 94: "Above prana, the light, / past light, the crystal. / Above crystal, the jade!" (654)

Terrell cites Yogi Ramacharaka's *Hatha Yoga*[70] as the source of Pound's knowledge[71] on yoga and attendant terminology, in an extensive note that defines *prana*, as well as giving background on Pound's routine yoga ritual at St. Elizabeths. Terrell also notes that the hierarchy given— from light, to crystal, to jade—represents symbolically the contemplative practice of Richard of St. Victor, which implies a progress made through meditation/contemplation toward a higher state. Ramacharaka explains *prana* as "the active principle of life," not to be confused with the personality or "Ego," but rather "a universal principle," found in all things, although *prana* itself is not matter.[72] Pound, caught up as he was in his ideogrammic project, would have found much to interest him in Ramacharaka's book, particularly concerning flux and flow: "There is nothing in absolute rest in nature. . . . Nothing is permanent in the world of forms. . . . Forms are but appearances—they come, they go, but the Reality is eternal and unchangeable."[73] This seems particularly apt when applied to the many forms the feminine divine takes for Pound: Aphrodite can become Kuanon can become Isis can become compassion, moving totally out of human—or even godly—form, while still true to some eternal reality.

What is significant here is Pound's increasing turn toward Eastern spiritualism, even Eastern occultism. Demetres Tryphonopoulos, while illuminating much of Pound's occult background in *The Celestial Tradition*, focuses almost exclusively on the Eleusinian mythos of what he sees as "the motif of palingenesis."[74] Kevin Oderman, too, argues for an impetus toward divine revelation; unlike Tryphonopoulos, however, he sees a stronger erotic component to Pound's ritual and vision.[75] This has interesting ramifications if Pound has any knowledge of Tantric yoga, something that seems quite likely given the titles listed in Tryphonopoulos's discussion of Ramacharaka, and his later discussions of occult influences prevalent among Pound's contemporaries. Tryphonopoulos argues that Pound may be "indebted" for several of his "occult ideas" to his readings of Ramacharaka's books, and notes that Pound and Dorothy Shakespear "are reported to have been reading *Advanced Course in Yogi and Oriental Occultism*" in 1910.[76] It is difficult to conceive of an "advanced course" in oriental occultism that would not include elements of Tantric yoga.

Oderman's analysis of Pound's use of the erotic to attain union with the mystic sounds uncannily like Tantric yoga, where "sexual experience is not *the* source of illumination but one source, nor is this just *any* sexual encounter, but one characterized by restraint, delay, and tension . . . . necessary rather than sufficient conditions for the success of the experiment."[77] The kundalini form of Tantric yoga, with its emphasis on raising kundalini—"the central psycho-physical power latent" in human beings[78]—emphasizes the slow raising of sexual energy from the base of the spine to the top of the skull, deferring sexual gratification, as one means of achieving union with the divine. Haridas Chaudhuri notes that Tantric yoga "is closely connected with the worship of God as the supreme Mother," and with the divine manifesting in two aspects, "archetypal masculine"—being—and "archetypal feminine"—becoming.[79] This dovetails neatly with Pound's use of various female figures to represent the divine, and his own quest to unite physically—sexually—with her/it. Such a reading also reifies the ideogrammic method, as being and becoming fuse, paralleling the meaning-in-process that is the ideogram. References to a union such as Chaudhuri treats are scattered—tantalizing clues—among various cantos: there is the "Sacrum, sacrum, inluminatio coitu" of Canto 36 (180); the "in coitu inluminatio" in Canto 74 (455); the "connubium terrae" of Canto 82 (546); and the veiled reference in Canto 82 to sex with Gea Terra (546), which Surette marks.[80]

As authors such as Surette, Miyake, Oderman, and Tryphonopoulos demonstrate, *The Cantos* are infused with movement toward mystic union. Surette maintains that Pound is attempting to articulate an Eleusis based on a "central rite . . . [of] coition."[81] This union is sought as a means of producing a revelation in the faithful, "an encounter with the divine, which mystically transforms the lives of the initiates."[82] Where Surette sees Eleusis only, a reading that takes into consideration the significance of Kuanon and the contexts of Buddhism, Daoism, and Eastern mysticism might see kundalini yoga as well, for Kuanon contains within one body the union of male and female, that collapse of binarism upon which Eastern mysticism is predicated: Daoism, with its emphasis on *yin* and *yang*, Buddhism with both being and becoming. In addition, Kuanon completes the East/West equation prevalent throughout *The Cantos*.

Given the Eleusinian elements of Pound's attempt to merge with the divine, the kundalini practice of Tantric yoga is the most obvious Eastern parallel to the Eleusinian rites. "[U]nion with the timeless" is total in kundalini practice,[83] with the additional benefit that the result of a "lawfully satisfied" sexual desire is a "growing interest in social welfare or humanitarian service,"[84] a critical element for an author who is trying "to make a paradiso / terrestre" (117/822). Within this context, Kuanon takes on an entirely different dimension: her appearance as daughter as well as mother reflects her dual role, partner in, as well as object of, desire. Paradoxically, her androgynous origins are also an asset: in one person she represents the union of male and female to which Pound aspires in his vision of the "connubium terrae." Using this reading, the often frustrating binary oppositions and the apparent inconsistencies of Pound's later fragments become less oblique—the poignancy of the last sections ("M'amour, m'amour / what do I love and / where are you?" [117/822]) is the grief of the lover for not only his beloved, but for his way home, his path to what lies beyond the narrow boundaries of the material world, his "bridge over worlds" (117/823). As Jean-Michel Rabaté argues, for Pound "The Greek cosmos and Chinese wisdom must be reunited in a new perception of rites and divinities," affecting "the harmonisation of the human world with the divine world." Rabaté draws attention to the plight of the inhabitants of Pound's "earthly paradise," who when forced to forgo their practice of free love, committed suicide: they "could not accept the new laws without despair." Such behavior demonstrates to Pound "that love is . . . a concrete force," one so powerful that to thwart it is to confer a death sentence.[85] It is this force that Pound attempts to invoke, attempts to establish as the governing principle in his own earthly paradise. And it is Kuanon who is the Eastern element fusing the Greek cosmos—Artemis, Ariadne, Aphrodite—with Chinese wisdom—her compassion, her protection, her motherhood, her feminine divinity—thus forging a new, ideogrammic female divine for Pound to pursue.

The poet Jane Hirshfield writes that the root word for both *Chan* and *Zen* is the Sanskrit *dhyana*, or "concentration." "In Western . . . etymology, we find a related concept," she explains, "*kentron*: the Greek word for the sharp point at the center."[86] So Greek links with Chinese with Japanese, the sharp point at the Western center becoming the focused meditation that lies at the Eastern heart of Buddhism. And Kuanon—Eastern female, mother/daughter/lover, Chinese/Japanese enigma—links with Aphrodite, with Pound's Eleusinian and Eastern mystic vision, the point at the ideogrammic center of *The Cantos'* sprawling pilgrimage.

NOTES

1. Akiko Miyake, *Ezra Pound and the Mysteries of Love* (Durham: Duke University Press, 1991), 3.

2. At least three critics engage Pound's use of Daoism and foreground both Pound and Buddhism and the similarities in his attitude toward the two religions. Hugh Kenner discusses Pound and Daoism in *The Pound Era* (Berkeley: University of California Press, 1971), 456, as do Reed Way Dasenbrock in *The Literary Vorticism of Ezra Pound and Wyndham Lewis: Toward the Condition of Painting* (Baltimore: Johns Hopkins University Press, 1985), 220–24, and Zhaoming Qian in *Orientalism and Modernism: The Legacy of China in Pound and Williams* (Durham: Duke University Press, 1995), 70–72, 104–8,

3. John Nolde, *Blossoms from the East: The China Cantos of Ezra Pound* (Orono, Maine: National Poetry Foundation, 1983), 430.

4. Thich Nhat Hanh, *Old Path White Clouds: Walking in the Footsteps of the Buddha* (Berkeley: Parallax, 1991), 131.

5. See Hugh Kenner, "Notes on Amateur Emendations," in *A Poem Containing History: Textual Studies in The Cantos*, ed. Lawrence Rainey (Ann Arbor: University of Michigan Press, 1997), 25. Kenner argues that when Pound uses variant names in *The Cantos* he is "recording the chain of transmission." However, in no text do I find Queen Maya referred to as "Nana." In many cultural traditions, *nana* is a

diminutive given to mothers, grandmothers, or women functioning in maternal positions. There would seem to be no other source to transmit.

6. Thich Nhat Hanh, *Old Path White Clouds*, 41.

7. Ibid., 40.

8. See Carroll F. Terrell, *A Companion to The Cantos of Ezra Pound* (Berkeley and Los Angeles: University of California Press, 1993), 54/167. References to Terrell will be made by canto and note number; e.g., note 40 to Canto 38 will be listed as 38/40.

9. Ibid., 54/169, 170.

10. See Nolde, *Blossoms from the East*, 152.

11. Leon Surette, *A Light from Eleusis: A Study of Ezra Pound's Cantos* (Oxford: Oxford University Press, 1979), 154.

12. Nolde, *Blossoms from the East*, 162.

13. See Sanehide Kodama, *Ezra Pound and Japan: Letters and Essays* (Redding Ridge, Conn.: Black Swan, 1987), 142.

14. See Jean-Michel Rabaté, *Language, Sexuality, and Ideology in Ezra Pound's Cantos* (Albany: State University of New York Press, 1986), 114.

15. Ibid., 99.

16. Surette, *A Light from Eleusis*, 155.

17. Kodama, *Ezra Pound and Japan*, 31.

18. Kenner appears to concur with this reading. He notes in *The Pound Era* that "[A] Confucian official might taoize on holiday, painting landscapes; a taoist might not govern" (3). A comparable argument may be made for Buddhism, according to Pound's reading.

19. See Roland Barthes, *Mythologies*, trans. Annette Lavers (New York: Noonday Press-Farrar, 1972), 94–95.

20. Kodama, *Ezra Pound and Japan*, 163.

21. See Qian, *Orientalism and Modernism*, 9ff., for an extended discussion of Binyon's influence on Pound's early exposure to oriental art and oriental perspectives.

22. Ibid., where this letter is quoted at some length on page 56, with an attendant footnote on page 189. In addition, I am indebted to Maureen Heher at Yale University's Beinecke Rare Book and Manuscript Library, who mailed me a photocopy of the original.

23. Letter from Ezra Pound to Homer Pound, dated December 5, 1913, YCAL, Pound Papers.

24. See Martin Palmer and Jay Ramsay, with Man-Ho Kwok, *Kuan Yin: Myths and Revelations of the Chinese Goddess of Compassion* (London: Thorsons, 1995). The full Chinese name for the Buddhist deity of compassion is Guanshiyin—"the One who Hears the Cries of the World" (Palmer and Ramsay, xii)—although she is more commonly known as Guanyin. According to Charles Eliot, *Japanese Buddhism* (London: Routledge, 1935), 349, the Japanese know her as Kwannon (the name Fenollosa uses); or she may be called Kannon (Palmer and Ramsay, xi). Pound's usage of *Kuanon* reflects a provocative conflation of the Chinese and Japanese/Fenollosa depiction of the Chinese and Japanese forms.

25. See Ernest Fenollosa, *Epochs of Chinese and Japanese Art: An Outline History of East Asiatic Design* (New York: Frederick A. Stokes, 1912), vol. 1, facing page 50.

26. Fenollosa, *Epochs*, vol. 2, facing 50. This would not, however, have been Pound's first encounter with the figure(s) of Kuanon.

27. See Akiko Miyake, "Contemplation East and West: A Defense of Fenollosa's Synthetic Language and Its Influence on Ezra Pound," *Paideuma* 10 (1981):542.

28. Fenollosa, *Epochs*, 2:107.

29. Fenollosa, *Epochs*, 1:29.

30. Fenollosa includes seven plates featuring Kwannon, either in sculpture or painting, in his two volumes.

31. Fenollosa, *Epochs*, 1:64.

32. Ibid., 1:107.

33. See Ronald Bush, *The Genesis of Ezra Pound's Cantos* (Princeton: Princeton University Press, 1976), 58.

34. Terrell, *Companion*, 74/210.

35. Fenollosa, *Epochs*, 2:49.

36. Ibid., 2:49.

37. Ibid., 1:124.

38. Palmer and Ramsay, *Kuan Yin*, 5.

39. Ibid., 7.

40. Ibid., 38.

41. See Nolde, *Blossoms from the East*, 155; Terrell, *Companion*, 74/46.

42. Terrell, *Companion*, 74/214.

43. Fenollosa, *Epochs*, 2:49.

44. Ibid.

45. See Bob Perelman, *The Trouble with Genius: Reading Pound, Joyce, Stein, and Zukofsky* (Berkeley and Los Angeles: University of California Press, 1994), 43.

46. Pound, "The Teacher's Mission," *LE*, 58-63.

47. Surette, *A Light from Eleusis*, 198.

48. Fenollosa, *Epochs*, 1:133.

49. Ibid.

50. Ronald Bush, "Quiet, Not Scornful? The Composition of the Pisan Cantos," in Rainey, *A Poem Containing History*, 188.

51. Ibid., 187.

52. Fenollosa, *Epochs*, 2:49.

53. Ibid.

54. Ibid.

55. See Miyake, *Mysteries of Love*, 52-53.

56. See Wendy Stallard Flory, *Ezra Pound and "The Cantos": A Record of Struggle* (New Haven: Yale University Press, 1980), 193.

57. Charles Eliot, *Japanese Buddhism* (London: Routledge, 1935), 60.

58. Ibid., 352.

59. See Philip Kapleau, *The Three Pillars of Zen* (New York: Weatherhill-Beacon, 1967), 170.

60. Ibid., 313.

61. Ibid., 338.

62. See Miyake, "Contemplation East and West," 544.

63. See Hélène Cixous, "Sorties," in *The Newly Born Woman*, ed. Catherine Clement and Hélène Cixous, trans. Betsy Win (Minneapolis: University of Minnesota Press, 1986), 67.

64. Ibid., 70.

65. See Trinh T. Minh-ha, *Woman, Native, Other: Writing Postcoloniality and Feminism* (Bloomington: Indiana University Press, 1989), 16.

66. Ibid., 38–39.

67. Cixous, "Sorties," 126.

68. See Edward Said, *Orientalism* (New York: Vintage–Random House, 1979), 6; emphasis added.

69. Cixous, "Sorties," 126.

70. See Yogi Ramacharaka, *Hatha Yoga* (Chicago: Yogi Publication Society, 1930).

71. Terrell, *Companion*, cites Ramacharaka 157–58 as his source for a note on 94/18, but gives no date of publication of this edition.

72. Ramacharaka, *Hatha Yoga*, 152–53.

73. Ibid., 159.

74. See Demetres Tryphonopoulos, *The Celestial Tradition: A Study of Ezra Pound's "The Cantos"* (Waterloo, Ont.: Wilfrid Laurier University Press, 1992), 4.

75. Kevin Oderman, *Ezra Pound and the Erotic Medium* (Durham: Duke University Press, 1986).

76. Tryphonopoulos, *The Celestial Tradition*, 66.

77. Oderman, *Erotic Medium*, 12; emphasis added.

78. Haridas Chaudhuri, *Integral Yoga: The Concept of Harmonious and Creative Living* (Wheaton, Ill.: Theosophical Publishing House–Quest, 1965), 57.

79. Ibid.

80. Surette, *A Light from Eleusis*, 213.

81. Ibid., 214.

82. Ibid., 221.

83. Chaudhuri, *Integral Yoga*, 58.

84. Ibid., 59.

85. Rabaté, *Language, Sexuality, and Ideology*, 289, 298.

86. Jane Hirshfield, *Nine Gates: Entering the Mind of Poetry* (New York: Harper Perennial, 1997), 7.

"Why Not Spirits?"— "The Universe Is Alive": Ezra Pound, Joseph Rock, the Na Khi, and Plotinus

EMILY MITCHELL WALLACE

The title is Poundian, for Pound was fascinated by the mysterious ways that people and their things and concepts are linked throughout history, for example, "Arab coins found in mounds in Sweden / under Fortuna" (103/756). Unexpected connections are a part of his complex technique that readers respond to with every human emotion from delight to disgust, depending on the curiosity and expansiveness of their minds. Perhaps twenty-first-century technologies will help scholars to see more of these links and connect "the tale of the tribe" with its readers in new and spirited ways.

In a rare moment of defense of his *Cantos,* Pound spoke of the "musical themes that meet each other." This is only four years before his death, in the 1968 interview with Pier Pasolini, in David Anderson's translation:

> *Pasolini:* Literary critics all agree that your poetry is extremely vast. It is as if your poetry covered an immense poetical territory. And it's true, for quotation after quotation . . .
> *Pound:* Chosen at random . . .
> *Pasolini:* Chosen at random? What? The critics or the quotations?
> *Pound:* They say they are chosen at random, but that's not the way it is. It's music. Musical themes that meet each other.[1]

If Pasolini's questions seem, inadvertently, comic, Pound, after a lifetime of such misunderstandings, remains calm and emphasizes the important point he wants to make. You will recall that Yeats, in *A Packet for Ezra Pound* (1929), famously describes the structure of *The Cantos* as a "Bach Fugue," with themes of "ABCD and then JKLM, and then each set of letters repeated, and then a new element XYZ, then certain letters that never recur, and then all sorts of combinations of XYZ and JKLM and ABCD and DCBA, and all set whirling together."[2] When friends asked Pound to explain Yeats's explanation, he remarked, in exasperation, that Yeats wouldn't know a fugue from a frog.[3] Nevertheless, Yeats does convey the complexity of the grand polyphonic structure of the poem.

For Pound the music of ancient dynasties included the Chinese language itself. He said to Angela Palandri, who is Chinese: "The Chinese tones are very musical. They make you sing. That's the way poetry should be in any language. . . . Yeats wanted to see all his poems set to music, as Kung [Confucius] set the *Odes* to music."[4] Pound's long poem is music for the ears, but this paper is about the music in it for the mind.

> *Pasolini:* . . . Confucius is the only great religious reformer who was not religious, whose philosophy was chiefly a practical philosophy, and I might even say secular. I would like to know how you include Confucius in your poetry which is, to the contrary—although it is very secular in its rhythm—enormously religious in its rationality. . . .
>
> *Pound:* Perhaps I found occasion to describe the Confucian universe as a "series of tensions."[5]

Mind music, literally, is in that "series of tensions," both of the Confucian universe and the Na Khi universe, themes that meet each other in the poem.

The Na Khi, one of fifty-six formally recognized ethnic minority groups among the three percent of non-Han Chinese,[6] emigrated more than a thousand years ago from Tibet to a border province called Yunnan in remote southwest China. The name translates as "South of the Clouds," and this province, the least visited in China, is one of the most pristine places of natural beauty on earth, and "the world's greatest treasure trove of temperate flowers and herbal plants."[7] Towering mountains, virgin forests, three great rivers, and flowering meadows surround the ancient villages and towns. Lijiang (also called Dayan), which has both an Old Town and a New Town roughly divided by Lion Hill, is the cultural center of the approximately 275,000 Na Khi people, who form the dominant group in a rich collection of tribal cultures, which coexist peaceably. One reason for the lack of strife may be the lack of rigidity in their religious beliefs. The Na Khi in their attitude toward religion, says Peter Goullart in *Forgotten Kingdom* (1955), are "in many ways similar to the Chinese who are not religious people *per se,* in the Western sense of the word. The Chinese believe simultaneously and sincerely in Buddhism, Taoism, Ancestral Worship (Confucianism), Animism, and willingly accept Christianity if need be." Goullart continues:

The Nakhi, likewise, had accepted Lamaism (Tantric Buddhism), Mahayana Buddhism, Taoism and Confucianism in addition to their ancient religion of Animism and Shamanism. To coin a phrase, they had a departmentalized belief, with each religion serving some particular need. Buddhism was useful in connection with the funerals and prayers for the repose of the dead. Taoism satisfied mystic and aesthetic cravings. Ancestor Worship was proper and necessary to keep up the contact with the departed. Animism was the recognition and definition of the unseen powers and intelligences in Nature and provided a method of dealing with them. Shamanism was indispensable for the protection of the living and dead from the evil spirits. On top of these religious beliefs they had inherited from their ancestors a deep-rooted and eminently practical Epicurean philosophy.[8]

Unlike the Chinese, however, in their attitude toward Christianity, the Na Khi were, Goullart says, "inconvertible."[9] They refused to abandon

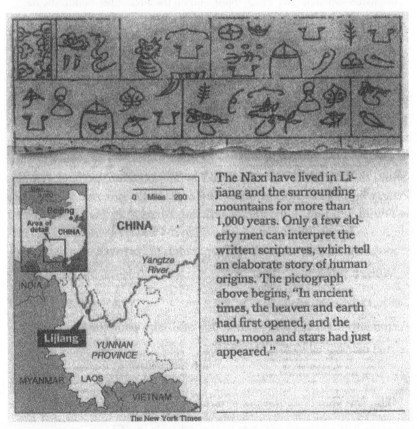

The Naxi have lived in Lijiang and the surrounding mountains for more than 1,000 years. Only a few elderly men can interpret the written scriptures, which tell an elaborate story of human origins. The pictograph above begins, "In ancient times, the heaven and earth had first opened, and the sun, moon and stars had just appeared."

Excerpt from an article by Eric Eckholm, "Dying Culture, as Seen through Aging Eyes," *New York Times*, January 5, 2000, A4.

their "close and intimate contact with the world of spirits."[10] To the Christian missionaries established in Yunnan, "All the séances and intercourse with the dear and helpful spirits were taboo. Ancestor worship was under interdict and so were all relations with the beautiful lamaseries and temples." The Na Khi were happy with their way of life and saw that "no area for hundreds of miles around" had "attained such prosperity and well-being as the Likiang valley."[11] So Likiang remained both a delightful place to live and "a haven for anyone interested in psychical research."[12]

According to Joseph Rock, the diversity of Na Khi religious literature "proves that it originated at different times and in different places":

> It is a composite religious edifice whose foundation rests primarily on primitive nature-worship (*vide* Mùa<u>n</u> ¹bpö), and on the ancient pre-buddhistic national religion of Tibet known as the Bön, of which it is in fact not only a part but a part which has survived among the ¹Na-²Khi in a purer form than can now be found in Tibet proper. ¹Na-²Khi religious literature has been influenced by Burmese Nat worship, Chinese Taoism, and finally Tibetan Buddhism; its core is however Bön with an admixture of aboriginal tribal shamanism.[13]

Pound heeded Rock's emphases and obtained one of the rare copies of Rock's 1948 article, "The ²Muan ¹Bpö Ceremony or the Sacrifice to Heaven as Practiced by the ¹Na-²Khi," published in *Monumenta Serica: Journal of Oriental Studies of the Catholic University of Peiping*. Many copies of the journal were destroyed by Communists; perhaps Achilles Fang, who was an associate editor and contributor, gave one of his copies to Pound. It is now in the library at Brunnenburg.[14] In *The Cantos* Pound alludes to ²*muan* ¹*bpo* in Cantos 98, and in 104 and 112 quotes from the ceremony, which is also called the "Propitiation of Heaven":

> Without ²muan   ¹bpo
>   no reality
>   (104/759 and 112/804)

Pound also describes a shaman in one of Rock's photographs:

> And the ²dto-¹mba's face (exorcist's)
>   muy simpático
>   (101/746)

The Na Khi ceremonies of propitiation and exorcism may seem superstitious in comparison with the elegant and aristocratic rites of Confucius, and, therefore, one might assume that the Na Khi universe is a musical theme that cannot meet the musical theme of Confucius and his world. That assumption would be wrong. Pound learned of the connection between the Na Khi and Confucius in Saint Elizabeths when reading Goullart's *Forgotten Kingdom* soon after its publication. The words must have leapt off the page:

> It was wonderful and extraordinary to hear the music which was played during the heyday of the glorious Han and Tang dynasties and, probably, during the time of Confucius himself. This musical tradition was one of the most cherished among the Na-khi and was zealously transmitted from father to son .... Their happiness was great and they did their best to express it in the

450   THE NATIONAL GEOGRAPHIC MAGAZINE

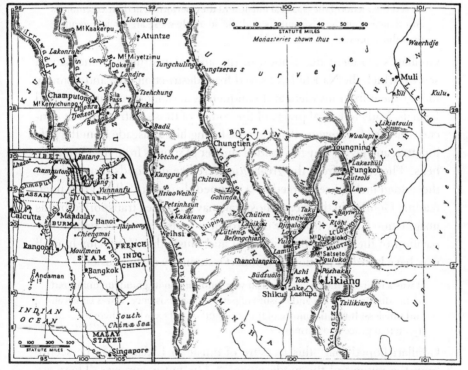

Drawn by Chas. E. Riddiford

MAP SHOWING THE YÜNNAN PROVINCE TERRITORY, WHERE A NATIONAL
GEOGRAPHIC SOCIETY EXPEDITION WAS AT WORK FOR TWO YEARS

Map of Yunnan Province, *National Geographic*, April 1925.

elegant and classical manner of their ancestors who had drunk deeply of Confucian idealism. The old Sage had always taught that music was the greatest attainment of a civilized man: and to music they turned to express the exquisite joy of living and to enhance the serenity of their old age.[15]

Goullart points out that "A great blow was struck to Chinese civilization with the loss of Confucius's own Book of Music. It was probably destroyed, along with other classics, during the great burning of books undertaken by Chin Shi Hwangti, builder of the Great Wall of China." Goullart maintains that a form of that music survives among the Na Khi:

> Yet it is impossible to believe that the tradition of that great music did not survive in some remote places. . . . Some esoteric Taoist monasteries have preserved fragments of the classical music and they perform it in their ceremonies and dances, but the instruments and the score they use are far less genuine than those preserved by the Na-khi.[16]

Goullart's eloquent description of the ancient instruments and sacred scores, which the Na Khi have saved from destruction time and again by hiding them from invaders and conquerors and, most recently, the Red Guards, leads to lyrical praise of the sound of those instruments in concert: "notes of unimagined sweetness, falling like a cascade from the jade lunettes, and giving way to a golden shower of sounds from the chromatic bells. The chords from the great *chin* were like diamonds dropped into the golden melody, reinforced by a stopped diapason."[17] The great poet, reading Goullart in the mental hospital, may have been transported by his imagination far away from the discordant sounds he endured daily to the pavilion of the apricot trees in Qufu and music that Confucius himself may have heard. A portion of Goullart's summary of the music:

> It was a recital of the cosmic life as it was unfolding in its grandeur, unmarred by the discordant wails and crashes of petty human existence. It was classical, and timeless. It was the music of the gods and of a place where there is serenity, eternal peace and harmony.[18]

Goullart hoped that "this treasure of music in Likiang may be secure from the ravages of the modern age."[19] The music survives. There are now four Na Khi orchestras performing on the ancient instruments or copies of them. The orchestra in Lijiang founded by Dr. Xuan Ke, whose family knew Dr. Rock, as they called him, and inherited some of his handmade furniture, is preparing to come to the United States to perform.[20]

Na Khi musicians in Lijiang

Pound would have considered the Na Khi respect for the "living fossils" of music from Confucius's time[21] a top recommendation of their character, and so he was receptive to many other details of *Forgotten Kingdom*. Goullart repeatedly praises the beauty of the Likiang valley and its mountains and rivers. At the end of his book Goullart notes that James Hilton's hero in *Lost Horizon* found his "'Shangri La' by accident. I found mine, by design and perseverance, in Likiang."[22]

Goullart describes Likiang as "an illusion of a miniature Venice"[23] of many canals and bridges, and says that the streets, "paved with stone slabs or stone bricks . . . were scrupulously clean," as were the canals, in which "the water rushed unceasingly crystal clear, and nothing but pebbles seen on the bottom."[24] One of the mountain streams flowing through the town is "Jade stream," as in Canto 112/804: "the clear discourse / as Jade stream." Goullart recalls that "Mountain youths, in the sheer joy of life, would dance through the street playing flutes like the pipes of Pan. They looked wild woodland creatures in their sleeveless skin jerkins and short skin pants."[25] "Merry girls . . . sat on the doorsteps . . . embroidering, in multi-coloured silks, the seven stars which every Nakhi woman, married or unmarried, wears on the back of her traditional sheepskin jacket. . . . These pretty circlets are about two inches in diameter. Formerly there were two larger circlets, representing the sun and moon, but they were now no longer worn."[26] Pound, relying on Rock's 1924 photograph, keeps "the sun and moon on her shoulders" (Canto 101/746).

Goullart's stories about "the world of spirits" in Likiang would have interested Pound because of his friends' "psychical research"[27] during his London years, and most particularly his memories of what he called the "spooks" of Yeats. Goullart says that to the Na Khi "The relationship between mankind and these many spirits was not considered hypothetical or conjectural but factual and authentic. . . . If there was an apparition, materialization or direct voice, people did not shrink from it but investigated the matter with sympathy and interest. In a word, a visitor from the unseen was treated as a person, with proper courtesy."[28] They also accepted the shamanistic belief that not only do the dear departed and the demons have spirits but also that the clouds and mountains and winds and trees and plants and lakes and springs and rivers and rocks each have a spirit.

Although Goullart says very little about Rock, other than a dramatic description of their final departure together in 1949 when the Commu-

Two canals in Lijiang, "The Oriental Venice." Top, photograph by Joseph Rock, 1947: "Crystal clear streams flow through the town in various directions" (*The Ancient Na-Khi Kingdom of Southwest China*, Plate LIII). Bottom, photograph by Gregory Harvey, 1999.

nists took over,[29] he expresses his profound admiration with a printed inscription: "This book is dedicated to / DR. JOSEPH F. ROCK." Goullart's dedication was sufficient to set Pound on the course of collecting and studying Rock's articles and books, and the theme of the Na Khi in *The Cantos* comes directly from Rock's scholarly studies, but Pound acknowledges a debt to Goullart in an early, unpublished draft:

> Rock's land and Goullart's
> paradiso;
> air blown into
> word-form[30]

Goullart's *Likiang* becomes *Li Chiang* in Rock and Pound. The biography of Rock by S. B. Sutton (1974) follows Goullart, not Rock, in spelling *Likiang*.[31] Today the town is called Lijiang. Whatever your choice of transliteration, the name means "beautiful river."[32] Pound reproduces the Na Khi words from Rock's writing exactly as Rock offers them. They look unpronounceable and are time consuming to copy with their superscript numbers (Goullart and Sutton omit these numbers), but when I showed a page of *The Cantos* to our Na Khi guide in Lijiang, he said jubilantly, "But here is Na Khi writing!" Our guide said that any of the transliterations for Na Khi are all right, Na-ki, Nak-shi, Na-shi, Na-si, Na-xi, Na-hi, with or without a hyphen. Rock usually uses a hyphen and the superscript numbers, ^{1}Na-^{2}Khi. Pound usually uses neither for this one word, Na Khi, but otherwise copies Rock carefully.

Much of what Pound knew about Joseph Frances Charles Rock as a person he gleaned from Rock's brief autobiographical admissions in the introductions to his books and monographs. In the preface to Rock's best-known work, the two volumes of *The Ancient Na-Khi Kingdom of Southwest China*, published in 1947 by Harvard University Press for the Harvard-Yenching Institute Monograph Series, Pound read:

> My predilection for Chinese characters made me begin the study of the Chinese written language at the age of 15. It created a desire in me to explore the vast hinterland of China and to learn to know its history and geography at first hand. It caused me to study the ancient Na-khi language, now no more in use, but preserved in the pictographic literature, which has at last given up its secrets. Thus equipped, I undertook the task of delving into the history of this fascinating and wonderful country, which I covered on foot and horseback from Siam to southwestern Mongolia. In the pages of this work, I describe the Na-khi region as it passed in review before my eyes: a wealth of scenic beauty,

marvellous forest, flowers, and friendly tribes. Those years of travel and the fellowship of the tribal people who accompanied me on my many journeys will remain forever among the happiest memories of my life.

I owe a debt of gratitude not only to the institutions and societies that made these explorations possible, but also to the faithful members of the Na-Khi tribe, fearless, honest and dependable at all times. To them, the success of my various expeditions is mainly due.[33]

Pound, like Rock, was fifteen when he chose his lifework: "I resolved that at thirty I would know more about poetry than any man living."[34] Probably Pound did not know that Rock had reddish blonde hair like Frobenius and himself, or that Rock had grown up in Vienna, a lonely boy whose Hungarian mother died when he was six, and her mother two weeks later, which deprived the child of maternal comfort and exposed him to the violent tempers of his father, who resented his bookish son's studies of languages and faraway places. Rock said that his childhood was more unhappy than David Copperfield's. However, his father worked as a steward for a nobleman, Count Potocki, and the Rocks lived in the count's house, where young Joseph developed an appreciation of fine food and good manners, and an air of urbane self-confidence, which later on, combined with his exceptional intelligence and curiosity and memory and prodigious hard work, brought him success in many fields, though, having no degree beyond secondary school, he lacked academic credentials.[35] Whatever a situation required, he taught himself or found an expert to teach him.

In September 1905 at the age of twenty-one Rock arrived in New York penniless and in poor health from tuberculosis. His assets were his character and his knowledge of languages; he knew German, Hungarian, Italian, French, Latin, Greek, Chinese, some Arabic, and he could read Sanskrit. He quickly learned English or American and spoke it almost without accent. Less than a decade later he was a success, in strong, good health from working outdoors, an American citizen, a tenured faculty member teaching botany (self-taught) at the College of Hawaii, and widely published with an international reputation among botanical scholars. His book *The Indigenous Trees of the Hawaiian Islands* (1913) is still considered essential in the study of Hawaiian botany. The same year this book was published, he took a leave of absence to travel around the world, briefly visiting China for the first time (seven and one-half hours in Canton and the high point, he said, of his trip). In 1919 he was promoted to the rank of Professor of Systematic Botany and determined to return to China. "In about a dozen years Rock achieved in botany what would take most ordinary men a lifetime."[36]

In 1920 Rock arrived in China for the second time and thereafter lived there as much as possible, gradually turning his obsessively thorough and original scholarship to focus on collecting, classifying, and translating into English the many manuscripts of Na Ki literature. His preface to his 1948 article "The ²Muan ¹Bpö Ceremony" begins:

> My first contact with the ¹Na-²Khi was in the spring of the year 1922. At that time I was Agricultural Explorer of the U.S. Department of Agriculture of Washington D.C. Later I continued under the auspices of the National Geographic Society of the same city. On my return to Li-chiang in 1927 from the Far Northwest of China, and Northeastern Tibet for Harvard University, I explored the regions to the northwest and northeast of it. In 1930 I again returned to ¹Na-²Khi land on my own, to devote my entire time to the study of the ¹Na-²Khi Literature. This I continued until the spring of 1943.[37]

For the National Geographic Society Rock made two expeditions, in 1922 and 1928, of several years each, and published in the *National Geographic* magazine ten substantial articles accompanied by superb photographs, many of which he developed in the field as he traveled. He introduced color photography (self-taught, of course) to the magazine, and made the pictures as important as the text.

Pound may have read some of Rock's articles in *National Geographic*, as well as a tribute to Rock by Gilbert Grosvenor, president of the National Geographic Society, who reported that on his first expedition Rock sent back large collections of seeds of spruces, firs, hemlocks, pines, junipers, blight-resistant chestnuts, and many rare species of primrose, larkspur, gentian, and other flowers. Complete sets of 493 species of rhododendrons collected by Rock in Yunnan were sent to Kew Gardens of London, the Royal Botanic Gardens of Edinburgh, Golden Gate Park of San Francisco, the botanic gardens of the University of California at Berkeley, and many gardens in the Puget Sound region and along the eastern seaboard. (In this context of seeds from China sent around the world, it does not seem odd that Pound repeatedly urged from Saint Elizabeths Hospital that his young publisher James Laughlin obtain seeds of the American sugar maple and send them to Italy for his daughter Mary and her husband to plant around the castle in Tirolo.) Rock also sent to the Geographic Society some sixty thousand sheets of herbarium specimens, and the skins of more than sixteen hundred birds and sixty mammals. Grosvenor reports that the specimens collected and prepared by this self-taught botanist and ornithologist and taxidermist reached the U.S. National Museum "in perfect condition," and everyone expressed "genuine approval."[38] During the expedition for Harvard, of almost two years, Rock sent plants and seeds to the Arnold Arboretum—Bruce Chatwin wrote that all the trees he liked best in the Arboretum bore Rock's name on their labels[39]—and birds to Harvard's Museum of Comparative Zoology.

For his field-work Rock needed substantial funding not only for equipment and assistants but also for twenty to two-hundred armed guards to protect him and his little group of helpers from bandits in the mountains. Rock's equipment included many weeks of food for the men and horses, tents and bedding for blizzard conditions, cameras and photographic supplies, guns, aneroid barometers, large quantities of special papers for blotting, drying, and packing the botanical specimens, other materials for the birds and mammals, and medical and dental supplies. Although Rock was, naturally, self-taught as both doctor and dentist, the Na Khi appreciated his skill and today display some of his instruments and tools, which we saw in a modest little museum at his house in Nguluko, a few miles north of Lijiang. Rock also traveled with a folding canvas bathtub, a phonograph and records of classical music, a folding table, linen tablecloths, fine dinnerware, and a Na Khi cook he had trained in European and American cuisine. Rock did not think of his arrangements as luxurious, but rather as essential for maintaining his identity and good health so that he could concentrate on his work.

The Na Khi evidently understood, having epicurean habits themselves, but in any case those who have accused Rock of living in luxury are mistaken. His house at Nguluko is neat and well built, but neither large nor elaborate. Now maintained by the Chinese government, it is a wooden structure built around three sides of a courtyard with the fourth side of the enclosure the outside stone wall of the stables. Rock's room, where he slept, studied, wrote, developed photographs (hanging the negatives to dry over his bed), is small and furnished with the same folding table and chair used on his field trips, and a large round brazier to provide heat. A picture of the room made when he was living there hangs in one of the theaters in Lijiang. The remainder of the house was used by his Na Khi helpers for the various tasks he assigned them. He observed that to pre-pare for his expeditions he had to be "a good housekeeper,"[40] and so he was, and, as usual, self-taught. The only apparent excess in his arrange-ments, aside from dining for a short time on gold plates given him by one of his hosts, was the breathtaking natural beauty of his surroundings. We approached his house on foot through a flowering meadow, stepping on stones to cross a little stream where a man was washing vegetables. We could see the mountain range, "the shining cliffs" that give Nguluko its name, and we were told that Jade Lake, which provides another name, Yuhu Village, is nearby.

In the heading for an article published in 1939 Rock identifies himself as "Research Professor in Oriental Studies, University of Hawaii. Membre Correspondant de l'Ecole Française d'Extréme-Orient."[41] As a true interdisciplinary scholar he could never get all of his activities into the same frame of reference, and other experts could judge his excellence only in their own specialities. James Wilhelm astutely notes that "Like Frobenius, Rock was interested in *total culture:* he did not divorce geog-raphy from linguistics from botany from anthropology from art; he saw all things in a vast cultural ideogram that in turn resembled Pound's own central ideogram."[42] During World War II Rock worked for the United States Army Map Service as Expert Consultant and Geographic Special-ist. After the war he became a research associate in linguistic studies, from 1945 to 1950, for the Harvard-Yenching Institute. His colleagues in Hawaii and at the Department of Agriculture and the Smithsonian con-tinued to ask for his advice and help. And the Central Intelligence Agency sent a person with security clearance to copy, with Rock's permission, portions of his diaries. Sutton says about Rock's record keeping:

> Every day that he traveled he made meticulous notes of compass bearings, landmarks, distances, altitudes, physical features, geological formations, botan-ical and zoological phenomena, agricultural patterns, and cultural oddities; the information was encyclopedic in quantity, succinct in quality. He also recorded vignettes of travel, encounters with bandits, meetings with chieftans, descrip-tions of villages, or whatever happened to distinguish one day from another.[43]

The integrity and intelligence of Rock's work shines through in every-thing he did. Although he had earned fame as a botanist and collector of rare plants, and celebrity as the *National Geographic*'s "man in China,"

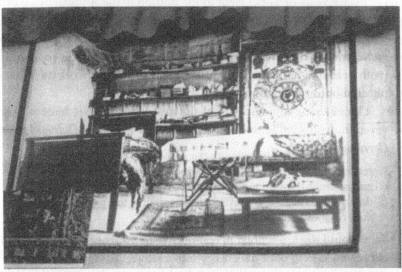

Displayed in a Lijiang theater are an informal snapshot of Joseph Rock and a photograph of his library-dining-sleeping-writing-photography room on the second floor of his house in Nguluko. Photographs by Gregory Harvey, 1999.

Rock chose as his major lifework a project that appeared at first to be unwanted and undoable. No one in the Western world knew anything about Na Khi literature, so how could there be any desire for it? Even for a genius at languages like Rock, the literature was unreadable without the help of a *dtomba* (or *dongba*), and few of them were left who knew what must be read into the texts from memory. "A great deal must be read which is not written and this rubric perhaps more than any other shows that the Na-Khi pictographs do not form a system of writing as we understand it."[44] Rock outlines some of the difficulties of translating this unique writing:

> The pictographic writing of the Na-Khi is a mnemonic one; only one, two, or three syllables of a phrase consisting of eighteen or twenty or more are written, the rest has to be supplied from memory. . . . very few indeed are the ²Dto-¹mbas who can read a text twice exactly the same. . . . I can only hope that Providence will grant me enough time to enable me to finish the task I have set myself to do.[45]

Even in translation, the proper names are mostly unpronounceable, except to someone like Rock. His position in China was often precarious because of almost continuous political and military turmoil and wildly fluctuating currency. And, as it turned out, he had to do much of the work twice. In 1941 four large volumes, with many photographs, waiting in Shanghai to be printed, were destroyed by the invading Japanese army. In 1944 "twelve years of work" went to the bottom of the Arabian Sea when the ship carrying two large trunks of his papers and photographs was torpedoed. Fortunately he had left in Washington a photostat of his Na Khi encyclopedic dictionary, which included a Na Khi Bön iconography (with brief biographies of all the major spirits), so that work on that complicated book could continue.[46]

The maddening immensity of the task Rock had set himself is conveyed in the following sentence from *The Na-Khi Nāga Cult and Related Ceremonies* (1952):

> It was my intention to give in this Introduction a complete resumé of the literature of the ¹Na-²Khi tribe, but since to do so would add another five hundred pages to this book, I have confined myself to that part which deals with their Naga Cult and other related ceremonies.[47]

Why would Rock, a scholar of compulsive thoroughness and rigorous accuracy, choose to pour his energy into a subject so difficult to grasp and be precise about? He wrote that "the Na-Khi believe that one thinks with

Sign on road to Rock's house in Nguluko, north of Lijiang: "Senic Spot / Former Residence of American Austrian Dr. J. F. Rock / Former Headquarters of American National Geographic Society's Yunnan Expedition." Photograph by Gregory Harvey, 1999.

Wall of stables, interior courtyard of Rock's house in Nguluko. Photograph by Gregory Harvey, 1999.

one's heart."[48] Confucius said something similar in suggesting that one must learn to read the tones of one's own heart in order to govern oneself before attempting to govern others (*Con*, 27–31). A man who had inherited the violent temper of his father, but who had taught himself the patience and endurance of a saint, Rock must have been thinking with his heart when he decided to devote his life to NaKhiology. He wrote in 1952:

> I contend that the translation of the entire ¹Na-²Khi literature, of which the present work is but a small fraction, will be indispensable to the proper comprehension of Bön literature, for I believe that the ¹Na-²Khi religious literature is in its greater part pure Bön. . . . If I live long enough, or if it will be possible to return to ¹Na-²Khi land in the not *too* distant future, the deciphering of the entire ¹Na-²Khi literature, so valuable in the study of Bönism, will still be possible.[49]

Rock's father had wanted him to be a Catholic priest, and Joseph's eventual response was an overwhelming interest in Na Khi religious literature, which led to the publication of some of his most important work in periodicals and books sponsored by Catholic organizations. One aspect of the Na Khi Bön paideuma that appealed to the botanist is the Na Khi reverence for plants and trees. Another of their beliefs that Rock liked is that evil came into the world through the incompetence and dishonesty of individual men, which implies the opposite belief, demonstrated by the extraordinary scope and depth of Rock's accomplishments, that good can come from the efforts of a competent and honest individual. In his study of Bönism the lonely Rock was in touch with something he never definitively articulated, but daily expressed by his actions, the Na Khi confidence in human ability to live in harmony with the natural world, and with one another.

Pound studied intently more than two thousand pages of Rock's published writing, selecting the poetry that "could *not be lost* by translation," and rejecting "effects . . . incapable of being translated,"[50] such as the chicken and animal sacrifices and the inexplicable ability of the dtombas to leap barefooted into bonfires, dip their hands into burning oil, hold a red hot plowshare between their teeth.[51] However, like the shaman's magic, Pound's efforts look effortless. He summarizes the catastrophe of the torpedoed ship in one line, and Rock's courageous perseverance in two:

> Mr Rock still hopes to climb at Mount Kinabalu
> his fragments sunk (20 years)
> 13,455 ft. facing Jesselton, Borneo

> (110/801)

The twenty years is Pound's prediction, quite close, as it happened, of when Canto 110 would appear in print after Rock's 1944 loss. Fragments from 110 were printed in two periodicals in 1963 (Gallup C1896), and the entire text of 110 was printed in 1965 (Gallup A85). Pound read about the sinking of the two trunks in at least four places, but I have not found Mount Kinabalu in Rock's writing or in Sutton's biography, which caused me to believe that Pound corresponded with Rock, and the letters had not yet been identified. Sutton believes not, but I have already found the first letter from Rock to Pound, dated January 3, 1956.[52] Only one year older than Pound, Rock died December 5, 1962, in Hawaii. Kinabalu, the youngest nonvolcanic mountain in the world, is rich in rare birds and plants, including 1,500 kinds of orchids. The natives in Borneo venerate it as the resting place of departed spirits and a dragon's home. The Chinese call it Son San—God's mountain.[53]

Pound quarried the poetry out of Rock, quoting so carefully that we can match dozens of gemlike descriptions and powerful incantatory images, from Canto 98 on, with Rock's words. John Peck and Carroll Terrell have eloquently shown us many of these matches.[54] Summarizing how the passages about the paradisical landscape of Na Khi land beautifully meet other themes in *The Cantos* "would add," as Rock would say, "another five hundred pages to this book." More briefly we can say that Rock's arduous and quixotic labors to bring the Na Khi to world attention succeeded far beyond anyone's dreams. At the entrance to the Old Town of Lijiang, a UNESCO (United Nations Educational Scientific and Cultural Organization) sign, dated "6 December 1997," proclaims that "The World Heritage Committee has inscribed the Old Town of Lijiang on the World Heritage List": "Inscription on this list confirms the exceptional and universal value of a cultural and natural site which requires protection for the benefit of all humanity." Pound's praise is elegantly specific:

> And over Li Chiang, the snow range is turquoise
> Rock's world that he saved us for memory
> > a thin trace in high air

> > > (113/806)

The Old Town of Lijiang survived an earthquake in February 1996. The New Town, built of twentieth-century cement, was leveled, but the Old Town, with its handsome wooden buildings of traditional Na Khi architecture, its cobblestone streets, and its many canals and wooden bridges, largely withstood the shocks. The government now encourages rebuilding in this region with native stone and wood rather than cement.[55]

The New Town, which is swiftly retaking shape with many luxury hotels for visitors, announces on a large billboard at its entrance that the Shangri-La of James Hilton's *Lost Horizon* (1933) was based on this area of "Northwest Yunnan Province." The quotation from the novel used on the billboard is enigmatic: "He liked the serene world that Shangri-La offered him, pacified rather than dominated by its single tremendous idea. . . ."[56] Although each person would probably describe that "single tremendous idea" differently, the billboard is not inaccurate. What no one has yet remarked, as far as I know, is that Hilton's fictional world of Shangri-La was heavily influenced by Joseph Rock's *National Geographic* essays. Hilton hints at his awareness of Rock's explorations of the tribal, border regions of China: "Strolling about Tibet isn't a one man job; it needs an expedition properly fitted out and run by some one who knows at least a word or two of the language."[57] And "He'd been travelling then for some American geographical society, with several colleagues, porters, and so on."[58] Hilton's borrowings from Rock are most obvious in his phrases describing the mountains, "the least explored range in the world," "never been properly surveyed," "rumors . . . about mountains actually higher than Everest."[59] Rock had dramatically titled an essay in 1930, "Seeking the Mountains of Mystery: An Expedition on the China-Tibet Frontier to the Unexplored Amnyi Machen Range, One of Whose Peaks Rivals Everest."[60] To Rock's chagrin, he soon realized that the supposed rival to Everest was forty-five hundred feet less than his first measurements, but he continued to stress that he was exploring unknown territory. His next essay, published a few months later, begins: "Strange as it may seem, hoary old China still holds within its borders vast mountain systems wholly unknown not only to the Western World, but to the Chinese themselves."[61] And "I marveled at the scenery, which I, the first white man ever to stand here, was privileged to see."[62]

The exact location of Shangri-La in the northwest part of Yunnan Province is disputed. Our Na Khi guide, who asked us to call him Michael (his professional name for Western tourists), is named Mu Shing Hong and is a descendant of the Mu chiefs who ruled the tribe for centuries and whose portraits can be found in Rock's *The Ancient Na-Khi*

Kingdom of Southwest China. Michael, in his twenties, unmarried, intelligent and witty, of tireless and disciplined energy, the best guide we have ever met anywhere, said that the name comes from a street in the Old Town of Lijiang, where he grew up, named Shangri, meaning serene, and *La* is Tibetan for mountain pass. Dr. Xuan Ke, the Lijiang conductor of the Na Khi orchestra that hopes to perform in the United States, points to an area some two hundred kilometers northwest of Lijiang, where Diqing is the country seat and where he, Xuan Ke, grew up, as having many more similarities to the descriptions in *Lost Horizon.*[63] Orville

Michael, the guide, in front of Stone Drum at Shih-ku (or Shigu), at the first bend of the Yangtze River. Photograph by Gregory Harvey, 1999.

Schell in *Virtual Tibet* (2000) complains of "Shangri-La Airport" in Zhongdian near Diqing, and an advertising campaign called "Shangri-La Found," as tourism ploys of the government.[64] I have seen no allusion to Shangri-La in either Rock or Pound, though they could hardly have been unaware of Hilton's 1933 book, which became a stupendous best-seller (Pound mentions Hilton's *Good-Bye, Mr. Chips*, 1934, in a letter of that year). However, Goullart's *Forgotten Kingdom*, written twenty-two years after *Lost Horizon*, announces at the end that Likiang is his "Shangri La," and earlier shows that the novel heightened his memories of a lamasery called Shangri Moupo:

> My favourite lamasery, however, was Yuenfoungze or Shangri Moupo gompa. It was the largest and most active lamasery in the Likiang district, and was set halfway up from the plain to the sacred peak of Shangri Moupo, whose 14,000 feet high pyramid dominates the city on the south side. It was very strange that, whilst the great snow peak of Mt. Satseto was only of local significance to the Nakhi, the smaller Shangri Moupo occupied a very prominent place in the Tibetan cosmology, being regarded as one of the sacred peaks of Tibet— the dwelling-place of the gods.[65]

Goullart describes the climb to the lamasery as "arduous" but "like a progress to paradise,"[66] and gives many wonderful details upon arrival, which parallel Hilton's descriptions, though he does not say that they are parallels. The Shangri Moupo lamasery is not mentioned in current guidebooks, and Michael did not know of it, which suggests that it may be one of the many lamaseries destroyed during the Cultural Revolution.

The movie *Lost Horizon* (1937), directed by Frank Capra with script by Robert Riskin, was as successful as the book. Schell skewers it, thus reminding us that efforts at creating a paradise or utopia, even a virtually fictive one, attract not only yearning but suspicions of implausibility:[67]

> Capra's $2-million *Lost Horizon* features a lamasery that looks like something Frank Lloyd Wright might have designed on a bad day for a Mormon golf club. Massive and white, Deco-modern with fountains squirting everywhere, Hollywood's Shangri-La was a curious and implausible pastiche of modernism, Orientalia, and generic fantasy that had precious little to do with the Potala—or anything else Tibetan, for that matter.[68]

This amusing, and abusive, lampoon of Capra's set is undercut by the picture of Potala Palace in Lhasa on the jacket of Schell's book, in

Terrace of multicolored Lijiang stones around a reflecting pool at Mu Mansion, Lijiang. Photograph by Gregory Harvey, 1999.

Fertile countryside near Lijiang. Photograph by Gregory Harvey, 1999.

which Potala in fact does appear "Massive and white. Deco modern" as in the movie. The photograph is copyrighted by China Tourism Press. The Hong Kong *China Daily,* July 3, 1999, reported that the newly and expensively restored Mu Mansion in Old Lijiang is now open to the public. Mindful of Michael's royal ancestry, we asked him to take us to this former residence of the Na Khi kings who had ruled Lijiang for almost five hundred years after leaving Tibet. Michael was as curious as we, as he also was visiting it for the first time. Covering six hundred acres, the many buildings feature the architectural styles of the Na Khi, Tibetan, Bai, and Han peoples, including traditional double-eaved roofs, lionlike stone animals standing at the gateway, and trees (magnolia and willow) more than eight hundred years old. A portrait of Confucius is on the first floor of Wanjuan Tower in the library. Locally Mu Mansion is called the "Forbidden City," like the emperor's palace in Beijing. What struck me as unusual, different, is a square paved with iridescent Lijiang stones and bordered by a large reflecting pool, all of which looks quite "Deco-modern." Whether this square is considered a Tibetan element of the Mu Mansion Michael could not say, but he saw nothing implausible about it. Nor did Michael express any doubts that he is living in Shangri-La.

Pound adheres to the solid reality of Rock's careful, scholarly observations and to precise quotation of Rock's Na Khi translations. Neither Rock, nor Pound even at his most lyrical, exaggerates or misrepresents the paradisical atmosphere of the Lijiang area. The landscape is beauty for the soul, the thirteen peaks of Jade Dragon Snow Mountain; the crested waters of Tiger Leaping Gorge where the Yangtze becomes so narrow that a hunted tiger was able to escape his pursuers by leaping across the turbulent waters to the other bank; the stately forests; the alpine meadows where Na Khi women, in their blue and red dresses and seven stars, dance together with Na Khi men to flute music; Black Dragon Lake (where Michael swam as a child) and its temple

> By the pomegranate water,
>> in the clean air
>>> over Li Chiang
> The firm voice amid pine wood,
>>> many springs are at the foot of
>>>> Hsiang Shan
> By the temple pool, Lung Wang's

the clear discourse
as Jade stream

(112/804)

The "pomegranate water," "Hsiang Shan" (Elephant Mountain), "Lung Wang's" (Dragon King's [temple and pool]), and "Jade stream" are taken from one brief paragraph in Rock's *Ancient Na-Khi Kingdom of Southwest China* (I, 173) or two short notes in "The ²Muan ¹Bpo Ceremony" (65), or both.

Our driver was a Na Khi woman, married and the mother of a young son. She was very beautiful and perhaps a few years older than Michael. He respectfully called her Mrs. Yong and asked us to do the same. We were

Mrs. Yong, the driver (facing camera), relaxing in the Old Town of Lijiang, which does not permit cars. Photograph by Gregory Harvey, 1999.

not told her Na Khi name. Mrs. Yong dressed professionally in slacks and jacket, and was punctilious in all her duties as driver. Michael explained to us that women are always better drivers than men. He did not define "better"—perhaps he meant swifter, more confident, for she barely slowed down to thread the car through a herd of water buffalo in the middle of the road. Na Khi women also manage the money, Michael said, because they are much wiser about money than men. The Na Khi men at their best, when married, care for the children but have time to be scholars, musicians, poets, painters, teachers. Or they may gamble, like our driver's husband, who kept her up all night at the hospital after he was wounded in a fight with other gamblers, as Michael explained to us the following morning. Some observers (not Goullart or Rock or Pound) call the Na Khi culture matriarchal, but this is not so, strictly speaking, because the rulers and warriors have always been male. However there is no question that Na Khi men are proud of their women and can be said to treat them as equals or superiors. Moreover, Michael surprised us by introducing me as a scholar, which we had assumed was a title reserved for men.

The only time Mrs. Yong forgot about her responsibility to us was when we were visiting a monastery, and a small boy threw a pebble at her brand new car, which caused a tiny dent in the fender. Na Khi women are passionate and aggressive, and soon a small village assembled around the rear of the slightly injured car to listen to Mrs. Yong and the attractive mother of the naughty boy hurl insults at each other. Michael, with a chuckle, said admiringly that Na Khi women also excel at invective. After an hour of name calling and curses Mrs. Yong accepted two hundred yuan (about twenty-four dollars) flung at her by the mother of the bad boy, and after ten more minutes of fierce verbal assaults, which protocol apparently required, the incident was over, and everyone serenely departed. Mrs. Yong did not apologize to us, though Michael did.

Michael, who had majored in mathematics at Kunming University, in Kunming, the capital of Yunnan, and who wants to teach mathematics in Lijiang, expressed skepticism about the ceremonial rites of his people. Nevertheless, he fondly recalled how his mother had summoned a dongba to exorcise evil spirits in his mind after he had almost died by accidental drowning. He had nightmares or could not sleep at all until the dongba came to Michael's house and forced the evil spirits to leave. A Na

Khi ceremony involving the spirits of the dead occurs at the lunar New Year, and Michael's father, who works in Shanghai importing German precision instruments for medical work, always returns to Lijiang for this ceremony. Michael shrugged his shoulders and said, "I don't believe these things, but they do work!" Michael took us to visit a dongba at home and asked him to pose for us in ceremonial dress. In the yard of the dongba's house was a much smaller wooden house, a Spirit House, Michael said, for homeless spirits.

A dongba in ceremonial dress of bright red, and wearing the ³K'o, a crown of papier-mâché or leather painted with images of Na Khi deities. Photograph by Gregory Harvey, 1999.

Every Na Khi woman, when dressed formally in the traditional way, used to carry the cosmos on her back, as Pound notes:

> With the sun and moon on her shoulders,
> the star-discs sewn on her coat
> at Li Chiang, the snow range,
> a wide meadow
> and the ²dto-¹mba's face (exorcist's)
> muy simpático
> by the waters of Stone Drum,
> the two aces
> Mint grows at the foot of the Snow Range
> the first moon is the tiger's,
> Pheasant calls out of bracken
>
> (101/746)

The sun and moon are no longer worn, as Goullart wrote in 1955, so Pound was thinking of the photograph taken by Rock in the 1920s. The sun and moon simply were not restored after several political upheavals forbidding native dress. However, the seven stars, intricately made of multiple cloth disks, have returned and appear on the back at the waist between the upper part of the cape, a band of indigo representing the night sky, and the lower part, a peplum of creamy silk or sheepskin symbolizing the light of day.[69]

Pound's lines about Stone Drum commemorate Na Khi men, who, though skilled at living peaceably with everyone, are fine warriors when forced into it. The town of Shih-Ku or Shigu, which means "stone drum," sits at the first bend of the Yangtze River. A large marble tablet shaped like a drum commemorates a sixteenth-century Na Khi victory over a Tibetan army. Michael translated the inscription for us. The beginning of the third part, titled "The Moon on the West River," chimes with Pound's lines:

> The chiefs leading a million brave soldiers, their majestic air like that of a tiger and of a plumed bird bent on exterminating, they struck and roared like thunder.[70]

Michael proudly posed, representing the victorious "ace," in front of the Stone Drum (see page 233).

Mrs. Yong's passion and fierceness in defending her car gives credence to the story of "The Romance of ¹K'a-²Mä-¹Gyu-³Mi-²Gkyi," hereafter referred to as Ka. Rock says that every young person knows the story of

PLATE 76. — NA-KHI WOMEN OF THE VILLAGE OF NV-LV-K'O

"With the sun and moon on her shoulders, / the star-disks sewn on her coat" (101/746). Photograph by Joseph Rock, 1924, in Ngulukö.

Two Na khi women in Lijiang. Photograph by Gregory Harvey, 1999.

Ka.[71] She is pregnant, and the parents of her lover reject her. Her own parents insist that she marry a man she does not love. She sends many loving pleas to her lover, saying that they belong together "like the turquoise and coral, like the oak and pine."[72] He invents excuses for refusing to meet her. She repeatedly fails to hang herself, for the spirits of nature do not encourage her. Finally she succeeds and eventually her lover finds her body in the mountains. Her body is dead but her soul can speak to him, and she tells him of her love for him and how he is to bury her body. He covets her jewels, and tries to take them, and she puts a rope around his neck. Rock describes a double ending:

> In our manuscript, the story continues. The rope which she puts around his neck only gives him illness; when he arrives home he is unable to move. He sends for a ²Llò-¹bbu, or sorcerer, who casts his horoscope. A dto-mba then performs the ²Har-²la-¹llö ceremony, and, after all the demons of suicide have been propiated, he regains his health. In the actual story as related by the Na-khi, she winds the rope with which she had hanged herself around his neck and he hangs himself on a bamboo.[73]

Michael said that of course suicide is against the law and denied that young people would think of such a fatal step now. The three of us took a chairlift up toward Mt. Satseto, near, according to the guidebook, "Love Suicide Hill." From the chairlift we looked down on many clumps of "the Artemisia so common in Li-chiang."[74] To Rock it was a herb called *Artemis a scoparia*, to Pound a reminder of a favorite goddess, "the wood-queen, Artemis" (91/632), a moon goddess, protector and hunter of wild animals, strict dispenser of justice, and one who holds beauty in her mind.

> The purifications
>   are snow, rain, artemisia,
>   also dew, oak and the juniper
>
>   (110/798)

In his account of the ²Muan ¹Bpö ceremony, Rock translates:

> The clean ²bbue (*Artemisia*) is searched for at the nine cross roads to chase the ³ch'ou. . . . Above the villages of the land, there, before any grass has sprouted, the ²bbue with the white roots and dark green foliage is born first, we use it to chase the ³ch'ou.
>   . . . the ²bbue was born before all other herbs, we use the ²bbue to lead the ²nder (sins) (away).[75]

After the chairlift we climbed through well-kept woodlands, for the Na Khi treat all trees with respect, to a large meadow with horses looking exactly

Woodland on the climb up Jade Dragon Snow Mountain (or Mt. Sateso).
Photograph by Gregory Harvey, 1999.

Alpine meadow halfway up Jade Dragon Snow Mountain. Photograph by
Gregory Harvey, 1999.

as in Rock's photographs. (Two tourist names for the Lijiang area are "Rooftop of the World" and "Land of Horses.") We continued climbing until we came to another alpine meadow where wooden platforms had been built for singing and dancing by several different minority groups. The Na Khi platform was first, and the dancers welcomed us with smiles and gestures to dance with them. We were the only Americans that day, and as the other visitors were Chinese families, some of whom asked to be photographed with us, we concluded that this excursion is regarded as simply a pleasant hike in a lovely place and a wholesome experience for the children. The tragic suicides of the past are not featured in any way, except by the name of the "hill" in English guidebooks.

Both Goullart and Rock placed much of the blame for the many suicides during their time on the dtombas who performed the ²Har-²la-¹llü, "the ceremony *par excellence* for the propitiation of these suicides":

> It all sounds most romantic and lovers, high-strung and credulous, will take that fatal step in the belief that they will live for ever young, in perfect happiness roaming with the wind and clouds, in the perpetual embrace of love, never to be reborn, never to be sent to an infernal region, but to live inseparably to the full in a state of eternal youth. Such is the picture painted by the dto-mbas in their book pertaining to the ²Har-²la-¹llü ceremony.[76]

Scene from ²Har-²la-¹llü ³k'ö ceremony. Photograph by Rock in his *Na-Khi Naga Cult*, 1952, Plate LIII.

Na Khi flute player and a group of young people in brightly colored Na Khi native dress dancing on a wooden platform in an alpine meadow halfway up Jade Dragon Snow Mountain. Photographs by Gregory Harvey, 1999.

Pound's statement that the dtomba performing the ceremony has a very sympathetic face may be edged with irony, for the dtombas used to make their living mainly from these ceremonies.

In Pound's unpublished parts of the *Drafts & Fragments* he gives many more details from the romance of Ka than appear in Canto 110, so there is no doubt that he read Rock's translation and commentary intently, and would have noted that Rock says that this ceremony, which is translated "Wind sway perform," is not necessarily for a suicide:

> Wind sway perform. The name has reference to the souls of departed who died by their own hands, *or who died unattended.* The Na Khi believe that it is imperative for someone to be present at the death of a person, for if anyone dies unattended, the soul becomes a roving spirit; such souls become the constant companions of the wind and the wind demons, cause hail-storms, illness, etc.[77]

The italics and underlining are mine, for I offer a different reading than the prevalent, dark interpretation of Pound's use of the story of Ka. Rock provides ample permission for Pound to use the wind-sway ceremony as he wishes, and suicide, I will argue, is not the focus, not even obliquely, that Pound chose. Canto 110 is the most polished of the final group, and by the final draft Pound had omitted all references to Ka, leaving the emphasis on the exotic Na Khi words for the ceremony of "Wind sway perform." For the poet the Na Khi ceremonies become metaphors for "thinking with the heart" about the spirits of departed or absent friends—"why not spirits?" (113/806). If there are hidden implications in the final cantos, they do not, I conclude, concern confession of a secret desire to commit suicide, but rather allude to the identity of the friends to whom he is paying tribute in his poem so that their spirits will not be troubled in this world or go into the next world *unattended* or unaccompanied by his love. These friends include, but are not limited to, Wyndham Lewis, 1957; Ernest Hemingway, 1961; H.D., 1961; e. e. cummings, 1962; Joseph Rock, 1962; William Carlos Williams, 1963; T. S. Eliot, 1965. The poem provides adequate clues to identify them, but what I wish to emphasize here is the elegiac tone of the final *Drafts & Fragments,* which is in the tradition of this prescription by a fourth-century Confucian scholar:

> In the funeral rites one adorns the dead as though they were still living and sends them to the grave with symbolic life. Entertained in life the dead were also entertained in the afterlife with radiating joy.[78]

From two funeral ceremonies described by Rock, "The ¹D'a ³Nv

Funeral Ceremony" and "The ²Zhi ³mä Funeral Ceremony,"⁷⁹ Pound
assembled a Na Khi blessing for the end of Canto 101 in *Thrones:*

> he perceived it:
> > The green spur, the white meadow
> > "May their pond be full;
> > The son have his father's arm
> > > and good hearing;
> > (noun graph upright; adjective sideways)
> > "His horse's mane flowing
> > > His body and soul are at peace."
>
> > > > > > (101/746–47)

The first fifteen lines of the final *Drafts & Fragments* offer blessings
from Pound's own repertoire. Serene beauty, punning exultance, playful
energy, and the healing powers of water "crest" with "panache":

> 1   Thy quiet house
> > The crozier's curve runs in the wall,
> > The harl, feather-white, as a dolphin on sea-brink
>
> > I am all for Verkehr without tyranny
> 5   —wake exultant
> > > > in caracole
> > Hast'ou seen boat's wake on sea-wall
> > > > > how crests it?
> > What panache?
> 10   paw-flap, wave-tap,
> > > > that is gaiety,
> > Toba Sojo,
> > > > toward limpidity,
> > > > > that is exultance,
> 15   here the crest runs on wall
>
> > > > > > (110/797)

So sublime are these opening lines, so filled with "radiating joy," that
we can only echo the question: "What panache?" What is the crest of the
wake of a lifetime? Gaiety, limpidity, exultance. "The crozier's curve" "in
the wall" of the "quiet house" (the cathedral of Torcello, as the canto later
says) resembles wave crests—"Hast'ou seen boat's wake on sea-wall /
how crests it?" The leaping dolphin also crests on the white wave crests.
The "boat's wake" matches the punning "wake exultant / in caracole,"
which yields another curve, a half-turn by cavalry or a Spanish dancer.
And the "paw-flap, wave-tap" of a small creature playing in the water also
creates a crest, a tiny one, but achieved in "gaiety" by the irresistible rab-

bits in the Kōzanji (High-mountain Temple) scrolls created by Toba Sojo (1063–1140) for the Buddhist monks on Mount Hiei near Kyoto. Pound wrote H.D., in February 1953, on a postcard of a section of the scrolls: "as Uncl Wm [Yeats] remarked: no picture containing rabbit has ever remained unsold." The scrolls, masterpieces in the "limpidity" of their drawing and narrative, a comic, irreverent parody of temple life, display "panache" like the leaping dolphin, running crozier's curve, turning caracole, and cresting waves.

The oldest meaning of "panache" is crest or plume of feathers, and it is the last word of *Cyrano de Bergerac*. Pound read Rostand's play in French class and imitated its poet-hero, William Carlos Williams recalled, by wearing a plumed feather in his hat for the entire academic year. Brian Hooker for his American translation (1923) chose "My white plume" as Cyrano's last words, but Anthony Burgess restored "panache" as the final word (1984) because it has no equivalent in English. It carries a symbolic weight, which "white plume" does not, of high spirits, courage against overwhelming odds, identifying crest, and "panache" is the one crown the dying Cyrano says he can take with him to heaven to offer his salute to God. Now we can see that cavalry "in caracole" may be wearing white plumes, or the dancer an ivory comb as her crest (a hidden tribute to Raquel Hoheb Williams).

"Harl, feather-white," hides another curve, a fish hook, for it is an artificial fly made from the barb of a feather. In the marble Byzantine reliefs in the Torcello basilica are two white peacocks, symbols of immortality, with perfect crest feathers for a "harl." Within the exquisite chimings of these opening lines is the white-haired poet meditating in the ancient church, itself a frail and evocative remnant of splendor. Blessed by the "crozier's curve," the old poet remembers beauty and gaiety and exultance, and sees the "harl, feather-white, as a dolphin on sea-brink." This is a stunning metaphysical conceit. Signifier of Neo-Platonism and its belief in Divine Unity, "a dolphin on sea-brink" also signals a future voyage from this world to another. The dolphin, with its extraordinary intelligence, keenness of vision and hearing, love of music, swiftness, playfulness, and kindness to humankind, is the lure or "harl" to lift the poet's mind and soul to "wake exultant" into thoughts of eternity. The oldest object in the cathedral is a small, marble tabernacle on the wall, a little spirit house, which has two dolphins and a scallop shell over its door, and at its base curving waves.

After these joyful opening lines, if Pound had wanted to hint of suicide, he would have used Ka's name instead of the ceremony's name and would not have chosen Dante's line for the murdered Paolo and Francesca, but lines for lovers like Romeo and Juliet, or Cleopatra, who did commit suicide. The wind links the Occident with the Orient, Dante's *che paion' si al vent'* (who seem so on the wind) with the Na Khi "wind sway," and the aural stress on "paion" (seem) is apt for the transition to the unusual questions now to be asked.

<pre>
15   here the crest runs on wall
         che paion' si al vent'
                        ²Har-²la-¹llü ³k'ö
         of the wind sway,
         The nine fates and the seven,
20   and the black tree was born dumb,
         The water is blue and not turquoise
         When the stag drinks at the salt spring
                        and sheep come down with the gentian sprout,
         can you see with eyes of coral or turquoise
25   or walk with the oak's root?

         Yellow iris in that river bed
                        yüeh⁴·⁵
                        ming²
                        mo⁴·⁵
30   hsien¹
                        p'eng²

         Quercus on Mt Sumeru
                  can'st'ou see with the eyes of turquoise?
                  heaven   earth
35   in the center
                              is
                           juniper
         The purifications
                  are snow, rain, artemisia
40   also dew, oak and juniper

         And in thy mind beauty, O Artemis,
                  as of mountain lakes in the dawn,
         Foam and silk are thy fingers,
                        Kuanon
</pre>

(110/797–98)

Two units of nine lines each describe two Na Khi ceremonial rites (17–25 and 32–40). In the middle is one line of English and five Chinese sounds explaining why the two ceremonies are needed. Before and after the two ceremonies are lines of delicate modulation showing musical themes meeting each other.

The only ²Har-²la-¹llü ³k'ö ceremony available to Pound was Ka's romance, though Rock makes clear there are many, many others he did not have time to transcribe. Indeed, over two hundred ²Har-²la-¹llü ³k'ö manuscripts are named in Rock's "Classified List" published three years after his death,[80] which are not all that exist. Each ceremony contains some of the same ritual elements but is regarded as unique. Rock also states that he is giving only part of the ceremony for Ka.[81] It is precious not only because it is the only ²Har-²la-¹llü ³k'ö that Rock published but also because it was done before World War II when the priests who best understood the pictographs were still alive.

For the final draft of 110 Pound retained these elements: the name of "wind sway perform" in its Na Khi form; the epithets for male and female (nine fates and seven fates, both "endearing names,"[82] says Rock); the innocence of nature—"the black tree was born dumb (was born without a mouth) . . . did not invite her (did not say)"; the autumn landscape ("the stag" and "the gentian sprout," last flower of the autumn); and, with insistent repetition, the questions: "can you see with eyes of coral or turquoise? / or walk with the oak's root?" The questions posed in the first ceremony are echoed in the second ("can'st'ou see with the eyes of turquoise?") with a tenderness matched by the question in the first fifteen lines ("Hast'ou seen boat's wake. . . ?"). Coral and turquoise are in Pound's youth, and in his "own myth" in Canto 2, written long before he knew of Joseph Rock, in which Daphne is turned not into a laurel tree but into coral (2/9). Turquoise holds the memory not only of mountain ranges and lakes but of the one turquoise earring Ezra wore as a fledging poet, which impressed his girlfriends, but alarmed the parents. There was also a coral necklace given by Dorothy Pound to Hilda Aldington when Perdita was born.

The questions about coral and turquoise and oak's root are transformed into an unexpected answer in the next line: "Yellow iris in that river bed." There is a verb in all the typescripts: "Yellow iris rise in that river bed." There is no evidence that Pound chose to omit "rise"; the deletion is a printer's or an editor's error.[83] The meaning comes through all the same. In the yellow iris resides the spirit of Kakitsubata (another "Ka"), a lady beloved of a poet who in the past had thought of her when he passed the iris marsh, so that now, in Pound's words from his introductory note to the play *Kakitsubata,* "the flowers are the thoughts or the body of her spirit." In the closing note to the play Pound writes:

> The spirit manifests itself in that particular iris marsh because Narihira in passing that place centuries before had thought of her. . . .
> The Muses were "the Daughters of Memory." It is by memory that this spirit appears, she is able or "bound" because of the passing thought of these iris. . . . she demonstrates the "immortality of the soul" or the "permanence or endurance of the individual personality" by her apparition.[84]

The spirit of the yellow iris is one answer to the Na Khi question: "can you see with eyes of coral or turquoise / or walk with the oak's root?" The body dies but the soul or spirit lives on, if only in memory, in thought, in a poem, or in some other special place or way, as in the iris rising "in that river bed."

After the yellow iris, a vertical arrangement of the sounds of five Chinese characters, without the ideograms to delimit their meaning, offers the reason for pondering the Na Khi questions. Using *Mathews' Chinese English Dictionary* and thinking with the heart, as the Na Khi do, one can see in the multiplicity of probabilities a range of emotions from elation to despair. The cluster of sounds may refer either to friends or reputation, and either may be a stream flowing, fresh as flowers, or as the whirling of dust. A friend (*p'eng*[2]) may be immortal, whisked away, former, deceased (*hsien*[2]) or in death tranquil or distressed (*mo*[4-5]) or of bright intelligence, again in death, in sleep, distant, intoxicated (*ming*[2]) in a place of moonlight, trees, and fast-flowing steam (*yuch*[4-5]). And so forth. The possibilities, though diverse and numerous, are finite within the context of the poem. The tones of the heart are sometimes hard to read, and Pound may have felt that multiplicity and uncertainty of meaning, even contradictory meanings, in this heart's field of five sounds would be more precise than the didactic simplicity of the way he must teach his readers Chinese. However, as there are uncertainties enough in understanding *The Cantos,* we are fortunate that Pound's grandson, Walter de Rachewiltz, asked his grandfather what the sounds meant and recorded the answer in the margin of a copy of *The Cantos* at Brunnenburg, and Hugh Kenner published it: "The brightness of the moon . . . there are no former friends."[85] This is the point of rest in the center of swirling, conflicting emotions: The moon is bright, my old friends are gone.

Canto 110 focuses not on the manner of death or ways of dying, but on ways of responding to the death of a loved one and to the possibilities of life after death, both of which Pound desires to accept without fear ("Arnaut"/T. S. Eliot: "I am afraid of the life after death"—29/145). Pound's friends died or will die "unattended" by himself, and for his own rightness of spirit, Canto 110 seeks to pay joyful and solemn tribute to their spirits, to their life after death in his memory, and in his poem. I can find no convincing way to see the diverse landscapes of Canto 110 as a "suicide night world" or as an "occulted" confession of "the imminent loss of his vision to a kind of suicide," as in John Peck's interpretation,[86] or as Pound's buried confession of a "suicide pact" with a sweetheart from whom he must otherwise be separated.[87]

Thoughts of suicide are denied to no one, least of all Pound, who in 1920 wrote "E.P. Ode pour l'élection de son sépulchre" (*P*, 185), and who told Desmond O'Grady in the early 1960s that he would not take an apartment in Rome on a high floor because "I might jump off."[88] Certainly Pound is aware that the romance of Ka is a suicide story, just as he knows that Paolo and Francesca were murdered, but his poem resists efforts to force from him a confession of thoughts of suicide. The rhyme emphasized in "che paion' si al vent'" and "²Har-²la-¹llü ³k'ö / of the wind sway" is *wind*. In probably the first elegy he wrote, "For E. McC,"[89] Pound says that "his dead friend is 'Gone where the grey winds call to you / . . . / Gone as a gust of breath'" (*A Lume Spento*, 61; *CEP*, 39). In another early poem, "Salve O Pontifex!" Pound writes of "the magian wind that is the voice of Prosephone" (*A Lume Spento*, 64; *CEP*, 42). In the final cantos Pound is reaching beyond the awareness of death, which Persephone brings, to an awareness of the hope of rebirth, which Persephone also brings. And "the wind also is of the process" (74/445). "The wind is part of the process" (74/455).

To make real and lasting his commitment to commemorating his friends, Pound completes the rites with the oldest and best understood Na Khi ceremony, the Propitiation of Heaven (²Muan ¹Bpö), in which "Quercus on Mt Sumeru" are the two oak trees "heaven" and "earth" on the holy mountain, and "in the center / is / juniper," the deity or God. Also part of "The purifications / are snow, rain, artemisia, / also dew, oak and the juniper." Rock says the ceremony is essential to the Na Khi because they believe that "if ²Muan ¹bpö is not performed, all that which we accomplished is not real; if ²Muan ¹bpö is not performed, we will not attain perfection like others."⁹⁰ Without this ceremony, "no reality" (112/804).

Pound risks still another exploration of the unknown. "Why not spirits?" (113/806). "That the universe is alive" (94/657), and we are always part of it, "That the body is inside the soul" (113/808), the soul is outside the body and immortal, means that "Soul melts into air, / anima into aura, Serenitas" (111/803). The celestial themes become prominent in *Section: Rock-Drill, 85–95* (1955), are developed further in *Thrones, 96–109* (1959), and cohere in *Drafts & Fragments of CX–CXVII* (1969), but they return to thoughts begun in youth. In *The Spirit of Romance* (1910) Pound writes of "our kinship to the vital universe, to the tree and the living rock":

> We have about us the universe of fluid force, and below us the germinal universe of wood alive, of stone alive. Man is—the sensitive physical part of him— a mechanism, for the purpose of our further discussion a mechanism rather like an electric appliance, switches, wires, etc. (90)

How magnificently, as Pound matured as a poet, did this idea grow and enlarge his universe so that he could recognize the kinship of his ideas with those of the Na Khi. In *Thrones:*

> and there is
>   no glow such as of pine-needles burning
> Without ²muan   ¹bpo
>   no reality
> Wind over snow-slope   agitante
>   nos otros
>   calescimus
> Against jade
>   calescimus,
>   and the jade weathers dust-swirl.
>
>   (104/759)

The phrase "agitante calescimus" is quoted, or misquoted, in *Rock-Drill* as "agitante calescemus" (93/648). It comes from the beginning of book VI of Ovid's *Fastii:*

est deus in nobis; agitante calescimus illo:
  impetus hic sacrae semina mentis habet.

[There is a god within us. It is when he stirs us that we glow.
It is his impulse that sows the seeds of inspiration.][91]

In his "Quotations from Richard of St. Victor," selected and translated in
1956, Pound makes explicit the connection in his mind between Ovid's
statement and one by Richard St. Victor:

Ignis quidquid in nobis est.
There is a certain fire within us.

  OVID: . . . est Deus in nobis, agitante calescemus illo.

(*SP,* 72)

From the beginning Pound had believed in a sacred order and in "a cer-
tain fire within us." He had always been "full of flames and voices" (7/27).
From the beginning he had regarded the universe with awe, and his amaze-
ment at the manifestations of divine order in the natural world, from the
veins of an oak leaf to the movements of the stars, had increased each year
of his life. He had written as early as 1910, "The keenly intellectual mysti-
cism of Richard of St. Victor fascinates me" (*SR,* 22), and in 1912, in "Psy-
chology and Troubadours," Pound cites his "Splendours of Paradise":

  Richard St. Victor has left us one very beautiful passage on the Splendours
  of Paradise.
  They are (he says) ineffable and innumerable and no man having beheld
  them can fittingly narrate them or even remember them exactly. Nevertheless
  by naming over all the most beautiful things we know we may draw back upon
  the mind some vestige of the heavenly splendour.[92]

A year later Pound again paraphrases, but without the word "splen-
dour," thereby unintentionally obscuring one of the sources for his later
significant use of that word in Canto 116 and in Heracles' statement
in *The Women of Trachis* (1956): "WHAT SPLENDOUR! IT ALL
COHERES!"

  Richard of St. Victor, who was half a new-Platonist, tells us that by naming
  over all the beautiful things we can think of, we may draw back upon our
  minds some vestige of the unrememberable beauties of paradise. If we are not
  given to mystical devotions we may suspect that the function of poetry is, in
  part, to draw back upon our mind a paradise, if you like, or equally, one's less
  detestable hours and the outrageous hopes of one's youth.[93]

Plotinus chooses a Greek word meaning "splendour" to describe the
primary Intellect, and he also describes those who do not have it:

There are those that have not attained to see. The soul has not come to know the splendour There; it has not felt and clutched to itself that love-passion of vision known to the lover come to rest where he loves.[94]

The glow of the burning pine needles and the "Wind over snow-slope agitante / nos otros / calescimus" in Na Khi land Pound interpreted as signs of the divine intelligence, as like the god within us. Not only Ovid and Richard of St. Victor are quoted to support this belief, but Pound also connects Plotinus to the glow of the pine needles in the later cantos. Plotinus, the first Neoplatonist and a philosopher of light, was a major teacher and mentor of Pound's youth, as shown by a sonnet in Pound's first book, *A Lume Spento* (1908):

PLOTINUS

As one that would draw through the node of things,
    Back-sweeping to the vortex of the cone,
    Cloistered about with memories, alone
In chaos, while the waiting silence sings:

Oblivate of cycles' wanderings
    I was an atom on creation's throne
    And knew all nothing but my unconquered own.
God! Should I be the hand upon the strings?!

But I was lonely as a lonely child.
I cried amid the void and heard no cry,
And then for utter loneliness, made I
New thoughts as crescent images of *me*.
And with them was my essence reconciled
While fear went forth from mine eternity.

"Lonely as a lonely child," Pound was comforted by Plotinus. Fifteen years later in another time of great need, Plotinus protects the poet, saving him, as they struggle together through a terrifying hell.

Pound's depiction of a contemporary hell is preceded, at the end of Canto 13, by an unusually lyrical quotation from Confucius about moral development, a quotation echoed decades later in the draft of Canto 115 published in *Agenda*:[95]

And Kung said, "Without character you will
    be unable to play on that instrument
Or to execute the music fit for the Odes.
The blossoms of the apricot

> blow from the east to the west,
> And I have tried to keep them from falling."

(13/60)

In the heaviest contrast possible, Pound's "hell cantos" open in a *luogo d'ogni luce muto,* a Dantesque place where all light is muted and men have lost "the good of the intellect" (*SR,* 129), a hell where the violent against self or others or God, and the brutish flatterers, hypocrites, thieves, evil counselors, etc., in the seventh and eighth circles of Dante's *Inferno* are reassigned their obscenely grotesque positions as the war "politicians," "profiteers," "perverters of language" "liars," and so on, of the 1914–18 war and its aftermath. This modern hell is inhabited by those who betrayed the sacred selfhood of the soldiers who "fought in any case" (*P,* 187). These betrayers are "the cowardly inciters to violence":

> the pusillanimous, raging;
> plunging jewels in mud,
> and howling to find them unstained

(14/62)

Eliot was only half right in seeing this hell as a place for "others" because the poet and his guide, Plotinus, are not merely observing hell, as Dante and Virgil did, but are themselves dangerously trapped, immersed in it:

> the welsh of mud gripped one, no hand-rail,
> the bog-suck like a whirl-pool

(15/66)

Reading the canto from which these lines are taken, one gradually realizes that the hell inhabited by the modern provocateurs of war is the same environment as the muddy trenches of the Great War. Poetic justice! The ordeal of the perilous escape of Plotinus and the poet transfers one's feelings to the ordeal of the soldiers engulfed by mud contaminated with the stench of slaughter and poison gas. The dreadful conditions, as Pound describes them, of the surreal mud are completely confirmed by a recent book, *Passchendaele,* about the Third Battle of Ypres, which ended on November 4, 1917.[96]

Plotinus, who holds the shield of Athena with the head of the Medusa on it, tells the poet, "Close the pores of your feet!" and "Keep your eyes on the mirror":

> Prayed we to the Medusa,
> petrifying the soil by the shield,

Holding it downward
      he hardened the track
Inch before us, by inch,
      the matter resisting

                                (15/66)

Pound's description, though conveying the sensory and psychic terror, takes its power from his refusal to describe directly the worst part, the shattered bodies and fragments of bodies in the mud. One way he does this is to show that the Medusa herself is reluctant to face this unspeakably terrible mud:

The heads rose from the shield,
      hissing, held downwards.
Devouring maggots,
      the face only half potent.

                                (15/66)

The theme of the difficult ascent, "the path wide as a hair" (93/652), to be found in Plotinus' *Enneads* and in Rock's accounts of his travels and in many places in *The Cantos*,[97] is here, as always, the way to salvation. Though the dangers presented are physical, they are also psychological and moral:

The serpents' tongues
      grazing the swill top,
Hammering the souse into hardness,
      the narrow rast,
Half the width of a sword's edge.
      By this through the dern evil,
now sinking, now clinging,
      Holding the unsinkable shield.

                                (15/66)

Afterward, "Plotinus gone," recovery is slow and agonizing for the poet, as it was for countless other survivors of the war: "Oblivion, / forget how long, / sleep, fainting nausea." And "Panting like a sick dog, staggered, / Bathed in alkali, and in acid." And "Swollen-eyed, rested, / lids sinking, darkness unconscious" (15/66–67).

The suffering continues in the next canto through changes of landscape, gradually modulating to the diverse voices and stories of the soldiers. The tone becomes cautious, matter-of-fact, sometimes grimly humorous, in this anthology of the absurdities, stupidities, and inhumane desecrations of the war. It is Richard Aldington who was put "in a trench

/ dug through corpses / With a lot of kids of sixteen, / Howling and crying for their mamas, / And he sent a chit back to his major: / I can hold out for ten minutes / With my sergeant and a machine-gun. / And they rebuked him for levity" (16/71). The hell/war cantos end quietly with the stoic, uninflected talk of soldiers on leave in London waiting to go to the front: "That they wouldn't be under Haig; / and that the advance was beginning" (16/75). No other single poem, including Pound's own *Mauberley*, offers such a range of experiences from the Great War, including the revolution in Russia, as Cantos 14 to 16, or is so humanely balanced between the extremes of rage at the needless loss of life and compassion for the soldiers who were ordered to their deaths, as if they were *only* cannon fodder, by generals who never visited the battlefields or the hospitals.

Of the survivors who never fully recovered from this war, Ezra Pound was one, for he vicariously shared the terror on the battlefields, grieved for the deaths and painful injuries, and observed the soldiers who "came home, home to a lie, / home to many deceits, / home to old lies and new infamy" (*P*, 188). Cantos 14 to 16 were written in Italy and Paris in 1922 and 1923 with painful deliberation after much listening and reading. They bear witness to profound psychic injuries.

Pound believed that it is the poet's responsibility to describe hell, which is not "funny," not "something to be joked about," but he also believed that the poet must avoid "hell obsession,"[98] must not concentrate on the absence of light. After the hell cantos, Pound never again tried to compose a whole linguistic reality out of the material reality of the mass destruction caused by modern war.[99] Never again did he call on the Medusa for help because like Ovid's Perseus (whose "delicacy of spirit" Italo Calvino commends),[100] Pound was aware of the Medusa's fragility. In the mirror the poet had seen that her face was "only half potent" (15/66) against the twentieth-century hell of the mass grave.

To speak more directly, if the Medusa is "only half potent" in facing the twentieth-century mass grave, how much more fragile are sentient human beings. John Keegan in *The Face of Battle* says that psychiatric breakdown was not even recognized during the first two years of World War I, and men were executed for "cowardice" and "desertion" instead of being treated for what the World War II physicians called "combat exhaustion." During the last two years of the 1914–18 war doctors could not avoid acknowledging "the multitude of 'hysterical conversion symptoms' (by which men lose the use of limbs, speech or sight rather than demonstrate straightforward displays of anxiety)," so they invented "the notion of 'shellshock' and treated the soldiers so affected in what were called N.Y.D.N. (Not Yet Diagnosed, Nervous) hospitals."[101] But many psychic injuries were never treated.

Hilton's hero, Conway, in *Lost Horizon* tells the High Lama in Shangri-La, "You can label me '1914–18.'" An English acquaintance, wondering about Conway's "veracity or his sanity," remarks that "people said he was a good deal changed by it [the war]." Conway's friend Rutherford replies, "There's no denying the fact. You can't subject a mere boy to three years of intense physical and emotional stress without tearing something to tatters. People would say, I suppose, that he came through without a scratch. But the scratches were there—on the inside."[102] In the late 1920s Yeats worried that Ezra's continued empathy for and active help to war-shocked veterans was harming him. Other friends, such as Joyce and Hemingway, expressed dismay in the 1930s at having to listen to Pound's obsessional ideas about how to achieve the economic reforms that would prevent a future cataclysm. Although these friends recognized that he was disturbed, they did not know how to help him, and besides, Pound continued to function much of the time with an appearance of vigorous and productive energy that sustained many other persons. But he had not recovered from the first war when the second exploded, and he went to pieces and lost his center:

> That I lost my center
> 　　　　fighting the world.
> The dreams clash
> 　　　　　　and are shattered
>
> 　　　　　　　　　　　　　　　　(822)

Pound's concept of centering comes not only from Confucius, and from Dante, who "believed in the 'melody which most in-centres the soul'" (*LE,* 442), but also from Plotinus, who said that striving to bring back the god in oneself to the divine in the universe places one at the center of oneself:[103]

Every soul that knows its history is aware, also, that its movement, unthwarted, is not that of an outgoing line; its natural course may be likened to that in which a circle turns not upon some external but on its own centre, the point to which it owes its rise. The soul's movement will be about its source, to this it will hold, poised intent towards that unity to which all souls should move and the divine soul always move, divine in virtue of that movement . . . . The soul is not a circle in the sense of the geometric figure but in that its primal nature (wholeness) is within it and about it, that it owes its origin to what is whole, and that it will be still more entire when severed from body. . . . [We] hold through our own centre to the centre of all the centres, just as the centres of the great circles of a sphere coincide with that of the sphere to which all belong. Thus we are secure.[104]

The return of Plotinus to Pound, or the return of Pound to Plotinus, who has not been seen or heard for eighty-three cantos since the perilous escape from the muddy hell of Canto 15, occurs at the same time as Pound's discovery of Goullart and Rock and the Na Khi landscape of paradise, the same year he translated Richard of St. Victor. What is new in Pound's thought after translating Richard in 1956 is acceptance not only of Ovid's statement that God is in us—*est deus in nobis* (98/705)—but also belief in Richard's statement that the human mind, the rational spirit, can be transformed by the divine Spirit of Love into its very likeness. This new acceptance enabled him to emphasize a related concept from Plotinus, who returns in Canto 98, the same canto affirming "est deus in nobis" and introducing the central ceremony of the Na Khi:

> Without ²muan ¹bpo . . . but I anticipate.
> There is no substitute for a lifetime.
>
> (98/711)

Pound later wrote to T. S. Eliot saying that Canto 98 marked an essential change: "But with no nerves left, broken mind, CAN I repair some of the harm I have done simple people? . . . my MONSTrous vanity, resisting up to Canto 98."[105]

The reappearance of Plotinus at first seems indeterminate, but he becomes a constant presence. The poet is slowly feeling his way forward to the full import of something wonderful and basically inexpressible:

> Anselm: that some is incarnate awareness,
>   thus trinitas; some remains spiritus.
> "The body is inside." Thus Plotinus,
> But Gemisto: "Are Gods by hilaritas";
>   and their speed in communication.
>   et in nebulas simiglianza,
>   χαθ' ὁμοίωσιν Deorum
>
> (98/705)

Canto 98 was published first in Italy in September 1958. Within the month the poet went to Torcello. The importance of the return of Plotinus is not clear yet, but is emphasized by repetition. In the second appearance of Plotinus in Canto 98, a key word is added, "soul":

> A soul, said Plotinus, the body inside it.
> "By Hilaritas," said Gemisto, "by hilaritas: gods;
>   and by speed in communication.
> Anselm cut some of the cackle, and relapsed for sake of
>   tranquillity.
>
>   (98/710)

Plotinus has reappeared in the company of Anselm and Gemisto, and a host of other worthies in other lines.

St. Anselm (ca. 1034–1109) is honored in succeeding cantos for his defense of democratic freedoms, his logic concerning the compatibility of faith and reason, and his rationality in discussing the Mysterium. Georgius Gemisthus Plethon (1355?–1450?), the Greek-Byzantine Neoplatonist philosopher, is often praised by Pound because under his influence Cosimo de Medici established the Platonic Academy in Florence for the translation and discussion of the rediscovered Greek manuscripts and because Gemisto's "gods come from Neptune, so that there is a single source of being, aquatic (udor, Thales etc. as you like)" for the ocean of the mind from which flows, in Neoplatonic terms, the light of the intellect (*GK*, 224). Sigismundo Malatesta understood that Gemisto's reverence for the qualities of water influenced Agostino di Duccio and his helpers in sculpting the beautiful bas reliefs in the Tempio at Rimini (83/548: "HUDOR et Pax / Gemisto stemmed all from Neptune / hence the Rimini bas reliefs"), and, in respect, Sigismundo brought the ashes of Gemisto from Greece and placed them in a sarcophagus on the outside wall of the Tempio. Pound adored the concept that the gods have "Hilaritas the virtuc *hilaritas*" (83/548), a mirth and rejoicing that has at its root a "sublime joy of wonder and intellectual love,"[106] and he cherished "speed in communication." The "mental velocities" of the gods (93/652) he compared to the speed and arrow-straightness of "the wing'd fish under Zoagli" (76/479) and to the grace and playfulness of dolphins: "Came Neptunus / his mind leaping / like dolphins" (116/815).

In 99, the next canto after the return of Plotinus, Pound comments disapprovingly on Plotinus' complaints about physical pain, though the poet is quick to add that Plotinus' physical suffering did not distract him from the main part of his vision, namely that the receptive human mind can be transformed by the divine mind:

> from Plotinus his bellyache,
> Though he still thought: God of all men.
>   The body is inside.
>
>   (99/720)

Thus in Canto 99 Pound affirms the essential Plotinian concept that the soul the body is inside of is the Soul of God, who is the God of everyone. This too is new in *The Cantos*, and the consolation it confers is immeasurable. "O God of all men, none excluded" (113/808) is a prayer of gratitude. Those members of the human race desiring peaceful coexistence with others can recognize that this concept rises above all partisan prejudice to say that *we* are all part of the same "intimate essence" (*SP*, 49).

In the next two cantos, 100 and 101, Pound adds more, in Greek and Latin. In 100 Plotinus' inquiry (for which Pound gives the Loeb citation) about whether one kind of love is a god or spirit and another also an affection is juxtaposed with a temple, suggesting the sacredness of this query, for Plotinus concludes that the mind in itself is most sacred and that affections are not separate from the mind.[107] This passage clearly contradicts Pound's youthful statement in "Axiomata," 1921, that "It is as foolish to try to contain the *theos* in consciousness as to try to manage electricity according to the physics of water" (*SP*, 49). The intelligence of the human mind and the ability to love others are the most sublime manifestations of the divine mind, and can reach anywhere, as light compenetrates water:

EX OUSIAS . . . HYPOSTASIN
III, 5, 3   PERI EROTAS
                          <u>III</u> hieron
nous to ariston autou
              as light into water compenetrans
that is pathema
              ouk aphistatai"

thus Plotinus
per plur diafana
neither weighed nor hindered;
aloof
1 Jan '58

(100/741–42)

In 101, Plotinus, in the company of Apollonius, who held "that the universe is alive" (94/657), Porphery, the biographer of Plotinus, and, again, Anselm, holds to his one vision, despite all the theories in which the mind can engage:

Apollonius, Porphery, Anselm,
Plotinus EN THEORIA 'ON NOUS EXEI
had one vision only

(101/746)

That one vision, again, is that the human mind can be transformed by the divine mind. Pound gives many examples of this process in 101, as experienced, even unknowingly, by others.

In 102 details of the Na Khi landscape merge with Plotinus:

AISSOUSIN,
the spirits,
Berenice, a late constellation.
"Same books," said Tcheou
they ought to be brother-like.
Crystaline,
south slope for juniper,
Wild goose follows the sun-bird,
in mountains; salt, copper, coral,
dead words out of fashion
KAI ALOGA,
nature APHANASTON,
the pine needles glow as red wire
OU THELEI EAEAN EIS KOSMOU
they want to burst out of the universe
amnis herbidas ripas

(102/750–51)

Flitting spirits at the beginning of this excerpt move about the Na Khi mountain landscape. The pine needles glowing as red wire and wanting to burst out of the universe follow Greek by Plotinus referring to something "unspoken," "secret, inscrutable, or unknown." This is a mystery meeting other mysteries. Perhaps Pound alludes to the "flight of the alone to the Alone," to the end of the ascent to the Good, when, in MacKenna's translation, "the essential man outgrows Being, becomes identical with the Transcendent of Being":[108]

> "They want to bust out of the kosmos"
>
>   accensio
>
>   (105/770)

Let us observe, simply, that the glowing of pine needles and the sound of the wind are indisputable signs that the universe is alive, and Pound understood that the Na Khi shared this belief. He found the concept of the living universe in Conybeare's translation of *Philostratus' Life of Apollonius:*

> Apollonius again asked which of the elements first came into being, and Iarchus answered: "All are simultaneous, for a living creature is not born bit by bit." "Am I," said Apollonius, "to regard the universe as a living creature?" "Yes," said the other, "if you have a sound knowledge of it, for it engenders all living things." "Shall I then," said Apollonius, "call the universe female, or of both the male and the opposite gender?" "Of both genders," said the other, "for by commerce with itself it fulfils the role of both mother and father in bringing forth living creatures; and it is possessed by a love for itself more intense than any separate being has for its fellow, a passion which knits it together into harmony."[109]

The poet's contemplation of the Light of the Soul outside the body leads, ten cantos later, to a moment of transcendent peace:

> Soul melts into air,
>
>   anima into aura,
>
>   Serenitas.
>
>   (111/803)

This is the experience itself, not an explanation for it, which accounts in part for the greater limipidity of the final group of cantos. Pound did not give up his books, as Prospero did, but he no longer quotes them as frequently. He thanks H.D. for the word she has contributed to this process, a word he retrieves from "pre-history":

> But for the sun and serenitas
>
>   (19th May '59)
>
> H.D. once said "serenitas"
>
>   (Atthis, etc.)

> at Dieudonné's
>> in pre-history.

(113/806-7)

The whole concept of which "serenitas" is the end result comes from the belief in—as Pound describes it, we should say the experience of—the human soul or spirit becoming a part of the Spirit of divine love, light, mind, soul, of the *Theos* or what we call God.[110] No person sincerely seeking this light will be excluded.

> For the little light and more harmony
> Oh God of all men, none excluded
> . . . .
> That the body is inside the soul—
>> the lifting and folding brightness
>>> the darkness shattered,
>>>> the fragment.

(113/808-9)

The paradisal moments of *serenitas* or of light shattering the darkness still came to the poet only in flashes: "For the blue flash and the moments / benedetta" (117/821). He imagines the light of the Na Khi landscape:

> In mountain air the grass frozen emerald
>> and with the mind set on that light
>>> saffron, emerald,
>>>> seeping.

(113/809)

All manifestations of the sacred order, however seemingly trivial, remained a source of wonderment: "How came beauty against this blackness" (116/816). Except for the paradisal moments, the darkness, the absence of light that he had feared and hated and worked to dispel, and the "darkness unconscious" that cannot be fathomed, also still remained part of earthly reality but, as twice before in his life, Pound's loneliness and fear are diminished by Plotinus. The poet no longer feels "excluded" from the divine mind and does not himself want to exclude anyone. With new humility, he gives up the vanity of trying to fight the world and accepts the poet's task as one of observation, as he had said in his youth. To be "God's eye" (113/810), "to 'see again'" (116/816), is the poet's responsibility. What splendour that "it coheres all right / even if my notes do not cohere" (116/817).

From Rock the poet learned that when hunting, the Na Khi know how to blend their voices into the sounds of the forest:

Ezra Pound & China

Na Khi talk made out of wind noise,
   And North Khi, not to be heard amid sounds of the forest
but to fit in with them unperceived by the game.

(104/758)

"Na Khi talk made out of wind noise." The Na Khi, with their ancient music that Confucius might have heard, and their reverence for the spirits of nature, are among the voices of the wind, the paradisal wind that the silent poet treasured in his old age. He may also have been remembering a comment by Laurence Binyon in *The Flight of the Dragon,* a book he reviewed in *Blast* in 1915: "The soul identified itself with the wind which bloweth where it listeth."[111]

I have tried to write Paradise

Do not move
   Let the wind speak
      that is paradise.

(822)

In the 1968 interview, "Breaking the Silence," after Pound explains that "*Spring and Autumn* is a book attributed by some to Confucius, who was anything but a war-monger," Pasolini asks about China.

> *Pasolini:* I want to ask you, Pound. You have never been to China on any of your travels?
> *Pound:* No.
> *Pasolini:* You've never been there. Is this a disappointment for you, not to have seen China, which inspired you so much?
> *Pound:* Yes, I have always wanted to see China. It's awfully late now, but who knows?[112]

Pound did "see" China in his poem. The American master who "tried to write Paradise" can be compared to a Chinese master described by Binyon as "the greatest of all Chinese masters,"[113] Wu Tao-tzu, who painted "as if a god possessed him and wielded the brush in his hand."[114] The emperor asked for a vast landscape on a palace wall. Wu Tao-tzu painted it, and while the painting was being admired, the artist clapped his hands and a cave in the painting opened and he disappeared into it. This was appropriate because a painting or poem was regarded as "the home of the artist's soul."[115]

NOTES

Acknowledgments: Many of the photographs in this article were made by my husband Gregory Harvey, to whom I also owe special thanks for being a matchless traveler. We appreciate the superb help of Katherine Fok, Barbara Chen, and Gerald Hatherly of Ambercrombie & Kent International, Inc., Hong Kong, in implementing details of our itinerary that made our travel throughout China in the summer of 1999 as smooth as silk. William McNaughton and his wife Marie Li Ying offered delightful hospitality in Hong Kong, and Bill has continued to share his knowledge about the Na Khi and China. I am grateful to Mary de Rachewiltz for generously sharing her knowledge of her father's friendship with Peter Goullart and Joseph Rock, and to Carroll Terrell for his vision and care in creating and editing *Paideuma, A Journal Devoted to Ezra Pound Scholarship*. My thanks also to Peggy Fox, vice-president of New Directions Publishing Corporation, Patricia Willis, curator of the Yale Collection of American Literature, and Zhaoming Qian, editor of this book, for their courteous encouragements; to Betsy Graves Rose for indispensable technical help; and to Amy Vaccarella of the Museum Library, University of Pennsylvania, for locating Schuyler V. R. Cammann's "Review of Joseph Rock's *The Ancient Na-Khi Kingdom of Southwest China*," *Far Eastern Quarterly*, 9, no. 4 (August 1950): 399–402. Harriet Provine, who climbed Mount Kinabalu in Borneo in 1985 (compare Canto 110/801), thoughtfully provided books and brochures about the mountain as well as visits to and books and articles about the Arnold Arboretum in Boston.

Three indispensable books about Pound, which I use constantly but do not cite in the notes are:

Robert J. Dilligan, James W. Parins, and Todd K. Bender, *A Concordance to Ezra Pound's Cantos* (New York and London: Garland, 1981).

Donald C. Gallup, *Ezra Pound, A Bibliography* (Charlottesville: Bibliographical Society of the University of Virginia and the University Press of Virginia, 1983).

Carroll F. Terrell, *A Companion to the Cantos of Ezra Pound* (Berkeley and Los Angeles: University of California Press, and Orono, Maine: National Poetry Foundation, 1984).

I am indebted to all Pound scholars, especially Hugh Kenner. As they are too numerous to list, I rely on the interconnections offered by scholars cited in these notes.

1. David Anderson, "Breaking the Silence: The Interview of Vanni Ronsisvalle and Pier Paolo Pasolini with Ezra Pound in 1968," *Paideuma* 10, no. 2 (Fall 1981):338.

2. W. B. Yeats, *A Packet for Ezra Pound* (Dublin: Cuala Press, August 1929); reprinted as the first essay in *A Vision* (October 1937; New York: Macmillan, 1961), 4–5.

3. Pound, "If Yeats knew a fugue from a frog, he might have transmitted what I told him in some way that would have helped rather than obfuscated *his* readers. Mah!!! . . . Take a fugue: theme, response, contrasujet. *Not* that I mean to make an exact analogy of structure. . . . All of which is mere matter for little Blackmurs and Harvud instructors *unless* I pull it off as reading matter, singing matter, shouting matter, the tale of the tribe." Letter 326, to John Lackay Brown, April 1937. *The Letters of Ezra Pound, 1907–1941,* ed. D. D. Paige (New York: Harcourt, Brace, 1950), 293–94. "Blackmurs," which is blanked-out in the book, is on the Paige typescript in YCAL.

4. Angela Palandri, "Homage to a Confucian Poet," *Paideuma* 3, no. 3 (Winter 1974):307.

5. Anderson, "Breaking the Silence," 339.

6. According to Bradley Mahew and Thomas Huhti, *Southwest China* (Hawthorne, Australia, Oakland, California, London, and Paris: Lonely Planet Publications, 1998), 50: Yunnan in the 1950s nominated 260 minority groups of which 25 were formally recognized. Of these the Na Khi are the dominant group.

Rock observed in 1947 that because the Na Khi are the largest group, "all the non Chinese people of the Li-chiang district, irrespective of family name, call themselves Na-khi, while the name Mo-so is resented" (Joseph F. Rock, *The Ancient Na-Khi Kingdom of Southwest China,* Harvard-Yenching Institute Monograph Series, 2 vols., xx, 554 pp., and 257 pp. of plates, plus four large maps by Rock folded into a pocket in the inside back cover (Cambridge: Harvard University Press, 1947), I, 181. Nevertheless, the Na Khi fiercely protect their identity—when I asked our guide about a person in another town claiming to be Na Khi, he replied, "No, no, NOT Na Khi!"

Representative of the difficulties that minority groups face in achieving official recognition, and of the confusion caused when several groups share a syllable (e.g., Na) in their name and are listed under the name of the largest group, whose customs they do not share, is a recent book by Cai Hua, Professor of Social Anthropology at the Institute of Sociology and Anthropology at Beijing University: *A Society without Fathers or Husbands: The Na of China,* translated from French by Asti Hustvedt (New York: Zone Books, 2001), distributed by The MIT Press of Cambridge, Mass., and London, England. Dr. Cai Hua notes that "Two westerners, an Italian and an American, have also vaguely noted the customs of the Na" (22), by whom he means Marco Polo and Joseph F. Rock. The word "vaguely" cannot realistically describe Rock's method of noting customs, for Rock's precise and abundant collection of facts and photographs and linguistic revelations are the opposite of vague, and he recognized that the Na have a history and customs very different from the Na Khi: "The Na were apparently not numerous but they had a religious literature and the name Na=black was perhaps given them by the Mo-so because they were darker skinned than the aborigines of the Li-chiang territory. . . ." (*The Ancient Na-Khi Kingdom of Southwest China,* I, 181). Rather, "vaguely" criticizes "value judgments" based on "fragments of the Na customs," because, according to Dr. Cai Hua, "Serious studies of the Na were simply not available until the 1960s" (24–25), and now the

Na, who number about 30,000, seek to claim their separate identity: "For more than a decade, the Na from Yongning have requested that the government, on every level from local to central, officially recognize them as an ethnic group distinct from the Naxi [i.e., Na Khi] of Lijiang. The People's Assembly of Yunnan Province has agreed to call the Na of Yongning Mo-so *ren* (Mo-so people) but not Mo-so *zu* (Mo-so ethnic group). To be considered an ethnic group, ratification by the central government is necessary" (37).

The important distinction to be emphasized here is that the Na are a matrilineal society, and the Na Khi have never been matrilineal, despite the immense authority and respect given to Na Khi women, who, as Pound notes, wear the cosmos on their back (101/746). The Na Khi are a matriarchate in some ways, but the kings, chiefs, and warriors of the Na Khi were male, and Na Khi husbands, content to share the cooking and child care and let women be in charge of business and finance and other practicalities, are free, outside their household duties, to devote themselves to music, poetry, art, philosophy, teaching, research, and scholarship.

7. Gerald Hatherly, "Yunnan, South of the Clouds," *Intrepid,* Spring 1997, 19.

8. Peter Goullart, *Forgotten Kingdom* (London: John Murray, 1955), 83–84. Goullart, a White Russian, lived in Likiang, as he called it, from 1940 to 1949.

Pound's daughter, Mary de Rachewiltz, told me that Goullart lived at Brunnenburg as a paying guest for over a decade, "was a 'comfort' to EP and visited him also in Martinsbrunn," the nearby clinic where Pound was hospitalized for depression. "Goullart came [to the castle] for the first time in January 1962 and stayed as p.g. through October and continued the pattern into the 1970s, i.e., when I no longer took p.gs. He died in the house of his friend Desmond Neill in Singapore on June 5th, 1978 ('talking in Russian and asking for Boris [de Rachewiltz, Mary's husband]')—the two had many interests in common. . . . In Brunnenburg he wrote *River of the White Lily: Life in Sarawak* and *Princess of the Black Bone: Life in the Tibetan Borderland.*" Goullart left his library of "about a dozen books, mostly by Joseph Rock, on China and Tibet," to Mary and Boris. Some of Goullart's letters to Dorothy Pound are in the Lilly Library, Indiana.

9. Ibid., 81.

10. Ibid., 142.

11. Ibid., 84–85.

12. Ibid., 148.

13. Rock, *The Na-khi Nāga Cult and Related Ceremonies,* 2 vols., xii, 806 pp., plus 356 pp. of plates and notes, Serie Orientale Roma 4 (Roma: Istituto Italiano per il Medio ed Estremo Oriente, 1952), I, 5.

14. Rock, "The ²Muan-¹Bpo Ceremony or the Sacrifice to Heaven as Practiced by the ¹Na-²Khi." *Monumenta Serica: Journal of Oriental Studies of the Catholic University of Peiping* 13 (1948):1–160.

15. Goullart, *Forgotten Kingdom,* 180.

16. Ibid., 180–82.

17. Ibid., 182–83.

18. Ibid., 183.

19. Ibid.

20. Dr. Xuan Ke's colleagues in Lijiang reported that he is working on the arrangements for travel to the United States, and he confirmed this in a telephone conversation with our guide in Kunming.

21. Lui Ju, the president of the Chinese Music Association, spoke in 1993 of the performances of Na Khi orchestras as the "living fossils of music."

In 2000 the Smithsonian published a book titled *Music in the Age of Confucius,* edited by Jenny F. So and based on an exhibition she curated in the Arthur M. Sackler Gallery, about a spectacular discovery in the Yangtze River Valley in central China near Leigudun, Suizhou, Hubei Province, about one hundred miles north of Wuhun. In 1977 soldiers found a Bronze Age tomb containing musical instruments, bells, zithers, drums, flutes, panpipes, "which can be dated," says Milo Cleveland Beach, "to about 433 B.C. and earlier" (7). Available at the exhibition was a CD-ROM, *Bells of Zeng Hou Yi* (Music Research Institute of China and Museum of Hubei Province, 1997), which says the bells come from the period when the craftsmanship of cast bronze bells had reached "perfection," which afterward was lost. Yi was the sovereign of the small state of Zeng, and the instruments in his tomb come from the Spring–Autumn and Warring periods (770–221 BCE). John S. Major and Jenny So say that the extensive inscriptions and illustrations on the instruments and other artifacts within the tomb form "the most complete written record of early Chinese musical systems" yet found, and the instruments are "the largest group of ancient musical instruments known, not just in China but in the entire ancient world. There is nothing like it from other ancient cultures in Mesopotamia, Egypt, India, Greece, Rome, or Mesoamerica" (18). Brenda Kean Tabor, "A Set of Bells Unearthed in China Is the Oldest Existing Musical Assemblage," *Smithsonian Institution Research Reports* 101 (Summer 2000):2, 6, remarks that this discovery "at the dawn of a period of renewed interest in scholarly pursuits in China, as well as a reopening of China to the West, was fortuitous timing." These commentators do not mention Goullart's belief that the Na Khi have preserved music that Confucius, 551–479 BCE, may have heard, so appropriate comparative studies are still to be made.

22. Goullart, *Forgotten Kingdom,* 218.

23. Ibid., 18.

24. Ibid.

25. Ibid., 36.

26. Ibid., 42.

27. Ezra Pound to his mother, Isabel W. Pound, London, November 1913, *Letters,* 25. And see note 94.

28. Goullart, *Forgotten Kingdom,* 142.

29. Ibid., 216–17. Our Na Khi guide showed us the field where Goullart and Rock were rescued by one of General Claire Lee Chennault's "Flying Tigers." My maternal grandmother, Emily Chennault, was related to Claire Chennault, so I checked the family history, and was surprised and thrilled to learn that the French Chennaults may earlier have been Chinese: "General Chennault told this story at a Chennault clan meeting a number of years ago. When he first arrived in China, he ran into a street scribe and asked if there were a Chinese symbol for the name Chen-

nault. The scribe replied, 'Oh, yes, centuries ago the name was "Shinado," meaning high tree. But Genghis Khan chased them all before him and they went into Europe to France.'" *Descendants of Estienne Chenault, 1991 Edition,* ed. Belle Montgomery Chenault (Cullman, Alabama, and Wyandotte, Oklahoma: Gregath Publishing, 1992), 252.

30. Pound, Notebook for "[THRONES, 23], 1957 November 8 [-1958 July 22]," described as Notebook 112 in *A Catalogue of the Poetry Notebooks of Ezra Pound* by Mary de Rachewiltz, assisted by Diana Ross, ed. Donald Gallup (New Haven: Yale University Press, 1980), 102.

31. S. B. Sutton, *In China's Border Provinces: The Turbulent Career of Joseph Rock, Botanist-Explorer* (New York: Hastings House, 1974). In *Charles Sprague Sargent and the Arnold Arboretum* (Cambridge: Harvard University Press, 1970), Sutton uses Rock's spelling.

32. Rock, *The Ancient Na-Khi Kingdom of Southwest China,* I, 172.

33. Ibid., I, vii–viii.

34. Pound, "How I Began," *T.P.'s Weekly* (London), June 6, 1913, 707: "I knew at fifteen pretty much what I wanted to do. I believed that the 'Impulse' is with the gods; that technique is a man's own responsibility. . . . I resolved that at thirty I would know more about poetry than any man living, that I would know the dynamic content from the shell, that I would know what was accounted poetry everywhere, what part of poetry was 'indestructible,' what part could *not be lost* by translation, and—scarcely less important—what effects were obtainable in *one* language only and were incapable of being translated."

35. Sutton, *In China's Border Provinces,* 27–30.

36. Ibid., 32–40.

37. Rock, "The ²Muan-¹Bpo Ceremony," 102.

38. Gilbert Grosvenor, "The National Geographic Society's Yünnan Province Expedition," *National Geographic,* April 1925, 462–98.

39. Bruce Chatwin, "Rock's World," in *What Am I Doing Here* (New York: Viking Penguin, 1989), 210. See also Stephen A. Spongberg, *A Reunion of Trees: The Discovery of Exotic Plants and Their Introduction into North American and European Landscapes* (Cambridge, Mass., and London: Harvard University Press, 1990), which refers both to the Chenault Nursery in the south of France (219) and Rock's triumphs (227–28).

40. Rock, "One needs to be a good housekeeper indeed to prepare for such a caravan": "The Glories of the Minya Konka: Magnificent Snow Peaks of the China-Tibetan Border Are Photographed at Close Range by a National Geographic Society Expedition," *National Geographic,* October 1930, 387.

41. "The Romance of ²Ka-²Mä-¹Gyu-³Mi-²Gkyi: A ¹Na-²Khi Tribal Love Story Translated from Na-Khi Pictographic Manuscripts, Transcribed and Annotated by Joseph F. Rock F.B.G.S.," *Bulletin de l'École Française d'Extrême-Orient,* vol. 39, 1939 (Hanoi, 1940), 1–155, plus appendix of photographs, 157–213.

42. James J. Wilhelm, *The Later Cantos of Ezra Pound* (New York: Walker, 1977), 170.

43. Sutton, *In China's Border Provinces*, 105.
44. Rock, "The Romance of ^{2}K'a," 77.
45. Rock, "The ^{2}Muan ^{1}Bpö Ceremony," 2–3.
46. It was published after Rock's death: *A ^{1}Na-^{1}Khi—English Encyclopedic Dictionary*, Part I, xliii, [1]–513, Plates I–XXVIII, each with a page of text, Serie Orientale Roma, XXVIII (Roma: Istituto Italiano per il Medio ed Estremo Oriente, 1963). Part II, *A ^{1}Na-^{2}Khi—English Encyclopedic Dictionary: Gods, Priests, Ceremonies, Stars, Geographical Names*, xxix, [1]–582, Plates XXIX–LVII, each with a page of text (1972). Both volumes are "Dedicated to the ^{1}Na-^{2}Khi Tribe of Li-Chiang" after the title page.
47. Rock, *Na-Khi Naga Cult*, I, 5.
48. Rock, "The Romance of ^{2}K'a," 47.
49. Rock, *Na-Khi Naga Cult*, I, 15–19.
50. See note 34. A list of Rock's publications is included in *Na-Khi Manuscripts*, compiled by Joseph Francis Rock, ed. Klaus L. Janert, 3 vols., 806 pages (Wiesbaden: Franz Steiner Verlag (GMBH, 1965), I, ix–x. This book published after Rock's death contains an introduction by Rock dated "Marburg, September 23, 1962." The three volumes describe Na Khi manuscripts originally in Rock's possession and now in the Staatsbibliothek in Marburg, Germany, and list some of the manuscripts deposited in Manchester, London, Paris, Leiden, Washington, Cambridge (Massachusetts), Greenwich (Connecticut), and in private collections. Many manuscripts were destroyed or stolen during World War II.

Many of Rock's botanical essays are omitted from the list of Rock's publications, probably because they are not about the Na Khi, including Rock's first essay for *National Geographic:* "Hunting the Chaulmoogra Tree," March 1922, 247–76.

51. Details of the shamans' feats are scattered throughout Rock's work. His amazement is most evident in his first essay about the Na Khi: "Banishing the Devil of Disease among the Nashi: Weird Ceremonies Performed by an Aboriginal Tribe in the Heart of Yunnan Province, China," *National Geographic,* November 1924, 473–99.

52. Rock, "The ^{2}Muan-^{1}Bpo Ceremony," 102; Rock, "The ^{2}Zhi ^{3}ma Funeral Ceremony of the ^{1}Na ^{2}Khi of Southwest China," *Studia Instituti Anthropos,* vol. 9, xv, 228 pp. and appendix of 21 pp. of plates and text (Vienna Mödling, Austria: St. Gabriel's Mission Press, 1955), ix–x; Rock, introduction, *Na-Khi Manuscripts,* vol. 1, xvi. The fourth place where Pound read of the destruction of Rock's work is in a two-page, handwritten letter from Joseph Rock in Hawaii to Pound at Saint Elizabeths, January 3, 1956, in which Rock summarizes his work for Pound in response to a letter from Professor Giovanni Giovannini of Catholic University of America to a Na Khi boy, Pao-hsien Fang, concerning Pound's interest in Rock's writings about the Na Khi. This letter is in a folder labeled "R-Miscellaneous" in the Pound Archive at Yale (YCAL, Mss. 43, Box 43, Folder 1830). Letters from Pound to Rock might be in the uncataloged papers of Rock at the Arnold Arboretum, Boston, and the Harvard-Yenching Institute, Cambridge. Letters from Peter Goullart to Rock might also be in these uncataloged papers. Goullart lived in Borneo for three years, off and on, between 1953 and 1961, and may have written to Rock about Mt. Kinabalu and discussed

it with Pound at Brunnenburg. Goullart's letters to Noel Stock from Borneo are in HRC, University of Texas at Austin, and he wrote about Borneo in *River of the White Lily: Life in Sarawak* (London: John Murray, 1965). On the dust jacket of that book is a photograph of Goullart and Pound seated on the terrace at Brunnenburg.

53. Tom Harrisson, "Kinabalu—Wonderful Mountain of Change," in *Kinabalu, Summit of Borneo,* ed. Datin Margaret Luping, Miss Chin Wen, and E. Richard Dingley (Sabah, Malaysia: Sabah Society, 1978), 26, 31.

54. John Peck, "Landscape as Ceremony in the Later *Cantos:* From the Roads of France to Rock's World," *Agenda* (Spring–Summer 1971):26–69; and Carroll F. Terrell, "The Na-Khi Documents I: The Landscape of Paradise," *Paideuma,* 3, no. 1 (Spring 1974):90–122.

55. Mahew and Huhti, *Southwest China,* 369.

56. James Hilton, *Lost Horizon* (1933; New York: Simon & Schuster Pocket Books, 1939), 190.

57. Ibid., 222.

58. Ibid., 225.

59. Ibid., 223.

60. *National Geographic,* February 1930, 131–85.

61. Rock, "Glories of the Minya Konka, Magnificent Snow Peaks of the China Tibetan Border," 385.

62. Ibid., 413. Other articles that gave Hilton unique information include:

Rock, "The Land of the Yellow Lamas: National Geographic Society Explorer Visits the Strange Kingdom of Muli, beyond the Likiang Snow Range of Yünnan Province, China," *National Geographic,* April 1925, 447–91.

Rock, "Experiences of a Lone Geographer: An American Agricultural Explorer Makes His Way through Brigand-Infested Central China en Route to the Amne Machin Range, Tibet," *National Geographic,* September 1925, 331–47.

Rock, "Through the Great River Trenches of Asia: National Geographic Society Explorer Follows the Yangtze, Mekong, and Salwin through Mighty Gorges, Some of Whose Canyon Walls Tower to a Height of More than Two Miles," *National Geographic,* August 1926, 133–86.

Rock, "Life among the Lamas of Choni: Describing the Mystery Plays and Butter Festival in the Monastery of an Almost Unknown Tibetan Principality in Kansu Province, China," *National Geographic,* November 1928, 569–619.

Rock, "Konka Risumgongba, Holy Mountain of the Outlaws," *National Geographic,* July 1931, 1 65.

63. Mahew and Huhti, *Southwest China,* 393.

64. Orville Schell, *Virtual Tibet: Searching for Shangri-La from the Himalayas to Hollywood* (New York: Henry Holt, 2000), 247.

65. Goullart, *Forgotten Kingdom,* 133.

66. Ibid.

67. See *The Faber Book of Utopias,* ed. John Carey (London: Faber, 1999), for excerpts from over one hundred descriptions of utopias, including *Lost Horizon.*

68. Schell, *Virtual Tibet,* 246.

69. Chatwin, "Rock's World," 207. This article introduced to the western world the engaging Dr. Ho, a Na Khi doctor, artist, and scholar, who as a child had known " 'Dr. Lock,' as the Nakhi remember him" (210). In the village of Baisha Michael introduced us to Dr. Ho, who served us tea and talked in excellent English not about "Dr. Rock" but about his own international fame in curing sickness with herbs.

70. Rock, "The Stone Drum Inscriptions of Shih-Ku," in *Ancient Na-Khi Kingdom*, II, 280–85.

71. Rock, "The Romance of ²K'a," 20.

72. Ibid., 4.

73. Ibid., 114.

74. Ibid., 98.

75. Rock, "The ²Muan-¹Bpö Ceremony," 35, 144.

76. Rock, "The Romance of ²K'a," 2–3.

Goullart also blamed the parents: "When a boy or a girl was missing from home for more than two days, the parents always suspected the awful truth. There was no time lost in organizing a thorough search . . . . The parents wailed and beat their breasts and began to make arrangements for the Harlallu ceremony. . . . Judging from their grief and lamentations, one would suppose that they would have been overjoyed to catch the children before the deed had been done. It was nothing of the sort. Were the lovers to be caught alive, they would be reviled and perhaps beaten to death by parents or neighbors from the necessity of saving face . . . [which] had precedence over parental love. It demanded blood sacrifices, in one form or another, irrespective of all other considerations. The lovers knew this only too well and took great care not to be found alive. If a girl's sworn lover had died far away from Likiang, she was honour bound to follow him into the grave" (*Forgotten Kingdom*, 155).

77. Rock, "The Romance of ²K'a," 5. "The kind of ²Har-²la-¹llö ceremony to be performed for a person depends on the manner of death" (7).

78. Copied from the label on two figures in the Chinese Sculpture Gallery in the Shanghai Museum, China.

79. Rock, "The ¹D'a ³Nv Funeral Ceremony with Special Reference to the Origin of ¹Na-²Khi Weapons," *Anthropos, International Review of Ethnology and Linguistics*, Vol. 50 (Fribourg, Switzerland: St-Paul, 1955):1–31; and "The ²Zhi ³mä Funeral Ceremony."

80. Rock, *Na-Khi Manuscripts*, ed. Janert, I, 35–40.

81. Rock, "The Romance of ²K'a," 13.

82. Ibid., 20.

83. The typescripts are at Yale and Harvard and Texas and in private collections.

84. Notes, *Kakitsubata*, in *The Classic Noh Theatre of Japan*, by Ezra Pound and Ernest Fenollosa (1916; New York: New Directions, 1959), 122, 130.

85. Kenner, "A Note on CX/788" [now CX/808 because of the addition of the two Italian cantos], *Paideuma* 8, no. 1 (Spring 1979):51–52.

Peter Stoicheff, in "CX/788 Revisited," *Paideuma* 12, No. 1 (Spring 1983):47–50, argues that "the multiple meanings, variously combined, lent an added resonance."

86. "Peck, Landscape as Ceremony," 50–60.

87. Massimo Bacigalupo, *The Forméd Trace: The Later Poetry of Ezra Pound* (New York: Columbia University Press, 1980), 467: "The allusiveness with which he presents the suicidal pact is an indication of its intimate relevance."

88. Desmond O'Grady, "Ezra Pound: A Personal Memoir," *Agenda* (Autumn–Winter–Spring 1979–1980):289.

89. The general assumption that "For E.McC" commemorates Eugene McCartney's death cannot be true because Mr. McCartney was alive for many decades after Pound's elegy was published. The young man who was Pound's "counter-blade under Leonardo Terrone, Master of Fence," and who was "Struck of the blade that no man parrieth / . . . / 'Gainst that grey fencer, even Death," was Ellicott McConnell. This information comes from a letter by Hilda Doolittle's and Ezra Pound's good friend Margaret Snively Pratt to Norman Holmes Pearson, July 4, 1973, YCAL.

90. Rock, "The ²Muan-¹Bpo Ceremony," 41.

91. Ovid, *Fasti,* Book 6, 5–6, Loeb Classical Library, 319. "Est deus in nobis" is twice quoted in Canto 98/705. The Loeb translation by Sir James George Frazer says: "There is a god within us. It is when he stirs us that our bosom warms; it is his impulse that sows the seeds of inspiration."

William McNaughton: "There is a god in us! under his influence we glow." *Paideuma* 3, no. 1 (Spring 1974):135–36.

Eva Hesse: "a god dwells within us, when he stirs we are enkindled." *Paideuma* 3, no. 1 (Spring 1974):136.

92. *Quest,* October 1912, *P&P,* I, 95, added in 1932 to *SR,* 96.

93. *New Age,* October 9, 1913, *P&P,* I, 184.

94. Plotinus, *The Enneads,* trans. Stephen MacKenna and first published in sections, 1917–1930 (London: Penguin, 1991), VI.9.4 pp. lxx, 540.

The edition that Pound would have read before MacKenna's translation and before he wrote the poem "Plotinus," published in 1908, would have been Thomas Taylor's 1794 translation from the Greek, which was issued in a new edition in 1895 (and reprinted for several decades after that), with a preface and bibliography by G. R. S. Mead. In London Olivia and Dorothy Shakespear introduced Pound to Mead, who became a friend, mentor, and publisher of Pound. An unexpected connection is Mead's essay, "The Way of the Spirit in Ancient China," which he published in *Quests Old and New* (London: G. Bell, 1913).

William French, in "For 'Gentle, Graceful Dorothy,' a Tardy Obit," *Paideuma* 12, no. 1 (Spring 1983): 89–113, gives a vivid account of ways in which the Shakespears, Olivia and Dorothy, helped Pound to gain "entrée to that potent world that would mark him and shape him for the rest of his life," and of how Dorothy's knowledge and shared memories of "the great London refulgence" and Pound's "mystical origins" encouraged and protected the poet at Saint Elizabeths and influenced his efforts "to write Paradise."

Guy Davenport observes that the Chinese "ideogram for *splendor,* which is placed in *The Cantos* as a motto for LII–LXXI, is composed of the radicals *light, wing feathers, and song bird.* The aesthetic controlling this ideogram is thoroughly

Chinese, but we can admire its style." *Cities on Hills: A Study of I–XXX of Ezra Pound's Cantos* (Ann Arbor, Mich.: UMI Research Press, 1983), 62.

95. Pound, Canto 115, *Agenda*, Autumn–Winter–Spring 1979–1980, 4:

The flowers of the apricot blow from the East to the West
I have tried to keep them from falling.

96. Nigel Steel and Peter Hart, *Passchendaele: The Sacrificial Ground* (London: Cassell, 2001).

97. Colin McDowell movingly explores this theme in "'As toward a Bridge over Worlds': The Way of the Soul in *The Cantos*," *Paideuma* 13, no. 2 (Fall 1984):171–200.

98. Hell not "funny," Pound to Felix Schelling, Paris, July 8, 1922, *Letters*, 180. Avoid "hell obsession," in "Cavalcanti," *Make It New*, 1934; reprinted in *Cavalcanti: An Edition of the Translations, Notes, and Essays*, ed. David Anderson (Princeton: Princeton University Press, 1983), 207.

99. Pound's attempt to describe in poetry the mass graves of World War II shows his fear of approaching this subject other than from a great distance:

do not seek among them your own men,
the blood you bring from thousands
who fall in mist and snow, in thousands,
and the flakes fall and melt
melt and fall the flakes   under April

This is Massimo Bacigalupo's translation from Pound's Italian "Drafts of 'Canto 75'" (YCAL), which Pound dates "14 Jan," the year being, Bacigalupo says, "probably 1945." This is the second draft, and both drafts bear some resemblance to lyrics composed by English poets at the beginning of the Great War before bitter knowledge made such superficial consolation wholly inappropriate. For Pound near the end of the second war, his attitude was of such despair—"that a war follows another, nothing matters"—and anguished forebodingness that this uncharacteristic prettification of the mass destruction reveals his fragility, his terror of total breakdown if he releases his deep emotions.

100. Italo Calvino, "Lightness," in *Six Memos for the Next Millennium* (Cambridge: Harvard University Press, 1988), 4–7.

101. John Keegan, *The Face of Battle* (London and New York: Viking, 1976), 334–36.

102. Hilton, *Lost Horizon*, 157, 229.

103. Plotinus, *The Enneads*, liii, lxxvi.

104. Ibid., VI.9.7, p. 544.

105. Carbon of letter from Pound to Eliot, October 1959, YCAL.

106. J. P. Migne, *Patrologiae Latina,* vol. 122, col. 121; Michael Shuldiner, "Pound's Progress," *Paideuma* 4, no. 1 (Spring 1975):78.

107. See Bacigalupo, *The Forméd Trace,* 391–92, for a more complete context for these lines.

108. Plotinus, *The Enneads*, VI.9.11, pp. 548–49.

In the exquisite lynx incantation at the end of Canto 79, "there is a red glow in the carpet of pine needles" (79/512).

109. *Philostratus: The Life of Apollonius of Tyana*, trans. F. C. Conybeare, Loeb Classical Library (1912), Book III, xxxiv, p. 309.

110. For a discussion of light read Carroll Terrell, "A Commentary on Grosseteste with an English version of *De Luce*" (and a facsimile of a Latin version), *Paideuma* 2, no. 3 (Winter 1973):449–70. Terrell considers the similarities of thought about light in Grosseteste, Plotinus, Cavalcanti, and Pound (449–55).

111. Binyon, *The Flight of the Dragon: An Essay on the Theory and Practice of Art in China and Japan* (London: John Murray, 1911), 27. Pound reviewed the book in *Blast* 2 (July 1915):85–86; *P&P*, II, 99.

112. Anderson, "Breaking the Silence," 339.

113. Binyon, *The Flight of the Dragon*, 48.

114. Ibid., 17.

115. Ibid., 85–86.

Poems

Beijing, Summer 1999

China, a world to have seen, a fervor.
He must have smiled on us all gathered there, the poet of *The Cantos*,
as we stood in awe in front of a mound of earth, covered with grass.
The soul of Confucius trapped for us to meet, make us stand still, then
wander off into the woods where his Odes still sing.

A tree in China has different voices.
Heavy with crickets, a legend woven with signs, it grows inside you
while you stand below it, it traps you for an instant and in that instant
you are incredibly old, exquisitely wise.
Gold glitters and temple roofs curl into tiny dragons, reverent myths
make you stand still and bow.
Someone special took me to Liulichang where I bought two tiny bamboo
     cages.
In each a cricket was trapped. Yet they still sing in captivity.
We climbed Pagoda Hill, up to the white dome, and there, in a blazing
afternoon, set them free.
One wandered off but the other stayed, and moved its slender feelers.
Inside me it sprang to stay forever.

How to tell
One cricket from
Another?
Two warriors on Pagoda Hill
As one set us free.

PATRIZIA DE RACHEWILTZ

登 泰 山

自 幼 頻 聞 遠 外 欽

快 登 今 日 丈 夫 心

大 河 不 息 連 黄 海

平 野 長 開 散 碧 岑

聳 立 雲 霄 疑 出 沒

眺 臨 塵 界 笑 浮 沈

幾 多 遊 子 幾 多 詠

視 古 元 來 猶 視 今

On Top of Taishan

From childhood I've heard of you and admired you;
Today I stand on top of you, being a true man.
The great river flows ceaselessly into the Yellow Sea;
The wide plain stretches out round verdant hills.
Rising into the clouds, you seem to come and go:
Looking over the world, you smile on its ups and downs.
How many songs have travelers sung about you?
To look into the past is but to see the present.

KIM JONG-GIL

地·第一

（他：商纣王）

黄昏　　　　　静
而生坛

　　宇　一个一个逃离
　　黄土盛大涌起
　　星宿沉天远方
　　静于中心
　　暴君的庭院坐着　石头累累如光

是这日子择定他，火择定他
反叛的莽原野性如吼，狼烟逼近
高台孤零零被弃像一尊巨鼎
松弛的膂力，宝弓鹰犬四散为暮色
邪一袭玉衣
他说，是死神　　　　　　：天命玄鸟
　　　　　　　　　　　　　降而生商

　　群山俯首这一张犁下
　　四季的种子
　　膨胀成一只将出土的蝉
　　夜一击　白杨脱身而去
　　像悬空腐烂的尸体
太阳享受他的祭祀，堕胎之血一池烈酒
泼洒于地女人背叛的翩翩舞蹈
太晚了，如今已没有一只杯子能举起
游夜之火折天之火，骸骨嘶嘶复仇的音乐

　　在云端盲目威严　这时辰空前
　　袭杀每一只飞鸟的嗅觉
　　预兆烧成琉璃瓦
　　零碎地死在周围
如水的静脉将引爆：兀立铜柱上炮烙的欲望
玩腻了心，漫天扬起耀眼的蝙蝠
当幽灵黄昏最后一道谕旨
通体透明地巡游碧空
他说，够了　　　　　　：天曷不降威
　　　　　　　　　　　大命胡不至

　　拾阶而上
　　脚掷进汉白玉的盘子哑口无言
　　被践踏的土　至高无上的土
　　黄　红　蓝　白　黑
　　聚于中心
　　推开一扇门　月亮翠翠深重

　　山上青烟袅袅
　　是积雪

EARTH 1 (KING ZHOU OF SHANG)

    Dusk
                      Stillness
    An altar is born

    Words   One by one escape
    Yellow earth surges massively
    Stars perish in the distance
    Tranquil at the core
    Sitting in the tyrant's court   Rocks radiate like circles of light
This day has chosen him, fire has chosen him
Rebellion's wildness howls ferociously, wolf smoke draws near
High platform solitarily abandoned like a huge tripod
Flaccid muscles, jade bow falcon hunting dogs disperse into evening colors
The jade suit
He says, is Death   *Heaven commands the swallow*
                              To descend and give birth to Shang

    Mountains prostrate before the plough
    The seed after four seasons
     Swells up into a cicada about to burst from the soil
    Night strikes   A white poplar is born
    Like a rotting corpse hanging in mid-air
The sun basks in the sacrifices presented blood of induced abortions a pool of potent wine
Splashing the earth the swirling dance of rebellious women
Too late, already not a wine cup can be raised
Night-wandering fires Heaven-beseeching fires, music of skeletons hissing revenge

    At the end of the clouds wanton grandeur   This unprecedented hour
    Slaughters the sense of smell in every bird
    Omens burnt into glazed tiles
    Die in fragments everywhere
Motionless veins like water are fuses: unmoving bronze pillars branded with lust
Tired of playing, the sky shakes forth a blinding flurry of bats
As the spirit at dusk gives the final command
It transparently infuses the jade heaven
He says: Enough   *Indomitable is heaven*
                                Omniscient its command

    Carried up stairs
    Thrown by the legs into a marble dish utterly mute
    Trampled earth   Earth ultimate and supreme
    Yellow   Red   Blue   White   Black
    Deaf at the core
    Pushing open a door   Moonlight's crimes in deep layers

    On mountains pure smoke curling
    Is piled-up snow

FROM "IN SYMMETRY WITH DEATH" SECTION OF 易 [YI] BY YANG LIAN,
TRANSLATED BY MABEL LEE (GREEN INTEGER, 2002)

Afterword
Kung Is to Pound As Is Water to Fishes

MARY DE RACHEWILTZ

"From Pisa to Taishan" was to be the title of my paper for the 1999 Pound conference, but now that the pilgrimage is over and I did not deliver it as a lecture, there seems little purpose in using the title of what had seemed important at Brunnenburg, but obsolete in China where the voice I deemed had a right to be heard was Ezra Pound's and not mine. So I thanked our hosts, Professor Jian Zhang in particular, and the convener and his organizing committee, and asked the audience instead to listen to the recording of Pound's reading of the Confucian Odes, remembering: "Sky, what words does the sky use?" (*Con*, 277) Confucius wanted to do without words, though his disciples protested. Pound said: "Words have left me. I did not choose silence, silence got hold of me."[1] It has taken me thirty years to understand that "silence" is the fulfillment of the "process." The Sky has claimed the Poet.

Thanks to Jeffrey Twitchell-Waas, our first visit in Beijing was to the Confucian Temple, and as I was looking at the seven-hundred-year-old cypress it came over me: "Trees die & the dream remains" (90/629),[2] also the line in an early poem: "Make-strong old dreams lest this our world lose heart" (*CEP*, 52, 77), and W. B. Yeats's admonition "In dreams begins responsibility."[3] There must have been strong dreams at the root of scholars gathering to honor China, Pound's China, and Pound in China.

In 1914 there was a plan for the Pound family to be reunited in China. Homer had been offered some kind of job by a missionary friend, but nothing came of it.[4] Perhaps it is just as well. We might not have the China Cantos, culled from de Mailla's *Histoire générale de la Chine*, or in fact the invention of Chinese poetry for the West, that is, *Cathay*, or Cantos 13 and 49, all written between the two terrible World Wars in Europe, as the poet was teaching himself Chinese with the Morrison and Mathews Chinese-English dictionaries, translating Confucius and living according to his teachings: Man standing by his word, with total candor and sincerity, making it new.

Had Pound not re-created China "in the wilds of the mind" even before writing the Pisan Cantos, in "the tent under Taishan" (74/457), an extended Pound family would not in 1999 have climbed the sacred mountain and visited Confucius's birthplace and burial ground in Qufu.[5]

The idea of having a meeting in China was voted down in 1991 in Brunnenburg, but during the next Pound conference in 1993 in Rapallo, Zhaoming Qian resolved to put the idea into action. "Sage men have plans" (99/715)—quietly persevering, he carried them out. William Mc-Naughton and others gave their strong support, and by 1997 the minds of the majority were made up and my own in a turmoil: so many interests, so many topics to pursue, from Cantos 52–61 to the "Sacred Edict" in Cantos 98–99. The series of tensions, between values of slowness and velocity that need to be resolved in order to "Build pen yeh" (99/717), was brought to rest by tuning in to the summons "begin where you are."

I asked myself, who from these mountains had traveled to China before me? Mostly missionaries. Hardly a suitable topic, given Pound's ambivalence, verging almost on hatred at times, toward converts and converters. Yet our local Pater Josef Freinademetz (1851–1908), to name but one—not to be found in *The Cantos*—spent forty years in China and became, like the great Matteo Ricci, "a Chinese among the Chinese," without losing that Euro-Catholic *joie de vivre* fitting into a system of morality unconnected with institutionalized religions. The nun in Genova hospital was not worried when Pound declared his credo to be Confucian. He liked her comment: "oh well; it's all one religion."

Preeminent among missionaries were the Jesuits: "the Jesuits brought in astronomy" is recorded as their merit in Canto 60 (328) and reiterated, somewhat reluctantly, in Canto 99: "(The Papist did help with the calendar)" (99/721). And yet, Pound's knowledge of China is derived mainly through texts written or translated by Jesuits, and their subtle influence runs from Canto 4 to the very end.

There is the ambiguity between Père Henry Jacque and Padre Jose Elizondo mentioned in the Pisan Cantos 77 and 79. Pound identifies the first in a letter to Professor Schelling in 1922 as "a French priest (as a matter of fact he is a Jesuit)" (*SL*, 180). Of the second we read in *Guide to Kulchur* that his name "was enough to get me a photo of the Cavalcanti ms. in the Escorial" (158). On his way to Spain from the Dampfer König Albert, he writes to his mother, May 2, 1906: "Brightest man on board a Dominican Monk from Ottawa Canada. . . . Raymond Roubeau of the freres precheures in co. of a funny kindly little German 'welt' priest and a bishop. . . . With M. Roubeau I talk French & English on Dante, middle ages." No Jesuit is mentioned.

One never asks enough questions when one is young. Memory or posthumous research can be faulty. Discretion practiced for too long may lead to permanent distortions. So far I have found no satisfactory answer for the identity of Père Henry Jacque, who "would speak with the Sennin, on Rokku" (4/16), thus introducing us to China and the spirits of nature or of the air, well in advance of Canto 13, presided by Kung.

Personally Père Henry Jacque takes me back to the hill of St. Ambrogio, where Pound walked and, in his own fashion, spoke with the Sennin. Every day he came up the *salita* to listen to Bach, Mozart, Vivaldi, and Janequin and then to read from the *Odyssey* in Greek and teach me the twenty different ways a line of *The Cantos* could be translated into Italian. He told me I should have three intelligent questions ready for him, and yet I never asked about Père Henry Jacque.

Was he a Jesuit he had met and was still alive in 1922? Or at least as real and as alive as Jacque Père was before he "OBIT, in Stratford 1616"? The pun on Shakespeare occurs in Canto 107 (777). It's the way the French might pronounce Shakespeare's name, and it is associated, through the mention of Le Portel, with Swinburne, who almost drowned, carried away by the current, actually not at Le Portel, but at Yport. Pindaric flights, one might call these fantasy links, yet they serve to remind us that the Cantos are not simply an epic, a poem containing history, but above all they are myth and music. Pound himself said: it's MUSIC. In Canto 4 we hear the swallow crying "'Tis. 'Tis. Ytis!" (4/14), as Swinburne's poem *Itylus* comes to mind: "Swallow, my sister, O sister, swallow."[6] Luminous sound-threads, phanopoeia and melopoeia, tie the poem together, and a Jesuit priest is part of the chorus. The beauty lies in the mystery of the metamorphosis occurring throughout the poem, where the birds write the tune:

> 8th day of September
> f　　f
> 　　　d
>
> 　　　　g
> 　　　write the birds in their treble scale

Terreus! Terreus!
    there are no righteous wars in "The Spring and Autumn."
                    (82/545)

The poet like "T'ao Ch'ien heard the old Dynasty's music / as it might be at the Peach-blossom Fountain" (84/558), although in reality it was "from the death cells in sight of Mt. Taishan @ Pisa" (74/447); and like Confucius, "seven days foodless in Tchin" in Canto 53 (53/273), Pound in Pisa "sang even more than usual" and, deprived of freedom, he remembered that "Padre José had understood something or other / before the deluxe car carried him over the precipice / *sumne fugol othbaer*" (77/486–87), adding layers and layers of meaning by quoting the line from the Anglo-Saxon *Wanderer:* one a bird bore away.

We are introduced to the layer technique, not much different from shoots fastened into the earth to strike roots while attached to parent plants—("learn from the green world")—precisely in Canto 4:

Ply over ply, thin glitter of water;
Brook film bearing white petals.
The pine at Takasago
    grows with the pine of Isé!
                    (4/15)

The boundaries between China and Japan are blurred at times, and Pound has interpreted the German verb *dichten* to suit his own purpose, that is, to mean *condense, charge with meaning.* Synchronize, synthesize, and listen to the sound of the clavichord's double strings. It is in the light of this *techne* that even the record of Catholic missionaries transpires in the Chinese History section. The best insurance against the wiping out of historical records is to remember names that made history. Among them Matteo Ricci, Grimaldi, Intorcetta, Verbiest, Couplet, Gerbillon, Bouvet, and others, above all Père Joseph-Anne-Marie de Moyriac de Mailla, *Jesuite françois missionaire a Pekin,* through whose eyes Pound has read the annals of the Chinese empire from its origin until its decline, when in Pound's version the MANDATE was transferred to John Adams in America.

The thirteen volumes of the *Histoire générale de la Chine* were published in Paris between 1777 and 1783. The most luminous figure is Emperor K'ang Hsi, much admired by Father de Mailla, who lived in China during the last years of his reign. Pound seems to give the Jesuits a higher

rank than the emperor intended, especially in the long passage devoted to
the treaty with the Russians, negotiated by Gerbillon and Pereira in 1689:

> and this was due to the frog and the portagoose
>> Gerbillon and Pereira
>> to Gerbillon in the most critical moment
> that he kept their tempers till they came to conclusion.
>
> (59/327)

The history of the Jesuits is complex and not always easy to decipher.
Pound relies on the luminous detail: at least on one occasion the Jesuits
acted as peacemakers; they introduced useful medicine, quinine; they
helped with the calendar, taught astrology, mathematics, and music;

> and Père Ricci brought a clock to the Emperor
>> that was set in a tower.
>
> (58/317)

The pattern shows a series of building blocks for a new civilization: "To
build the city of Dioce whose terraces are the colour of stars" (74/445).

Civitate Dei based on an earthly paradise, or vice versa—

> "Can you tell the down from the up?"
>
> (27/132)

At the end of the Cantos Pound says: "I tried to make a paradiso / ter-
restre" and "I have tried to write Paradise" (117/822), thus conferring on
his epic not only music and mythology, but also a religious dimension
where "God is that one man love another."

The emperor K'ang Hsi came to the throne in 1662 at the age of seven.
In 1664 the regents, on false testimony, removed the German Jesuit Adam
Schall from his position as president of the Tribunal of Mathematics, and
most of the missionaries were put in prison. Because this measure was
triggered by the corruption of the eunuchs, Pound's fury against eu-
nuchs, hochangs, foes, Buddhist sects is clearly colored by Father de
Mailla's resentment, though it seems to become more virulent in Cantos
98 and 99, where the text of the Sacred Edict follows the translation of
the American missionary F. W. Baller, prepared for the Presbyterian In-
land Mission in 1907.

Pound was always seeking positive elements to infuse into a new cul-
ture, a new economic order that would make wars obsolete. The China
Cantos lead up to the core of the poem, the John Adams section, and the
line continues in Cantos 88 and 89, where we are again reminded that it

takes time, time to learn, to think, to meditate, to contemplate the patterns in nature:

> To respect the vegetal powers
>   Or "life however small" (Hindoustani).

. . . .

> Père Henri Jacques still
>   speaks with the sennin on Rokku,
> "These people," said Mr Tcheou "should
> be like brothers. They read the same books."
>
> (88/602)

> To know the histories
>
>   to know good from evil
>
> And know whom to trust.
>
>   Ching Hao.
>
> Chi crescerà
>   (Paradiso)
>
> (89/610)

Canto 89 not only links up with Canto 99 of *Thrones*, the "Sacred Edict," and the total light process, through the two quotations from Dante's *Paradiso* ("chi crescerà" and "non disunia") but ties in also Jefferson, the Adamses, Jackson, Van Buren, Thomas Hart Benton, and many others who may grow in our affection, or not, as the case may be, if we study the history and learn whom to trust in order to "make paradise" in this world.

> Till the blue grass turn yellow
>   and the yellow leaves float in air
> And Iong Cheng (Canto 61)
>   of the line of Kang Hi
> by the silk cords of the sunlight
>   non disunia.
>
> (99/714)

In the Pisan Cantos we read:

> To study with the white wings of time passing
>   is not that our delight. . . .
>
> (74/457)

Thus we have the passing of one season into another: the blue grass turn yellow. The passing of generations: Yong Cheng, mentioned in Canto 61, son of K'ang Hsi, all flowing together in a river of light toward *sinceritas.* A sincerity that speaks to the common people, expressed by the Greek words *koine ennoia,* meaning "the thoughts of the people."

> With splendour,
>> Catholicity,
> Woven in order,
>> as on cords in the loom.

(99/715)

At the opening of the China Cantos we have in capital letters the sign-posts: "between KUNG and ELEUSIS" (52/258), with the warning in the following canto: "Kung and Eleusis / to catechumen alone" (53/272). I prefer to read the signs differently from Pound scholars who stop at the Greek mysteries. *Catechumen* is indeed a Greek word, but it was used for the early Christians. Between the Confucian teachings of right conduct in this world and the pagan mysteries and mythologies lies the luminous road toward catholicity, the inclusive religion that is not Catholicism as practiced and expressed by Padre José Elizondo in Canto 81:

> "Hay aquí mucho catolicismo—(sounded
>> catoli*th*ismo)
> y muy poco reliHion"

. . . .

> That was Padre José Elizondo
>> in 1906 and in 1917
> or about 1917.

(81/537)

At a first reading, *The Cantos* may appear like a labyrinth with innumerable entrances. Both the "Taught and the not taught" (53/272) may find themselves on false roads, but the labyrinth is concentric, as was the enigma in the looking glass and Dante's schema. Pound used Dante as his guidebook, but he did not find the road to China in Dante. Although Marco Polo and Dante were contemporaries, they traveled in opposite directions, and Ignatius of Loyola, the founder of the Jesuit order, was not yet born. Padre Matteo Ricci came to China in 1581; Father Andrew White went to America on the Maryland in 1634. Always and everywhere the Jesuits have been both lauded and defamed, even feared because of their universalism. The hardest blow was the condemnation by papal decree of the "Chinese rites," which admitted certain traditional practices. To me it seems that what Matteo Ricci and his companions have not been

able to achieve has found a solution in *The Cantos* through a cosmothe-
andric experience, leading to SPLENDOUR, blending insights from the
East with those of the West:

> i.e. it coheres all right
>> even if my notes do not cohere.
>
> (116/817)

At this point it will appear obvious that my interest in Jesuits in China
would have been out of place, that my original idea of asking if within the
walls of the imperial palace there was any trace left of the church estab-
lished in 1693 at the expense of the emperor K'ang Hsi would have been
not only a breach of etiquette, but totally irrelevant after my visit to the
Confucian Temple. What mattered in Beijing was the meeting with Chi-
nese and Korean scholars, as well as poets and artists interested in
Pound's work, and the assurance that Confucius is held in great respect.
I was told that a golden statue of Confucius has been commissioned by
the present government, but I dared not ask if gold meant gold or merely
gilded, though I confess to a certain amount of embarrassment at the
thought of Aaron's golden calf.

What holds is said in Canto 54: "Kung is to China as is water to fishes"
(44/285). To which I would add: Kung is to Pound as is water to fishes.

EDITOR'S NOTES

1. See Donald Hall, *Remembering Poets: Reminiscences and Opinions: Dylan
Thomas, Robert Frost, T. S. Eliot, Ezra Pound* (New York: Harper and Row, 1978),
183: "I did not enter the silence; silence captured me."

2. Abbreviations for Pound works and page numbers in parentheses are added
by the editor.

3. Yeats, *The Poems*, ed. Richard J. Fenneran (New York: Macmillan, 1983), 100.

4. F. T. Song, an official of the newly formed Republic of China, on a visit to
Philadelphia, offered to get Homer Pound a job in China. To this Ezra Pound re-
sponded in his letter of January 4, 1914: "China is interesting, VERY" (YCAL). Two
weeks later Mr. Song traveled to London and made the same offer to Ezra, who
wrote in his letter of January 19, 1914 to his father: "We may yet be a united family"
(YCAL).

5. In 1968, during an interview for an Italian documentary, Pound expressed his
regret for not having been to China. When asked, "Is this a disappointment for you,
not to have seen China, which inspired you so much?" he replied, "Yes, I have al-
ways wanted to see China. It's awfully late now, but who knows?" (*P&P*, 10:317).

6. *The Complete Works of Algernon Charles Swinburne*, ed. Edmund Gosse
and Thomas James Wise (New York: Russell and Russell, 1968), 1:187.

Contributors

BARRY AHEARN, Professor of English at Tulane University, is the author of *Zukofsky's "A"* (1983) and *William Carlos Williams and Alterity: The Early Poetry* (1994). He is also the editor of *Pound/Zukofsky: Selected Letters* (1987) and *Pound/Cummings: The Correspondence* (1996).

RONALD BUSH, Drue Heinz Professor of American Literature at Oxford University, UK, is the author of *The Genesis of Ezra Pound's Cantos* (1976) and *T. S. Eliot: A Study in Character and Style* (1984). He is also the editor of *T. S. Eliot: The Modernist in History* (1990), (with Elazar Barkan) *Prehistories of the Future: The Primitivist Project and Culture of Modernism* (1995), and *Claiming the Stones/Naming the Bones: Cultural Property and the Negotiation of National and Ethnic Identity* (2002).

WENDY STALLARD FLORY, Professor of English at Purdue University, is the author of *Ezra Pound and "The Cantos": A Record of Struggle* (1980) and *The American Ezra Pound* (1989).

CHRISTINE FROULA, Professor of English, Comparative Literary Studies, and Gender Studies at Northwestern University, is the author of *A Guide to Ezra Pound's "Selected Poems"* (1983), *To Write Paradise: Style and Error in Pound's "Cantos"* (1984), and *Modernism's Body: Sex, Culture, and Joyce* (1996).

BRITTON GILDERSLEEVE, Director of the Oklahoma State University Writing Project, is the author of *The Privilege of Breath* (2002). Her work has appeared in *Early American Literature, Tulsa Studies, Bulletin of Bibliography, Paideuma, Calyx,* and *Spoon River Poetry Review*.

KIM JONG-GIL, a Korean poet, translator, and critic, has translated classical Korean poems in Chinese into English (1987).

PETER MAKIN, Professor of English at Kansai University, Japan, is the author of *Provence and Pound* (1978), *Pound's Cantos* (1985), and *Bunting: The Shaping of His Verse* (1992). He is also the editor of *Basil Bunting on Poetry* (1999).

Contributors

IRA B. NADEL, Professor of English at the University of British Columbia, Vancouver, is the author of *Biography: Fiction, Fact and Form* (1984) and *Joyce and the Jews: Culture and Texts* (1989). He is also the editor of *The Letters of Ezra Pound to Alice Corbin Henderson* (1993) and the general editor of *The Cambridge Companion to Ezra Pound* (1999).

ZHAOMING QIAN, Professor of English at the University of New Orleans, is the author of *Orientalism and Modernism: The Legacy of China in Pound and Williams* (1995) and *The Modernist Response to Chinese Art: Pound, Moore, Stevens* (2003). He is also the editor of *Annotated Shakespeare: The Sonnets* (1990).

MARY DE RACHEWILTZ, daughter of Ezra Pound, has authored *Ezra Pound, Father and Teacher: Discretions* (1971), *I Cantos* (1985), and *For the Wrong Reason* (2002).

PATRIZIA DE RACHEWILTZ, granddaughter of Ezra Pound, has translated into Italian the fairy tales and poems of Paul de Musset, E. E. Cummings, and Kenneth Grahame.

HONG SUN, Professor of English at Renmin University of China, has edited *An Encyclopedia of World Poetics* (1999) and authored *A Comparative Study of the Chinese and American Educational Systems* (1993) and *Myth and Reality in the Rural and Urban Worlds: The Literary Landscape in American and Chinese Regional Literatures* (1997).

EMILY MITCHELL WALLACE taught at the University of Pennsylvania, Swarthmore, Curtis Institute of Music, and Yale University before becoming an interdisciplinary scholar of poetry and visual culture. Author of *A Bibliography of William Carlos Williams* (1968) and many essays about Williams, Pound, H.D., and Marianne Moore, a recent monograph is "Saffron Honey: A 'Love Song' by William Carlos Williams" (2001).

YANG LIAN, a Chinese poet with numerous collections in Chinese, is currently resident in London. His most recent books in English translation are *Where the Sea Stands Still* (1999) and *Yi* (2002).

Index

Index